I0820783

PRAISE FOR
THIS CAR SUX!

"In *THIS CAR SUX!* Randy Pressgrove does an exemplary job of colorfully describing the process of getting an automobile from manufacturing through to the brand delivering it to dealerships and into the driveway of its new owner. *THIS CAR SUX!* is a delightful romp through something that touches everyone's life in some form or fashion. Whether you are a veteran of the business, just entering the craziness and wanting some perspective as you try to learn the ropes, or just an average person wanting to know what goes on behind the scenes, *THIS CAR SUX!* will have you earnestly turning the page to see what shenanigans the car business serves up next. You too may find yourself intrigued, curious, and perhaps tempted, as many of us have been, to wonder what it would be like to be a part of the dynamic story of the modern auto industry."

—*JOHN SZYMANSKI,* VICE-PRESIDENT, HOLMAN AUTOMOTIVE GROUP

"In an age of e-commerce and doorstep delivery, the car dealership is a clunky anachronism. Randy Pressgrove is our old-school car-guy guide to this strange and disappearing world, full of war stories and warnings of what to look out for when you go in search of that new car smell."

—*DAN ALBERT,* AUTHOR OF *ARE WE THERE YET?: THE AMERICAN AUTOMOBILE PAST, PRESENT, AND DRIVERLESS*

"Every year, millions of Americans dive into the wild world of car shopping—a process that evokes emotions ranging from 'this is exciting!' to 'I'd rather be getting a root canal.'

In this entertaining and eye-opening book, Randy Pressgrove, an insider with over forty years of automotive industry experience under his belt, takes readers on a ride through the inner workings of the car world. From assembly lines to showroom floors, he reveals what really goes on behind the scenes, and trust me, it's not all shiny paint jobs and free coffee at the dealership.

With sharp insight and a storyteller's flair, Pressgrove dishes out the good, the bad, and the 'did-that-really-happen?' of an industry that's been both roaring and sputtering over the decades. If you've ever bought a car, sold a car, or been baffled by the whole process, this book is your backstage pass to the automotive circus."

—DON HUGHES, **FORMER EXECUTIVE, VOLKSWAGEN OF AMERICA**

"Randy Pressgrove's tenure in the auto industry spans decades filled with industry changes, manufacturer bankruptcies, and a global pandemic. He has had a ringside seat to the ups and downs of the industry, witnessing firsthand the good times, the bad times, and the crazy times! His story is filled with a plethora of colorful characters who are emblematic of the wild world of cars. If you work in this business, you know it is in your blood, it is never boring, and you've never 'seen it all.' With Randy's witty repartee and knack for storytelling, *This Car Sux!* will take you along on the ride of his career. Buckle up and enjoy!"

—EILEEN CUMMINGS, **REGIONAL SALES DIRECTOR, STELLANTIS FINANCIAL SERVICES**

TALES AND TIPS FROM A LIFE OF *WHEELING & DEALING*

RANDY PRESSGROVE

amplify
an imprint of Amplify Publishing Group

www.amplifypublishing.com

This Car Sux!: Tales and Tips from a Life of Wheeling and Dealing

The author has tried to recreate events, locales, and conversations from their memories of them. In order to maintain their anonymity in some instances, the author has changed the names of individuals and places, and may have changed some identifying characteristics and details such as physical properties, occupations, and places of residence.

For more information, please contact:
Amplify Publishing, an imprint of Amplify Publishing Group
620 Herndon Parkway, Suite 220
Herndon, VA 20170
info@amplifypublishing.com

Library of Congress Control Number: 2025905072
CPSIA Code: PRV0825A
ISBN-13: 979-8-89138-634-1

Printed in the United States

To Jim Seidel, my first boss at Mazda—
who taught me most of what I needed to know
about the business.

CONTENTS

PROLOGUE

"This car sux!"

More than once, these three words have been uttered in exasperation by remorseful buyers. Not surprisingly, this statement is often true, particularly in the case of a shoddily assembled automobile. More often than not, however, the source of a remorseful buyer's regret is the buyer himself. You see, the big mistake a lot of people make is that they do not arm themselves properly to negotiate with some of the slyest—or, in some cases, sleaziest—individuals known to humankind. Information is power. If more customers would prepare themselves with the available information regarding automobile models, customer incentive programs, financing options, and—above all—dealer tendencies, practices, and attitudes, they could mitigate any subsequent remorse.

Let's face it, car dealerships are not philanthropic institutions, and car dealers, like all businesspeople, are in business to make money. An uninformed, unprepared, unsophisticated customer is a car dealer's lawful prey. When you embark on a hunt for a car, you might actually become the hunted. Car salespeople become very adept at spotting and capitalizing on an easy mark. However, some prior research, ready cash in hand, a clear knowledge of what you want, and a firm resolution to achieve your goal can make the car-buying experience vastly more endurable, if not enjoyable.

In this book I make a sincere attempt to offer a fuller understanding of the retail car business. I examine the manufacturer's, dealer's, and customer's roles in the process and how these roles eventually affect you, the consumer. Specifically, we'll look closely at the factory, the dealer, the government, and you. And we'll explore the history of how all these entities combine to make the car-buying experience either a jolly rotten exercise or an efficient, if not actually enjoyable, one. Since I've spent forty-two years in the business, I will also share pertinent anecdotes from my life to enliven the journey.

I originally trained at the University of St Andrews in Scotland as a medievalist, with the idea that I was going to be a high school history teacher or a professor of Latin and medieval studies at a small college. When I returned home to Memphis, Tennessee, I encountered little demand for a medieval scholar, so with five dollars in the bank, I found myself at Liberty Chrysler-Plymouth—as perhaps the only parts counterman with a graduate degree in Scottish medieval history in America. I learned quickly that the only guys making money at a Chrysler dealership in the middle of the worst recession since World War II were the car salesmen (and yes, back then only men sold cars). Thus, I began selling cars, and to my surprise, I actually enjoyed the job. Even my classical European education proved useful: long hours of study had made me a quick learner, and within a year I began working for the Chrysler Corporation directly. And so began my very long affiliation with the car industry, working in sales and dealer development with Mazda, Toyota, Volkswagen, Audi, Porsche, and Kia. Along the way, I was fortunate enough to have some fulfilling assignments in Canada, Germany, Japan, and even a stint as a director with a large private distributor of Toyota in Saudi Arabia.

During that time, because I have a pretty good memory, decent powers of observation, and an ear for a good story, I accumulated a sizable cache of automotive anecdotes from colleagues, customers, and dealership employees. As my mental storybook grew over the years, I would often say to someone, "I'm going to put that one in my book!" I began to make this joke with increasing frequency, to the point that one day when my partner and I were driving to a car show in New Jersey and I said, "That's going in my memoirs," she took out her laptop and said, "Okay, buster, start talking!" Over the next year and a half, I spoke my story aloud as she transcribed. This book is the result of our collaboration—an honest effort to detail the inner workings of the retail car business, its relevant history, and how all these factors colored my personal and professional experiences. I hope it proves useful.

CHAPTER 1

BASTARDS, BANDITS, AND BOZOS (PART I)

Most adults who have purchased a car in the affluent post–World War II American economy have had the dubious pleasure of visiting a car dealership. My experience of forty-two years indicates that a portion of these encounters involves chicanery, duplicity, or even actual fraud on the part of dealership employees. Sometimes the visit results in the purchase of a "lemon," a purchase price far in excess of the customer's wherewithal, or worse, outright thievery.

True, a car salesperson, finance person, service adviser, or mechanic is entitled to earn a living. However, the extent to which retail dealership personnel pursue that endeavor can become the source of many a customer's woe. Regrettably, many customers add to the bitterness of their experience through poor preparation. The worst time to visit a car dealership, whether new or used, is when you absolutely, desperately need a car. Not surprisingly, an average customer's financial wherewithal falls to its lowest point at these precarious times; hence, that moment is the exact one in which the needy customer is most vulnerable.

Similarly, the general American throwaway mentality works against proper maintenance of their automobiles, usually the second-most costly purchase they will make in their adult lives. Changing the oil and getting repairs done on the manufacturer's recommended maintenance schedule can minimize more extensive and costly repairs down the road. The old saw about a woman being taken advantage of by a car dealer or a mechanic is, in reality, dwarfed by the actual times an average, cogent, intelligent male is taken for a ride on a car deal or an engine job.

To sum up, no one—absolutely no one—is immune to the charms of an unscrupulous car person. Car buying, or any other applicable trip to a car dealership, whether new or used, ranks right up there with a trip to the local DMV, the US Post Office, or the dentist in terms of desirability. Here's why:

In America, unlike in Europe, the automobile has been an essential mode of transportation since the end of World War II. At any one time, an excess of one hundred million automobiles travel the road. Simply put, unless you live in a large city with reliable public transportation, you *need* a car. Furthermore, the automakers, dealers, and government have conspired to foster the notion that you also *need* the newest, shiniest, most luxurious model car you can ill afford. Toward that nefarious end, the dealers—and more specifically, their salespeople and finance specialists—are most happy to oblige.

The salesperson will serve their own best interest by building as much "value" into a car deal as possible. That padded value is the source of their income. Since most salespeople are paid on gross, which is the difference between the actual cost of the car to the dealer and the transaction price, the dealer incentivizes the salesperson to add equipment and accessories to the car. Sometimes, unless a customer is very wary, a salesperson can structure a car deal that entails a model price thousands of dollars above what the customer had budgeted or had deemed willing to pay, regardless of budgetary constraints. Accessories are another delightful tool used by dealerships to sweeten the deal . . . for them. Items such as undercoating, window tinting, pinstripes, Gentex mirrors, seat protectors, and monster mats are, in the end, not so much customer *needs* as they are dealership profit builders.

Let's take a particularly egregious item: the "protection package," which is marketed by a particular Toyota distributor as a "vehicle protection package," wherein the seventeen-digit vehicle identification number is electronically etched into every pane of glass on the vehicle. The idea is that if your car were stolen and parted out (disassembled and sold for parts), investigators acting on your behalf—or more accurately, on behalf of your insurance company—could trace the vehicle and perhaps rat out the automotive malefactors. Never mind the fact that if your vehicle is stolen and parted out, you're pretty much screwed anyway because insurance almost never pays the actual value of the car. Accordingly, you're stuck without a car, fighting with the insurance company over an appropriate amount of compensation *and* still having to buy another vehicle. So if the vehicle is, in fact, stolen and parted out, what good is the "protection package" to a customer? By the time the purpose of the package manifests itself, you're already a loser.

To be sure, the package may include items other than glass etching. These additions might entail bumper rub strips applied after delivery to the dealer, some kind of sealant for the exterior paint, and perhaps bumper reflectors. The whole idea, however, exists solely to increase the transaction price. The "protection" ploy works marvelously, and the package sells more often than not.

But let's get back to the actual negotiation. Let's say you have settled on a particular model with a particular price in mind. Let's also assume that you already own a car, which you will be trading in for your new car. One of the first actions a salesperson will take, regardless of what model you have settled on, is to ask what you are trading in for the new model. Be prepared to hear (1) a price on a new car somewhat higher than you expected to pay and (2) an allowance for your current car considerably lower than the value you apply to it. In the salesperson's mind, even if the value you apply to your used car is lower than what the salesperson suggests, they will attempt to screw that price down even further.

In a classic retail car transaction, real negotiation begins at this point in the process. In a matter of seconds, the salesperson has mentally structured a transaction based on your perceived desire for the model you want, as well as their perception of what they can get your trade-in for and what the dealership can subsequently retail it for. For a layperson unschooled in the art of negotiation, the ensuing give-and-take can make for a long afternoon of back-and-forth. To further muddy the water, the salesperson will ask you what other money you wish to put down on the new car. This extra ask is just gravy for the salesperson because in most cases, unless your trade-in is an abominable bomb, the trade-in value should cover the down payment.

Okay . . . at this point, let's assume that between the price of the new car, the value of your trade-in, and whatever other money you have to put down, you have arrived at a transaction price. You may think that you have finished for the day. In reality, in many cases a tougher negotiation has just begun. Next, the salesperson may say to you, "This is really a great deal and so advantageous to you that I need to take this to my manager." At which point they will excuse themselves and disappear into an unknown recess of the dealership. Keep in mind that, by this time, the salesperson has already asked you for the keys to your trade-in so the used-car manager or appraiser can properly assess the value of your trade.

After a decent interval, usually the length of time it takes to smoke two unfiltered cigarettes, the salesperson will reappear with a somewhat hangdog look on their face. They will seat themselves behind their desk, fold their hands before them, and possibly say, "I really fought for you for this deal. This is a car we really need to move. However, I'm fighting two issues. Number one, my manager says we need another $200 to make this deal work, and number two, your trade-in is very nice, but it's worth about $500 less than what we had figured into the deal." The salesperson will make this speech with the tone and solemnity of a country preacher.

At this exact moment, you should require the keys back to your trade-in. You should then politely ask that your old car be brought back around to you. In a firmer tone, you will inform the salesperson that you are leaving the showroom immediately. The unruffled salesperson then might say that they will have to locate the keys to your car and that this task might take a while, which is when you should demand to see their manager. Since most salespeople prefer that a manager not enter the negotiations at this early juncture, they will probably then make an obviously concerted effort to locate your trade-in and present you with your keys.

However, another scenario could be that the manager appears as you stand up to leave, introduces themselves with a toothy smile and a firm handshake, and reiterates that they really want to do business with you, saying, "Can't we figure out how to get this deal done today?" You should then state that you know the terms under which you will complete the transaction and that you will brook no further delay. If you really want to twist the knife, say, with the utmost courtesy, you really don't want to waste any more of their time or, more importantly, your own. The upside of this second scenario is that, faced with a resolute customer with a broomstick up their backbone, the manager will agree to your terms, and you can complete your transaction. The downside is that by agreeing to meet your terms, the manager has now exposed you to the most tortuous aspect of the car-buying experience.

How so, you ask? Well, if you are financing the balance of the transaction that is not covered by the down payment and the trade-in allowance, you will now meet with the dealership's finance specialist. Make no mistake, the job of the finance manager is to wring every remaining nickel from your pocket, wallet, and bank account. Here's a good illustration:

Let's say you're buying a midsize family sedan, and the final agreed-upon price is $30,000. Let's say your trade-in allowance is $5,000 for that 1999 Toyota Camry with 160,000 miles on it. You have decided to put down another $1,000 in cash. You thus have a $6,000 down payment on a $30,000 purchase, or 20 percent down. Therefore, the final total financed is $24,000. The finance person is going to take this transaction to a lender, who will give *them*, not *you*, the most favorable terms.

The most common terms offered for an installment auto loan are thirty-six, forty-eight, or sixty months. Many lenders are willing to stretch an installment loan out to seventy-two or, in some cases, eighty-four months with local banks or other financial institutions. Keep in mind that the longer the term you pick, the lower your monthly payment will be. Since 1980, the average price of a new car has climbed from about $5,800 to as much as $30,000. A thirty-six- or forty-eight-month contract entails a monthly payment that is somewhat more than the average customer can afford, hence the onset of longer contracts. Be aware, though, that if you're paying $250 per month over seventy-two months, you are paying much more interest than in a shorter-term contract. The second downside is that, unless you are a particularly frugal and mindful person, you will not keep this new car for that length of time.

Additionally, the dealer often incentivizes the finance manager to sell you a vehicle protection plan. Not a vehicle protection plan like glass etching but rather an extended warranty, which is alleged to cover most unexpected vehicle repairs. Such a plan is extremely limited, very expensive, and, frankly, not worth the money paid. Dealers prefer to sell plans other than those sponsored by the manufacturer, especially those that they have developed on their own or that are underwritten by their own or dealer association's insurance company. Because a major engine failure can run up into thousands of dollars, most of these plans will have all sorts of rules and deductibles that will be fail-safes for the dealer in the event of a major claim. Accordingly, the costs of these protection plans vary widely and can add thousands of dollars to the transaction price of your car. As few of these claims are ever actually paid, these extended warranty plans mean enormous profit to the dealer and hundreds of dollars in commissions to the finance manager.

The finance manager may try to sell you other trinkets of travail. For example, if the salesperson hasn't already tried to sell you a tinted windshield, tire sealant, fabric protector, Gentex mirrors, a trailer hitch, or some other must-have item, the task will fall to the finance manager. We can trace the original reasons for the high-pressure hawking of such automotive impedimenta. Thirty years ago many cars were sold as "basic" models. In fact, not until the early 1980s did conveniences—such as cassette players, antilock brakes, air-conditioning, power windows, power door locks, steering, brakes, antennae, and leather seats—become standard items on many cars.

About that time the auto manufacturers got smart: they figured out that since many people seemed to like these items and their application on the basic model cars provided additional income, the manufacturers could ostensibly bundle many of these bells and whistles into "option" packages that carried higher prices. (We'll talk more about this practice in chapter 9, "It's Nice to Have Options.") Consequently, a lot of add-ons that used to be installed by dealers became "standard" on the cars from the factory, eating into a dealer's share of the pie. No wonder extended warranties and low labor-intensive items such as sealants and undercoating became so popular: as dealers' profit margins sunk from about 14 percent in 1980 to about 8 percent today, the dealers rightly figured they had to compensate for that loss in some effective but inconspicuous way.

Now back to how the customer pays for all this "additional value." Many new-car dealers have arrangements with their manufacturer's "captive" finance sources (financial institutions owned by or affiliated with the car manufacturers) that allow them to use that captive's programs to finance retail car deals. Many times the captive finance source will offer the same monthly installment terms we discussed earlier. They also will pay the dealer a small markup, usually called "finance reserve," for the privilege of financing the deal.

As a customer, you should understand that if you elect to finance your car deal through the dealer, (1) you will be paying, at minimum, a slightly higher rate for the same term you can get through the bank or your own credit union, and (2) your own credit rating could determine not only how your car deal is structured but also the rate you actually pay or how much additional money you have to put down. As an ongoing sore point, some captive finance sources contend that certain dealers will send them only high-risk, low-quality deals while directing higher-quality deals to another manufacturer's captive finance source or to a local or regional bank offering the dealer a higher finance reserve. We will deal more with captive finance sources in the chapter "Held Captive (Part I)," but for now you should understand that the auto manufacturers build the car you are buying and thus have a major impact on how you buy it.

Consumers certainly can find other ways to acquire a car, most of which are especially less egregious than the ordeal I have just described. Leasing is the most common and popular alternative. A lease allows you to take possession of a car only for the amount of time specified in the lease contract. The closed-end lease at thirty-six months has become the bedrock of most sales strategies, particularly in the Northeast. In a lease, especially in the manufacturer's supported program, you will pay a security deposit, which can range anywhere from $1,000 to 10 or 12 percent of the vehicle's capitalized cost. Sometimes the first month's lease payment is included in the down payment, often referred to as "due at signing." Thereafter you will pay a set amount per month—let's say $369 for a midrange sedan. At the end of the lease term, you have the option of (a) turning the vehicle in at the dealer and walking away from the lease, less any lease turn-in costs or nickel-and-dime fees for damage, or (b) purchasing the leased vehicle for the residual, which is the capitalized cost of the vehicle less three years' depreciation calculated, of course, by the leasing company. If you are using a manufacturer's supported lease through the manufacturer's captive finance company, the captive usually will be more than happy to finance the purchase for you under terms similar to those we detailed before.

However, throughout most of the United States, across all brands, models, and price classes, the good old retail purchase is still the mainstay of the retail automobile business. With the aforementioned exception for the Northeast, including New England, the straight retail purchase is still a customer's preferred method of acquiring an automobile. Yet leasing remains a very important tool, offering a viable alternative to the straight purchase.

By now you're probably wondering where this chapter's title actually comes into play. For all the honest brokers in the retail automobile business—dealers, sales managers, general managers, salespeople, and finance persons—the majority are well-meaning, competent, hardworking guys and gals who are simply there to make a living. The sad part is, the law of averages dictates that a high enough percentage of retail dealership employees are expressly intent on merely separating you from your money. The worst players use the most outgoingly obnoxious, egregious, and unethical, if not downright illegal, means possible. These select few have earned the epithets in this chapter title: bastards, bandits, and bozos.

Knowing this background material when you walk into a dealership will help you understand why you should be fully informed when buying a car. You should have reasonable ability to recognize a truly well-intentioned features/benefits analysis and discern it from a shameless upsell job. The dealer carries an enormous amount of overhead between facilities, occupancy, and personnel expenses; in fact, the dealer may be on the hook for as much as half a million to a million dollars before they even open the doors or sell a car. Accordingly, the dealer is highly motivated to entreat all employees to fight for every last dollar they can squeeze out of a car transaction.

General managers, sales managers, and salespeople are similarly motivated. Whereas today most dealers have more than one dealership and may also be involved in a myriad of other businesses, retail employees usually don't have that luxury. A general manager is usually paid a nominal salary by the dealer, plus a commission based on the dealership's total gross. This amount usually includes used cars, parts, service, and body shop operations, if a dealer does indeed have a body shop. Since a new-car department generates transaction costs that are often higher than those of all the other departments, a general manager's focus will naturally be on you, the new-car customer—the biggest source of their gross.

Furthermore, the general manager supervises a sales manager, who usually oversees only the new-car sales department. In smaller stores and markets, a sales manager might also have responsibility for the used-car department. As dealerships have become fewer and larger and the demands of the business have become more complex, a sales manager responsible for both the new and used departments is rare. Also, sales managers generally work too many hours and too hard to have much outside income. In essence, the main source of livelihood for a new-car sales manager is you, the consumer.

A retail salesperson is even more inclined to squeeze every nickel out of a new-car deal than the general manager or the dealer. Even today the new-car salesperson almost always works on straight commission and receives no other income from the dealership. Over time most dealerships have developed group plans that cover items such as medical and dental insurance and sometimes even vision. However, these plans generally are less favorable than the plans large corporations' benefits departments can offer. Quite often a dealership pay plan can change depending on business conditions, the desirability of vehicles offered, or simply the dealer's whim. For example, when Japanese-imported cars skyrocketed in popularity in 1979 and throughout most of the 1980s, many dealers, recognizing the potential profits offered by the imports, instituted what came to be called "pack."

Pack is a catchall term for additional dealer profit. In the early 1980s, with the increasing desirability of most Asian import cars, dealers realized that they could charge hundreds, sometimes even thousands, of dollars more than the manufacturers' suggested retail price (MSRP). As vehicle pricing remained mostly unregulated at the time, not much could be done to stop a dealer from "packing" additional profit onto the car.

Consumers fed up with the domestic manufacturers' gas-sucking, poor-quality, oversize sedans and coupes gladly forked over hundreds of dollars in excess of the MSRP for highly sought-after Hondas, Toyotas, and Datsuns. So brazen did the packing practice become that dealers actually pasted what came to be known as "addendum stickers" below the standard

Monroney labels, or basic price tags, on the windows of new cars. Sometimes these addendum stickers even declared the amount of the pack, such as $500 for undercoating (actual cost to dealer, usually about $15 worth of chemicals); a phantom safety package of $100, which included nothing at all; and $1,000 additional dealer margin.

This practice got an unintended boost when the Japanese Ministry of Economy, Trade and Industry agreed to voluntary import restraints in the early 1980s. The supply of high-quality Japanese cars became so constrained that even some of the most scrupulous and ethical dealers jumped on the bandwagon. With Japanese competition artificially restricted, many domestic dealers adopted the shady pack practice. At the same time, domestic manufacturers such as General Motors (GM), Ford, and Chrysler raised the MSRPs. For example, a Buick LeSabre, which would have cost $7,500 in 1981, might then have a transaction price to the customer of $9,000 in 1984. With raised prices, at first the pack constituted a mere $200 or $300 addition to the published price of the car and went straight to the dealer's pocket. The salesperson who sold the car did not share in this windfall; rather, the salesperson received a commission of usually 20–25 percent of the difference between the pack and the gross profit in the transaction.

Dealer profits per car soared, and with them the demand for more product. The Japanese discovered they could not grow their business unless they established manufacturing in America. By 1987 Toyota, Nissan, Honda, and Mazda all had plants operating in the United States. The quality of the US-produced products rivaled that of the imports. With the increased availability, most of the import car shortages disappeared. The prices got more competitive for all brands, and sales incentives, which previously had been used only in the most desperate situations, began to become a vital part of the retail automobile business. By the time of the 1992 recession, incentives had become an expected part of the transaction process. Even with intermittent downturns in the business, most notably in 1992, 2001, and 2008, none of these recessions kept the most aggressive dealers from profiting from car retailing.

To summarize thus far, over the past thirty-five years, the retail car business has brought out the best and the worst in the people of its domain. While strong ethics and honesty made the best of the retail automobile dealers even better, the temptations presented by business conditions and market forces proved too irresistible to the worst-intentioned players. When the business grew very strong, even the manufacturers gave into avarice. Unfortunately, the bastards, bandits, and bozos are still in the car business, still out there preying on uninformed customers.

In this first chapter, I have stressed the importance of not only reliable information but also situational awareness. I have also described how you can take as much control as possible of the car-buying experience. To those ends, I have explored the different tools, such as purchasing and leasing, available to help you acquire a new car without too much torture. In the next chapters, I will explain the nuances of these tools in even more detail, provide a thorough overview of how new-car financing developed in the industry, and show how these tools can be deployed in your personal experience at the dealership. These tools are the province of financial institutions, such as banks and captive finance sources. You will learn that while most dealerships want to separate you from your money, financial institutions can be valuable allies and honest brokers in ensuring that you can tailor your car purchase to your preferred terms.

CHAPTER 2

HELD CAPTIVE (PART I)

Unless you are extremely wealthy, chances are, you will buy or lease a car "on time." That is, you will finance your purchase through either a bank or a credit union, or even more likely, if you are purchasing or leasing your vehicle through a new vehicle dealer, you will be financing through the dealership's captive finance source.

Years ago the Big Four (General Motors, Ford, Chrysler, and American Motors) realized that the availability of easy credit vastly contributed to the increase in new vehicle sales. Accordingly, these companies chartered and funded the establishment of finance arms affiliated with their brands, specifically for financing new-car sales. The move soon proved a prescient initiative on the part of the original equipment manufacturers' ever-opportunistic sales executives in view of the rising costs of new vehicles.

In the postwar automotive boom, the GI Joes came home triumphantly from World War II, and businesses and cities expanded to service the ever-growing economy. These new additions to the American workforce needed reliable transportation to travel to their new jobs (which had been quite recently, and successfully, filled by the industrious women left stateside). In an era when the average husband's salary was $9,000 per year and the average cost of a new car was $2,000, captive finance companies provided a mechanism to bridge the gap between a 20 percent down payment and the balance of a new-car purchase price.

A war veteran, working-class average Joe with his eye on a 1959 Fairlane could put down $500, an extraordinarily large amount of money in those days, and submit an application for the balance of $1,500 through his Ford dealer to the Ford Motor Credit Company. Provided that Average Joe could prove his employment tenure, his ability to pay his other household bills, and a stable longevity at his current address, Ford Motor Credit would advance the dealer the money for the balance of the purchase. A smiling salesperson would pose with Average Joe and his smiling wife and baby, presenting the young, happy family with a set of keys to the aforementioned Fairlane.

This basic scenario still plays out today, but the choices for dealerships and customers are so much greater now. In addition to the captive finance companies, most retail and even commercial banks are in the car-finance business. Similarly, hundreds of smaller, less well-known but highly reputable finance companies are in the retail automotive business as well. Over time nearly all of them, except some of the more persnickety larger banks, have cultivated a major industry within the industry—the special finance market.

Since even the least creditworthy buyers still need transportation, this industry within the industry gladly does business with this segment of the population. And since dealing with this segment of the market entails greater risk, the stakes for the customer are higher, particularly in the form of higher interest rates. Everyone knows that the higher your credit score, the more favorable your loan terms will be. This premise applies to buying a car, whether new or used, as much as, or more than, it applies to purchasing a home. Because many credit-challenged customers are also chronically short of ready cash, a larger portion of the purchase price of an automobile will be financed.

Generally speaking, today's average customer will need a credit score of 600 or above to get truly favorable loan terms. A customer with a credit score of 650 can still reasonably expect to get a rate of only a few points above prime over a term of thirty-six, forty-eight, or sixty months. A customer with a much lower credit score will have the double whammy of a still-considerable down payment and, to make the transaction more affordable for them, a contract term of sixty, seventy-two, or even eighty-four months. While these terms lower the monthly payment, they also vastly increase the overall cash outlay by the customer over the term of the contract. This paradox creates secondary problems for the customer. Unless a car is exceptionally well maintained, the likelihood of even a quality, well-built, new car lasting seven years or more is suspect.

Similarly, if the credit-challenged customer is purchasing a used car (or "pre-owned" in modern parlance), this dynamic plays out sooner. Since the car is now in the possession of a customer who is less able to afford preventive maintenance on a regular basis, the less well-cared-for car will break down far earlier than the expiration of a seventy-two- or eighty-four-month contract. What then? The most likely scenario is that the customer takes the dented, smoke-belching, ten-year-old used car back to the dealer to trade it in for something a little more functional. More problems arise because the old trade-in doesn't have a lot of value to throw against another used-vehicle purchase, and unless the customer's financial fortunes have changed significantly, they may still be sporting a credit score that is less than "fair."

The cumulative effect of this process is that in trading in the old car, the customer still has an unpaid balance on a seventy-two- or eighty-four-month contract of several thousand dollars. The only way he can get "mobile" again is by rolling the unpaid balance into a new contract on the newly purchased car for perhaps an even longer term. Thus, buying a car becomes an unrelenting downward spiral that, for many credit-challenged customers, is probably impossible to overcome.

Interestingly enough, the secondary credit market also holds perils for dealers. While this market is undoubtedly profitable, it also has the effect of taking a customer, creditworthy or otherwise, out of the new-car market for several years. Additionally, an endless parade of customers from a dealership's finance manager to a bank, credit union, or captive finance company does little to instill great relationships between the dealership and its finance sources. Based on over a year of experience in the captive finance side of the business (Volkswagen Credit and Audi Financial Services), I contend that the captive looks more favorably on a dealership that consistently offers high-quality paper representing creditworthy customers as opposed to high-risk, delinquent portfolios.

For the sales arm of the manufacturer, the secondary finance market, along with the products its captives develop to service said market, constitutes a mixed blessing. Some dealers actively cultivate the secondary market and make it their stock-in-trade and eventually do a thriving business with it. However, while the manufacturers like the volume such business generates, they privately deplore some of the more unglamorous aspects of it: customer complaints detailing excessive interest rates, rolling unpaid loan balances into new loans, and the assortment of added warranty or protection products included in the deal. More than anything else, the manufacturers worry about unwanted publicity and the negative impacts the preoccupation with the subprime market can have on some of their dealers.

As of this writing, not much change seems forthcoming: As mentioned before, even less-than-creditworthy customers need reliable transportation. Given the risks at stake, the banks, captives, and finance companies have to charge higher interest rates to subprime customers. That said, many of these same institutions make billions of dollars in the subprime business. Customers themselves most often are thankful to have a car, despite burdensome interest rates, hefty monthly payments, and the weight of such debt notwithstanding. Also, as stated earlier, the manufacturers love the additional volume, which the dealers need to achieve the manufacturers' objectives. Therefore, as long as all these factors are in play, the subprime finance market will remain an integral part of the business.

CHAPTER 3

HELD CAPTIVE (PART II)

In the previous short chapter, I reviewed the benefits and hazards of dealing with a dealership's finance department. I also offered a brief overview of "captive finance companies"—the credit companies set up by the manufacturers specifically to finance the sale of their name-brand vehicles from the dealership to the customer. However, what a lot of people do not know is that the dealers themselves depend greatly on these same companies to finance their wholesale purchase of new vehicles from the factory to have new-car stock on their lots. This concept is called "floor planning." In this chapter I will focus on that particular part of the business, which is absolutely critical for a new-car dealer to actually, well, stay in business.

Not surprisingly, most dealers are, if not wealthy, at least relatively well-to-do. They have the captive finance sources to thank for their prosperity. Like most adept businessmen, the dealers have perfected the art of using "OPM," a.k.a. "other people's money." Let me explain.

Before the end of World War II, the general business environment was mostly one of a cash condition. The Great Depression and the memories of what it did to the US banking system were still very much top of mind for everyone, from the smallest businessman to the highest levels of the government. During World War II, America's auto industry converted from vehicle production for consumer use to military production. For example, most of Chrysler's plants—which had formerly cranked out Dodge, DeSoto, Plymouth, and Chrysler sedans and coupes—switched over to tanks and two-and-a-half-ton trucks. Similarly, Ford expanded its Willow Run Plant west of Detroit, dedicating it solely to the production of B-24 four-engine heavy bombers for pounding German, Italian, and Japanese military and industrial concerns into dust.

Across the country, smaller "feeder" plants, which formerly had produced automotive components to contribute to the thunderous maw of the giant assembly plants, retooled to manufacture ammunition belts, shell casings, rifles, a dazzling array of machine guns, steel army helmets, belt buckles, cannon barrels, propeller blades, and heavy-caliber shells. Yet with the war's end, all these plants converted back from war production to manufacturing consumer goods, including automobiles. No passenger cars had been produced in the United States since February 1942, and sixteen million men and women veterans then returning from the war were in dire need of transportation. The manufacturers had a ready market more than willing to buy their products. In the first six months of 1946 alone, over eight million people reentered the US labor market. They had to have some way of getting to their new jobs—or in the case of those vets taking advantage of the new GI Bill of Rights, getting to their college classes.

But . . . the war had steadily driven up the prices of everything. GIs returning from the war could collect $20 per week for as much as a year until they found solid, permanent employment. When they did find permanent employment, such proved to be steady, reliable, and lucrative work. Remember that during this time a motor vehicle constituted a much larger percentage of a worker's compensation than it does today, so much so that most of these vehicles had to be financed. At first, financing remained under the auspices of local banks. However, now that the United States had become the richest country in the world, an American worker with some time in his job, several hundred dollars in the bank, and a steady paycheck could usually get a loan from a bank for a motor vehicle.

Over time, and with the rising prices of cars, credit gradually became the most common method for someone to acquire a car. Even with the commercial credit industry still in its infancy, the entire US business landscape began to change. Because of the lack of production during the war years and the vast demand for transportation fueled by cheap gasoline, the automobile sector simply started to boom.

Because most banks that had weathered the Depression and World War II were small local banks, the automotive executives began to realize two major factors: First, the banking sector, in addition to financing cars, also became busy financing the affluent society. All those GIs back from the war had bought homes that they had to stuff with appliances, furniture, and that new marvel of communication, televisions. Second, a healthy competition for capital arose. Everyone wanted and needed money. The automakers themselves required more and more cash, as some of the auto plants that produced the most popular cars had not been refurbished or retooled in years. The demands of the growing motoring public included bigger, faster, roomier, sportier cars, ones that the older plants were not equipped to produce.

At Ford, the chaos engendered by Henry Ford's last days had left the company in a precarious position. To get more throughput, the company had to refurbish its existing plants and build new ones. As the company hemorrhaged cash, young Henry Ford II was convinced by his board and investment advisors that the only way to fund the needed expansion was to take Ford Motor Company public. The result bloomed beyond the wildest dreams of the Ford family, its investment advisors, and the board. Ford's initial public stock offering in 1955 raised over $600 million, an extraordinary amount of money in any era but particularly impressive in 1955.

This windfall allowed Ford to establish the Ford Motor Credit Company at about the same time that GM recognized and decided to act on the same need for credit availability for its customers. At GM, the need for financing became even more critical than at either Ford or Chrysler. In those days GM held about a 60 percent share of the US market and needed a mechanism to get its customers into all those vehicles. Thus, the idea of the General Motors Acceptance Corporation (GMAC) was born.

Chrysler came to this party somewhat later. Ranked third among the manufacturers, it generally sold about two million Plymouths, Chryslers, DeSotos, and Dodges per year. As the business grew (along with prices), Chrysler learned the benefit of credit purchase. By the early 1960s, Chrysler had made arrangements with the Commercial Credit Company for the financing of retail car deals. Some years later, Chrysler formed the Chrysler Credit Corporation. Because of a major recession in the last part of 1957 and into 1958, as well as a major slowdown in 1961 and into 1962, the automobile manufacturers realized that the portfolio of their respective credit affiliates needed to expand beyond retail car deals. In fact, during the recessions, dealers' banks often would not even allow dealers to order new cars.

If dealers couldn't buy cars, the plants would have to be shut down, which meant no revenue. Hell hath no fury like a car guy with no money. Accordingly, the financial experts at the manufacturers' credit companies developed financing programs to enable dealers to purchase cars from the manufacturers. The new programs lessened the dealers' dependence on banks and increased the manufacturers' role and control of the retail automobile business. Now a manufacturer could not only offer a dealer programs to help retail cars and trucks but also provide an alternative to the banks. For example, by the mid-1970s, over half of GM's six thousand dealers had some type of financial arrangement with GMAC.

As we learned earlier, the practice in which the manufacturers' credit companies finance dealers' inventories has been dubbed "floor planning." Once the plant ships the car to a dealer, the manufacturer generates an invoice and bills the dealer's captive finance source for the price of the car. The captive sets a floor plan limit, which dictates how many cars a dealer can finance with the captive, and prescribes daily limits on shipments.

For example, a dealer's floor plan is usually the amount dictated by sixty days' worth of inventory. In some cases an additional thirty days' financing is available to account for vehicles on their way from the plant to the dealer. Every month the captive finance source bills the dealer for the amount of interest incurred on his sitting inventory. Higher interest rates mean bigger monthly finance costs for the dealer. The captive's financial arrangement with the dealer calls for the dealer to pay off the invoice amount of the car to the captive, usually within a couple of days of the vehicle's retail sale. As the captive finance sources behave much like banks in thought process, woe betide the dealer who fails to pay off a car after a customer has bought it. In essence, the captive actually owns the cars until the dealer sells them.

This system worked quite well until the next catastrophic downturn. After the February 1979 Iranian revolution, the world economy plummeted. Gas prices shot up to over $1 per gallon from about sixty cents. As a result, powerful inflationary pressures pushed interest rates to over 21 percent by the end of the year. Many dealers failed under the weight of the interest charges applied by their captive finance sources. Therefore, the most visible effect (to consumers) of the captive finance source's benefits became the new *retail* finance services. To move cars at retail, the manufacturers demanded retail finance options. The captive finance sources—Ford Motor Credit Company, Volkswagen Credit, Chrysler Capital, Toyota Financial Services, Nissan Motor Acceptance Company, and others—now offer competitive interest rates on vehicle purchases, and in many cases they also offer leasing programs. Leasing offers an attractive alternative because a three-year closed-end lease can be much less expensive than financing a vehicle purchase for thirty-six or seventy-two months, as discussed in the previous chapter.

However, new-car financing is not the only service that the captives offer to dealers. Often a dealer will elect to finance their *used*-car inventory with the same captive that finances the new-car inventory. The captives realize that banks often loan money to dealers to finance their dealership buildings and also offer capital loans. Dealers often have all their business tied up with their captive finance source. To compete with banks, the captives cut deals with multifranchise dealers that include great discounts and other more favorable terms if a dealer affiliates all his competitive dealerships' business with a single captive finance source.

Single-source financing affects the price you pay for a car and the interest rate you may pay on the loan. From the dealer's standpoint, single-source financing makes for good business because it enables the dealer to shop their entire portfolio and play one finance source against another.

The banks, never fully removed from the retail automotive finance business, meet the challenge of the captives by creating their own automotive lending specialty divisions, sometimes luring employees from the captives to come work with them. The banks generally offer the same types of financing facilities as the captives. Sometimes they are even more competitive than the captives. However, for the most part, the banks pull out when a major recession hits or if they sustain unacceptable losses from dealers with bad portfolios, poorly performing brands, or bandits for finance managers.

The captive finance sources must operate differently. They are beholden to their manufacturer, literally "captive" to the brand, and remain in the automobile finance business for the long haul. Remember, the captives are chartered and created by the manufacturers; banks are more independent, and if they choose to get out of the automobile finance business, they can continue to finance commercial enterprises outside the automotive industry. For example, when business declines and the brands need to maintain production, the manufacturers may gently remind the captives whose brand name appears on their paychecks, and the captives may take the hint and allow some dealers to accept more cars, which may take their inventory levels to 120 or 130 percent above the floor plan limit. Ordinarily, a captive will suspend a dealer's floor plan if the inventory exceeds the dealer's established limit.

For example, when sales of large American-made cars screeched to a halt as gas prices nearly doubled in response to OAPEC's oil embargo in

1973, the extra floor plan room enabled dealers, if willing, to accept more shipments from the manufacturers. This practice did not quite repeat itself in the aforementioned 1979–1982 recession; that economic event proved much too severe, and the captive executives, with memories of the 1973 debacle, actually cut off most dealers' floor plan lines when they hit their established limits. Hence, a deep industry downturn resulted, from which dealers, manufacturers, captives, and the general economy only began to recover halfway through Ronald Reagan's first presidential term. From a historical perspective, 1980–1981 marked the apex of high interest rates. The crisis also marked the beginning of a more sustained cooperative spirit between the dealers, the manufacturers, and their captives.

In result, wholesale flooring accommodations aside, the financing of automobile dealers has become almost always profitable for almost everybody in the industry. As dealers have learned to function largely on OPM (from the banks and the captives), the business of extending credit to dealers through capital loans and real property mortgages has become almost as profitable as "flooring" new and used cars. Likewise, as dealers have expanded their holdings in the years since the 2008 recession, the demand for credit, with the easy terms offered via historically low interest rates, has fueled a rash of new dealership construction. Existing dealer acquisition of less successful dealers—who simply did not possess the economies of scale, required personnel, or the sophistication of operations to remain competitive—has also increased.

As I have mentioned before, the captives are much like banks in thought, so when manufacturers insist on "jamming" dealers with cars, some captives grumble about the excess inventory. I recall a 1979 incident in which a Chrysler Credit branch manager exploded at a Chrysler zone manager's suggestion that the captive extend enough credit to a large Dodge dealer in Memphis to accommodate the shipment to the dealer of a couple of dozen extra cars. "You, dummy, you can't be serious," the branch manager fumed. "Choke off this guy's wholesale line and we'll see who the real dummy is," the zone manager retorted. Fortunately, such incendiary exchanges, and the actions they engender, are almost unheard of today.

I offer two final notes on captive finance sources here: one from the customer angle and one from the dealer angle. From a customer's point of view, retail captive financing offers a big plus—whether the customer leases or buys, the rates are usually as competitive as those of the banks, and the customer makes one payment a month in the same amount for twenty-four, thirty-six, or forty-eight months. From a dealer's point of view, a captive finance source serves simply as a tool, a means to an end. While most dealers cultivate a close relationship with a captive, a dealer remains a dealer, and a bank or other source offering to do business at a floor plan interest rate of a quarter or half percent less than the captive will always be an option.

Dealers are businesspeople. Some (but not all) will play off one potential floor plan source against another. One of the oldest dealer tricks in the book involves applying to the manufacturer's captive finance source for a floor plan. The dealer will add that if the captive comes to the table with a good rate, the dealer may throw the captive all their automotive business, including floor plans for other franchises, capital loans, used-car flooring, and even mortgages. The captive offers up what is called a "terms and conditions" sheet, which lays out the provisions, including the interest rate, for available credit to the dealer based on getting all his business. Many times, the dealer, after securing these terms from the captive, will go to another lender, usually a large commercial bank, and ask the bank to meet or beat these terms.

Then it's hell to pay for the dealer. The account manager for the captive, who has been working hard to secure the dealer's finance business, will not be happy. Let me share an illustrative example: One regional manager of a captive finance source, a good friend of mine for many years, had a New York–area dealer take his finance business to a large regional bank *after* the captive finance regional manager had endeavored for several months to secure the dealer's business for the captive. The regional manager, justly livid, later described the dealer's jilting to me. At the end of the conversation, she exclaimed, "I want that SOB's balls on a fork!" This is all to say that the car industry is known for both its colorful language and its cutthroat competitiveness.

In fact, the industry is so over-the-top competitive that as of this writing, in late summer of 2021, with interest rates at historic lows, banks now realize that to grow their business, they have to actively acquire new business. A bank will shave as much as a quarter percent off their normal deal if it means getting a forty- or fifty-million-dollar book of new business. Banks love earning a plum account from a captive. Since business is business, the captive will continue to finance retail deals with the dealer, as money is green regardless of whether it comes from a new-car deal or a used-car deal. If the retail customer is a good business risk, the captive will take the deal. However, captives have memories longer (and sharper) than elephants—the sting of having been spurned by the dealer for a bank remains long after a retail deal is booked. Further, dealers complain all the time about captives who turn retail finance down if the captive begins to receive "edgy" or less favorable deals. In such a case, the captive will not-so-gently remind the dealer that business is (indeed) business, and the captive is just doing "good business" by not accepting a riskier deal.

In short, a dealer does business with the captive to solidify the relationship with the brand, and as long as the captive's rates on floor plans, capital loans, and real property mortgages are competitive with the bank's rates, a dealer will continue to do business with the captive. Moreover, a dealer realizes that providing branded retail financing for their customers helps tie the customer to the brand as well. For their part, the captives know that preserving a relationship with a dealer, particularly a dealer who has more than one location with the brand, remains essential to further growth. As long as business is aboveboard and money's earned in the transactions, both dealer and captive stay happy. An obviously harmonious relationship between the dealer and the captive also binds the customer to the brand.

CHAPTER 4

BUY A CAR, GET A . . . LET ME CHECK ON THAT . . .

Wary consumers have long associated car dealers, car salespeople, and the industry as a whole, practically since its inception, with games, gimmickry, and shenanigans. Yet, immediately after World War II, such buffoonery became mostly unnecessary. With car supplies low and consumers desperate for transportation, the plants powered back up to full production to meet the now-booming demand. Other factors, such as transportation infrastructure and new marketing techniques, boosted the industry as well. President Eisenhower and Congress had authorized the building of the vast interstate highway system, and the new medium of television heavily advertised Fords, Studebakers, and "See the USA in Your Chevrolet." With such focus, the US car industry didn't need a lot more inducement to drive sales. Access to the open road, and not safety, occupied the minds of most eager consumers.

However, safety actually led to the first recognized incentive program. In the 1956 model year, Ford developed several key safety features to differentiate their brand from the much more popular Chevrolets. Ford General Manager Lee Iacocca promoted the new padded dashboard of the '56 Ford by announcing a program called "56 for '56." For fifty-six dollars down and fifty-six dollars per month, a customer could drive off the lot in a new '56 Ford. Ford sales ramped up, and Iacocca began a meteoric rise through Ford's executive ranks. Iacocca's 1956 idea became the first modern-day automotive incentive program.

Yet in early 1958, two events conspired to crack the invincibility of GM, Ford, and Chrysler, historically known as the Big Three. First, American Motors Corporation (AMC, the fourth-ranking automotive manufacturer) and upstart imports such as Volkswagen (VW) offered smaller, more economical, lower-priced models. Concurrently, a nasty recession made those same new models very attractive to consumers suffering their first real economic hit since the end of the Second World War. In response, GM, Ford, and Chrysler took two actions, neither of them very effective. First, they began to offer their own smaller, lower-priced cars to chase the imports. Second, and counterintuitively, they only half-heartedly promoted these vehicles in marketing and incentives. They just couldn't get their arms around how to push the new, smaller offerings. Hearts and minds remained loyal to the big land yachts with tons of options and high prices. Big cars meant big profits; small cars meant small profits. This dictum proved true when (1) the new small cars offered by the domestics sold poorly, and (2) the recession eased by early 1959. In fact, the most famous oversize symbol of automotive excess was the 1959 Cadillac Convertible—at 5,030 pounds and $5,453, it proved to be the longest, heaviest, and most expensive mass-produced car in American history.*

In addition, 1961 heralded better economic times, a new young president who fostered a positive, aggressive outlook, and an economy that had revved back up after the 1958 recession. The sixties seemed an era of promise and optimism. Chrysler dealers still speak fondly of the brand's 1961 product line, which looked great and sold well under competitive

---

* "1959 Cadillac," Automobile Catalog, https://www.automobile-catalog.com/make/cadillac/series_6200_1959-1964/series_6200_1959-1964_convertible/1959.html#gsc.tab=0.

pricing. The improvement trend continued for all domestic brands throughout the first part of the 1960s. In fact, for all across the industry, domestic brands sales and profits had soared, and the highways had improved so much that nobody had much to complain about. Quality began to suffer, but Americans had become so enamored with cars and the open road that nobody saw the steady but slow creep of VW and the other imports. Toyota and Nissan had begun to import cars into the United States in the late fifties and early sixties, but generally their quality proved so bad, the performance of the cars so poor, and their size so laughably small that no one paid much attention to them. In fact, an industry joke at the time, which also persisted into the sixties, declared that if you scratched the paint on a Toyota door panel, you would see the Budweiser label beneath.

VW, which had been steadily gaining ground in the United States since the late 1950s, represented a very small percentage of vehicle sales into the mid-1960s. But the tough, durable, enduring little Beetle, even today, continues to maintain its initial cult following among a significant segment of the car-buying public. The VW Beetle—cheap, economical, and so different from the domestics—became almost a point of pride among its fans. Similarly, the undersized, underpowered Datsuns, Toyotas, and Renaults of the day also proved quirky enough to gain a substantial following. During this time the domestic manufacturers granted bigger and better contracts and concessions to their respective United Auto Workers (UAW) units. Naturally, these costs made their way into increased prices for American cars and trucks. The relatively weak German mark and Japanese yen exacerbated the pricing issue. Depending on the model, a VW Beetle, Toyota Corona, or Datsun 510 could cost just over half the price of a midsize Chevrolet, Ford, or Dodge.

Through the mid-1960s, the US car market remained strong enough for GM, Ford, and Chrysler to basically ignore the imports. This attitude prevailed even through the debilitating 1970 strike by the UAW against GM. But even after the strike ended, VW and the Japanese imports continued, if ever so slowly, to gain significant inroads into the US car market. In fact, in

1972, VW retailed over 571,000 cars and buses in the United States.* Still, the domestic manufacturers hardly looked over their shoulders; on the whole, the imports constituted barely a blip on their radar screen.

But the warning signs hovered there for anyone who wanted to see them. The automobile industry had been rolling along quite profitably, almost oblivious to the reasons why. The American market, fueled by a postwar boom (both economic and baby), three-dollar-per-barrel oil, and industrial expansion brought on by the Vietnam War, suddenly got a jolt. In October 1973, Arab states suddenly attacked Israel, and when Israel, with American support, successfully repelled the attacks, the enraged Arab states, particularly those aligned with the Organization of the Petroleum Exporting Countries, struck back at America in their fury with an oil embargo.† Almost overnight the price of gasoline in the United States more than doubled, rising from twenty-seven cents per gallon to over sixty cents per gallon. GM, Ford, Chrysler, and AMC were caught flat-footed. With each manufacturer, the product lineup overflowed with huge gas-guzzling cars, which, at best, got twelve or thirteen miles per gallon.

With no contingency plans and new models with any semblance of fuel economy in their lineups, by mid-November 1973, the domestic manufacturers found themselves with hundreds of thousands of unsold, unwanted cars. Worse yet, production plans for all the manufacturers entailed much of the same. The generous contracts that the manufacturers had negotiated with the UAW contained clauses that either prohibited or made very difficult the closure of car plants. Early 1974 hurt the manufacturers tremendously. A powerful inflation, driven by the oil price increases and the fumbling

---

* "1961 to 1972—Boom and Crisis in the One-Product Business," Volkswagen-Group.com, https://www.volkswagen-group.com/en/volkswagen-chronicle-17351/1961-to-1972-boom-and-crisis-in-the-one-product-business-17357#.

† "Arab Oil Embargo," Britannica, https://www.britannica.com/event/Arab-oil-embargo; "Oil Shock of 1973–74," Federal Reserve History, https://www.federalreservehistory.org/essays/oil-shock-of-1973-74#:~:text=October%201973%E2%80%93January%201974&text=The%20embargo%20ceased%20U.S.%20oil,a%20barrel%20in%20January%201974.

economic policies of the Nixon administration, pushed the country into a deep recession, the worst one since 1958. With no choice but to incur the wrath of the UAW, all the domestic manufacturers chose to close their auto plants. Further, with acres of unsold cars sitting on open lots in the Rust Belt, the domestic manufacturers resorted to a tactic that only five years before seemed unthinkable—they began to offer significant discounts or incentives on most of their models.

Chrysler, the worst-hit manufacturer, demonstrated the most outwardly visible signs of the desperate times. Stuck with tens of thousands of cars sitting axle deep in the mud, Chrysler offered direct $400 rebates on most of its models. Chrysler's pitchman and star of their television commercials, Joe Garagiola, instantly recognizable because of his work with Major League Baseball, provided a credible face in the otherwise almost-carnivalesque atmosphere of hopelessness embodied by the severe circumstances enveloping GM, Ford, Chrysler, and AMC. By current measurements the $400 incentive seems laughably low, but at the time an average Dodge, Plymouth, or Chrysler cost about one-eighth the price of a new car today. In those days the manufacturers measured sales every ten days, as well as in monthly increments. Ford and GM, noticing the uptick of Chrysler sales, and with their own hordes of unsold cars, had no choice but to jump on the rebate bandwagon.

To an extent, the strategy worked. Sales increased, and the more consistent flow of customers back into dealer showrooms provided a welcome respite in the worst part of the recession. Slowly the economy began to improve, and the shuttered plants came back online as the sales freefall abated, with some models actually beginning to sell fairly well. Although some of the new models exhibited terrible design and manufacturing flaws (e.g., Chrysler Corporation's Plymouth Volaré and Dodge Aspen shot right out of the gate with deplorable paint and rust problems), the market stabilized to a point that the manufacturers could actually call some workers back to the job.

Nevertheless, the underlying fundamentals of the business had been shaken to the core. While most other consumer prices moderated, the price of fuel, which for decades had hovered around three dollars per barrel, remained high relative to historical standards. Gradually consumers became accustomed to the higher prices at the pump. By early 1976 the manufacturers, stung by the higher fuel prices and poked and prodded by the government to increase fuel economy standards, went ahead with downsized versions of their most popular models. Across the board, the weight of large- and medium-sized cars was decreased by 450 to 700 pounds. While the manufacturers gradually rolled back incentives, the discount mindset instilled in customers by the vehicle offers remains to this day. "Get a car, get a check"—Chrysler's clarion call of 1975—became a catchphrase in the industry for years.

The incentives had kept the wolf from the manufacturers' doors, but the side effects had pummeled the industry. The manufacturers, whose cash flow had been stymied when the plants closed and no cars were shipped to the dealers, had to deal with the double whammy of weak balance sheets and the enormous cash drain of the incentives. Some of the worst years for the industry in terms of profitability were 1974 and 1975. Incentive payments literally ate the hearts out of the manufacturers' finances. The manufacturers rolled out their 1977 offerings only by massive cost cutting, selective layoffs, and torturous plant closures.

Not that the new, downsized 1977 models were gems. The manufacturers were still spooked by the memory of their inefficient large cars, and they overreacted. I remember when GM shortened the Cadillac Fleetwood for 1977 by an average of about twelve inches. At Ford, the effects of the product downsizing program on the Lincoln Continental, Town Car, and Ford Crown Victoria induced customers to practically turn up their noses when viewing the cars in the showrooms. Chrysler's new Diplomat, LeBaron, Volaré, and Aspen looked like chopped-off versions of the same old cars. They appeared so appallingly ugly and unreliable that the only people who bought them were the customers who had postponed purchases in the recession and had to have some type of transportation.

However, the fall of 1976 brought on a marked improvement in the economy and a national election. Gerald Ford had the misfortune of presiding over the worst economy in almost twenty years. The voters remembered, and Jimmy Carter defeated Ford to become POTUS on January 20, 1977. At the same time, the 1977 models gradually began improving the fortunes of the manufacturers. Carter's new economic policies notwithstanding, people wanted big, new American cars. Aside from pickup trucks, they bought 1977 and 1978 Pontiac Bonnevilles, Chevy Caprices and Impalas, Lincoln Continentals, and Ford Crown Victorias. Even Chrysler enjoyed modest success with their large R-body cars. The 1979 Chrysler Newport and Chrysler New Yorker sold well and offered a level of luxury that Chrysler had not seen since the Imperial line of the early 1960s. They garnered enough profit per unit to allow Chrysler to limp into 1979 with the same old product plan, the same old outdated plants, and the same old tired workforce and mindset. And in the meantime, Americans had gotten quite accustomed to sixty-cent-per-gallon gas. Indeed, those who forget history are doomed to repeat it.

Then in the first quarter of 1979, the shah left town. The Islamic revolution forced the shah of Iran, Shah Reza Pahlavi, from the throne. Twenty-five years of misery, social upheaval, and too-close association with Western (i.e., American) ideals and culture fomented a mass wave of protest, exacerbated by Islamic fundamentalism. Terrified by Ayatollah Khomeini's return to Iran after years of exile in France, the shah fled. The events roiled the oil market—Iran's instability and its location at the eastern extremity of a region long susceptible to social and political unrest negatively affected Western markets. Accordingly, the price of oil shot up immediately, and with it the price of just about everything else.

In an eerie repeat of the gas crisis of 1973, panic ensued. Motorists queued up for expensive, scarce gas. The auto manufacturers struggled to adjust production and, once again, resorted to incentives in the form of rebates to move thousands of suddenly unwanted gas-guzzling behemoths. The turmoil affected all the domestic manufacturers. Suddenly no medium- or large-sized car or pickup truck held any appeal for the motoring public. At the same time that $1.27-per-gallon gas made these American cars undesirable, thousands of small Japanese imports from Toyota, Datsun, Honda, Subaru, Mazda, and Isuzu flooded the docks in Philadelphia, New York, San Francisco, and Los Angeles. These foreign models became the hottest tickets in the new-car world. Besides being much smaller and much more fuel efficient than American cars, the marked disparity between the Japanese yen and the American dollar made them much cheaper than American cars.

Hence, the American manufacturers offered rebates, the only way they could stay viable. By December 1979, for example, Chrysler offered as much as $2,000 off some of its larger cars. Also, by late 1979, because the more expensive oil had a catastrophic effect on the economy as a whole, the entire industrial complex in the West declined. Fueled by higher oil prices, powerful inflation again devastated the economies of the Western European countries and the United States. By December 1979, interest rates in the United States exceeded 21 percent, even as Paul Volcker, chairman of the Federal Reserve, attempted to rein in inflation, which soared to over 13 percent by the beginning of 1980. For the automobile manufacturers, a business bloodbath ensued.

With plants closing and rebates taking a chunk out of what meager revenues the auto plants generated, the manufacturers suffered a catastrophe that made the recession caused by the Arab oil embargo six years earlier look like a picnic. In fact, by December 1979, Chrysler had gone hat in hand to the government for $2 billion in loan guarantees. Accordingly, the Chrysler Corporation Loan Guarantee Act of 1979 helped save the company. The highest level of management also helped save the company when they decided to continue with car rebates.

Even later, milder recessions produced similar results. The 1992 recession provides a good example. GM, Ford, and Chrysler survived the major recession of 1979 but grew fat and complacent in the intervening years. With voluntary import constraints in place beginning in 1981, domestic manufacturers felt emboldened to raise prices and curtail product improvement plans. With profits pouring in to stoke continued complacency, the domestics found themselves ill-prepared for the recession of 1992. Again in 2000 and 2001, powerful recessions driven by the events of 9/11 and the dot-com bubble brought automotive retailing to a screeching halt, whereupon the domestics led by GM again relied on rebates and other incentives. The downturns of 1992 and 2000–2001 only solidified the prevailing attitude engendered by the 1979–1982 recession.

As a result, if anyone today wants to see the net effect of the great automotive recession of 1979, just take a look around. Gas is well over three dollars a gallon on average. All cars are considerably smaller than they were forty years ago. The Japanese, who held only around 20 percent of the car market in 1979, control about half of the car market now. After 1979, the automotive world changed drastically and not necessarily for the better.

The recession produced two grim jokes that made the rounds in the awful winter of 1979–1980. One recounted the story of the Dodge dealer in a major metropolitan market in the Midwest whose dealership was failing. He could not keep up with the interest payments to Chrysler Credit on his floor plan. All his inventory consisted of huge St. Regis sedans that got lousy mileage and vans that he could not even give away. In despair one night, he knelt beside his bed, folded his hands, lowered his head, and prayed, "O Lord, please make me the largest import dealer in a major metro market." When he awoke the next morning, he was the largest Dodge dealer in Yokohama. The other joke featured two salespeople having a smoke in the employee lounge of another Chrysler dealership fallen on hard times. One said, "Hey, did you hear about the new demonstrator vehicle for Chrysler dealers? It has no seat and steering wheel." Intrigued, his companion asked why. "Because," said the first salesperson, "the dealers have all lost their asses, and they don't know where they're going."

CHAPTER 5

THE DEALERS (PART I)

In my opening chapters, I hit hard on the dealers, with some justification. Everyone, it seems, has had some experience with a car dealer. Sometimes that experience has been negative. In fairness, however, car dealers rank among the most highly successful businesspeople in American industry. In view of the capital they risk, the people they employ, the services they offer, the tax base they provide to local governments, and their other contributions to the community, automobile dealers exemplify the epitome of successful entrepreneurship.

In truth, the American car dealer proves somewhat of an anomaly in the global automobile business. Throughout most of the rest of the world, automobile manufacturers control the distribution of their vehicles through carefully selected distributors, some of whom are in the actual employ of the manufacturers. These distributors, in turn, may select subdistributors, subject to the approval of the manufacturer's local or national sales company. The manufacturer retains almost complete control of the distribution channel. Through its distributor network, a non-American manufacturer may assume responsibility for distribution, advertising, marketing, repair services, and the resulting warranty expenses.

By contrast, the American dealer is an independent businessperson tied to the manufacturer by a franchise agreement. Unlike most other automotive retailers worldwide, the American car dealer finances their own operations, makes their own hiring decisions, erects their own facilities, negotiates their own financial agreements, and assumes responsibility for all legal and regulatory compliance of their own free will and accord—and all done at their own very considerable risk. A dealer manages the sales of their representative makes and models within a defined geographic area, sometimes a collection of census tracts as defined by the US Census Bureau or, in the cases of some luxury manufacturers, by zip codes. Although the manufacturer may closely monitor dealers' sales performance in their assigned area of responsibility, the dealer alone must strongly, aggressively, and successfully represent their brand in that locale. Over the years, as the automobile business has grown, so, too, has the wealth and influence of the American car dealer. Certainly, the dealer has had help along the way. The vast network of state motor vehicle commissions, state dealer associations, state legislatures, and dealer lawyers has mostly successfully fended off the more high-handed and egregious attempts by the manufacturers who want to control almost every aspect of a dealer's operations.

We may call the American car dealer a rare breed, indeed. When the automobile business began in the early twentieth century, many different kinds of individuals tried their hand at the infant trade, but they shared some common traits. From general store owners and shopkeepers to bankers and farmers, the business just seemed to attract a certain kind of individual: men possessed of almost-demonic energy, a sense of fierce independence, and an insatiable desire to experiment. Many, with meager funds, even less business experience, and in many cases no knowledge of accountancy, succeeded by sheer force of will. Many of the industry's founders, with their world of innovative ideas and institutions upon which the car business still runs today, started with less than a dollar in their pocket but an overwhelming desire to excel in the industry. Today's American car dealer still embodies the character, cunning, and courage of those who blazed their trail one hundred years ago.

Moreover, the American car dealer has been able to adapt—and adapt quite well. We often hear the repeated phrase "born salesman" in any discussion of the American automobile business. And the vast majority of American car dealers through the years have been superb salespeople. Given the proliferation of companies with competing models that seemed to spring up instantly through the first couple of decades of the last century, any dealer who survived had to be tough, savvy, competitive, and imbued with a keen sense of avarice. Some of the companies and nameplates lasted no more than a couple of years, while the American car dealers not only survived but also thrived. Practically on their own, they adapted themselves to be, in addition to salespeople, mechanics, bookkeepers, parts merchants, and retail psychologists. These inventive salespeople quickly learned how to get a customer behind the wheel.

As the business grew and its functions became more specialized, the dealers not only hired people to help them grow but also taught them the specific disciplines required to succeed in this strange, new, but exciting business. Throughout the 1920s, as cars became bigger, more complicated, and more expensive, the various disciplines within a dealership began to take on different characteristics. For instance, dealers hired bookkeepers and accountants to keep track of revenues. Eventually, these folks also had to learn a modicum of business planning to pay the store employees, vendors, and banks. The banks could prove particularly persnickety, and dealers relied on highly trained employees to cultivate as amicable a relationship as possible.

Similarly, the enthusiastic mechanics of the day, who tinkered with all manner of machines, from bicycles and motorcycles to rail and ship engines, overcame the electrical, mechanical, and hydraulic challenges presented by the automobiles of the early 1900s. The less talented among them learned successful parts procurement and sales. And as car sales volume increased to a point where dealers could no longer handle the sales function themselves, the new-car salesperson evolved to relieve their load.

After an initial shakeout and wave of mergers in the early 1900s to the early 1920s, dealers remained fiercely loyal to the brand—or brands—that had brought them the best success. Ford, which had largely revolutionized not only the retail car business but also American industry itself since 1908, still reigned supreme. GM, created by an uneasy alliance of mergers under Will Durant, made considerable inroads to Ford's dominance primarily through its volume Chevrolet Motor division. Chrysler, founded in 1925 and augmented in 1928 by the addition of the Dodge Brothers organization, rounded out the top tier of car companies. During this time, just before the Great Depression, the dealer alliances with manufacturers really began to take shape. A smattering of luxury marques retained a toehold in the American car business. Auburn, LaSalle, Studebaker, and Cord most readily come to mind. By the late 1920s, however, the future configuration of automobile representation in the United States had already taken shape. For example, to this day there are still Ford dealerships that remain in the same family almost one hundred years after their establishment. Similarly, many GM and Chrysler Corporation dealerships retained loyalty to their respective brands well into the 1980s.

Accordingly, brand loyalty became a primary goal for both manufacturers and dealers. To this end, the manufacturers rewarded their franchised dealers by supplying a steady stream of gradually improving new models, along with support in the way of special tools and technical expertise. Case in point, Ford's rollout of the Model A, though long overdue, helped revive and accentuate a loyalty to the brand that had been sorely tested by Henry Ford's dogged adherence to the Model T. The Model A's innovations proved vital to the success of the brand.

During the Depression, dealers became essential to the industry—perhaps more so than at any other time in history. As production, sales, and overall business practically ground to a halt, the determination and bravery of the franchised dealers set the standard for the automakers. Dealers who survived the Depression were lucky enough—or unlucky, as the case may be—to face World War II. American car dealers weathered one storm, only to face another. By the end of February 1942, automobile production in the United States ceased. As discussed in an earlier chapter, factories that had produced Plymouths, Fords, Chevrolets, DeSotos, and Pontiacs now built B-24 bombers, Sherman tanks, Browning automatic rifles, and two-and-a-half-ton trucks. American manufacturers would not make nonmilitary motor vehicles again until 1946.

To survive, American car dealers turned to used cars, despite being in short supply as a result of the just-ended Depression; car repair, which proved precious work for the same reason; bicycle repair; and secondhand parts sales. Tire repair offered another particularly lucrative sideline, as rubber grew scarce because of Japanese incursions into the rubber-producing countries of the South West Pacific area. What rubber could be obtained went to military uses. A typical tire by 1943 might have as many as a dozen patches.

Not surprisingly, the car dealers who survived the war, hardy as they were, found their ordeal, in some ways, just beginning. After the war, manufacturing plants needed time to switch from war production to car production. Transportation-starved customers aggressively bargained for the new cars, never mind that these "new" models were only updated versions of the 1942 models. Many a new-car dealer launched his fortune in the heady days of the postwar period. Customers, easy to please, paid top dollar, and the automobile business entered into a "golden" phase that continued into 1957.

As noted in a previous chapter, the inception of the interstate system, leaner and more efficient production systems (some brought about by the war), a more affluent and eager population base, and government encouragement combined to make automobile retailing a sure bet. The system and situation fed into each other. More cars sold and on the road meant more service business, more parts sold, and more used cars available. The trend for wealthy, ubiquitous, and influential automobile dealers reached full throttle during the 1940s and 1950s. What happened next helped fuel, however inadvertently, the perception of the car dealer as a money-grubbing, self-absorbed, and less-than-scrupulous individual. As cities grew, the dealers' traditional downtown locations became too small, too dated, and too inefficient to handle the growing volume of car sales and service requests. Cars were also larger, necessitating more room for display and storage. The automobile manufacturers, understanding the popularity of their product, the potential for growth, and the lure of the suburbs, alternately cajoled and encouraged dealers to spend big bucks to buy land on the ever-outwardly expanding fringes of established markets on which to build larger, more efficient (and, by the way, more expensive) dealerships.

The dealers bore all the very considerable expenses of such enterprises in those days. The dealers grumbled, but they grumbled all the way to the bank. As the facilities grew, so did everybody's profits. If size begat volume, volume begat profits. For the manufacturers, the sheer profitability of the dealers made the leap to the suburbs in big, shiny new facilities worthwhile. The bigger dealers began to squeeze out the smaller, older, and less efficient operators who had refused or politely declined the automaker's entreaties (or, in some cases, demands) to move. As the suburbs grew and the downtown business districts declined, the dealers who remained downtown never had a chance; the economies of scale available to the dealers who had moved to new locations quickly began to overwhelm their urban competitors.

The new suburban dealers soon enjoyed the good life. Basic economic principles came into play: As the manufacturers built and shipped more cars, the dealers sold those cars (at handsome profits), and as those cars came back for service, not only did the dealers make much more money, but doing business required much more money as well. Maintenance of the new facilities, acquisition of expensive service equipment, the hiring of additional staff to conduct business, and servicing the debt on the money borrowed to operate all created enormous demands for additional capital. If the old saw "the more you have, the more you want" was ever true, it was never truer than in the life of a car dealer.

Just as the dealers became much more prosperous, they also became much more pecuniary. During most of the 1950s and 1960s, sales boomed, and the dealers took it almost for granted that each month and each year would be better than the one before. At the same time, they became much more acutely aware of the forces that chipped away at their hard-earned fortunes. At first they attuned their senses more to the general costs of doing business: payroll, real property mortgage, personnel and training costs, and interest on all the borrowed money they had on the line. Add to that list overhead—advertising expenses, utilities, taxes, fees imposed by the manufacturers for things such as signage, parts, and the ever-growing myriad of other little expenses that they periodically assessed. The recession of 1957–1958, which proved significant enough to induce the manufacturers to be much more wary of the vagaries of the economy, also instilled in the dealers a high sense of propriety for preserving their earnings.

Slowly the focus of the dealers shifted from the general cost of doing business to maximizing every opportunity to make a buck. This much more aggressive drive for profits gave rise to the well-known caricature of the successful car dealer with white shoes, a loud plaid sports coat, and a porkpie hat. Throughout the 1950s and 1960s, dealers generally remained hardworking, if inordinately driven, entrepreneurial businesspeople—more successful and wealthier than other types of businessmen but nonetheless more compelled to succeed by the simple exigencies of their profession. Even in those days, automobiles represented the second-largest expense for most American families. In fact, from the late 1940s through the mid-1970s, an automobile purchase represented a bigger proportion of a family's total household budget than it does today.

Suddenly, as the economy grew and technology afforded families the opportunity to buy refrigerators, stoves, televisions, and other appliances, the dealers had competition for disposable consumer income. Additionally, the arrival of imported cars augmented the proliferation of car models by the domestic manufacturers. By 1955, Germany's VW had gained a significant toehold in the American market. Though on a much smaller scale, Renault, Toyota, and Datsun did the same, although collectively their volumes represented a tiny fraction of the overall US automobile market. Yet their very presence drove the competition to protect the interests of domestic dealers. Again, after the 1957–1958 recession, the domestic manufacturers added smaller, if ill-conceived, models to their product offerings. Despite their degraded quality, these new offerings helped replace dwindling sales of the larger, more profitable cars that the dealers had depended on for years for the bulk of their profits. Of all the newer models, both foreign and domestic, only the VW Beetle and the Ford Falcon really retained any staying power in the American car market.

Despite the instability of the market, American dealers continued to show resilience and perseverance. Most of the domestic car dealers, regardless of brand, survived the late-1950s recession with panache. These dealers entered the next decade well positioned to take advantage of the economic boom that ensued during the Kennedy administration and Vietnam War. In short, the lessons of the recession and the general wariness fostered by the arrival of imports only strengthened the dealers' determination to thrive and prosper.

Concurrently, the automobile manufacturers, while applauding the profitability of their retail networks, noticed that their retail partners were becoming richer and richer. The manufacturers soon began passing even more operational costs onto the dealers, namely interest on inventory financing, as well as marketing and warranty expenses. Given their focus on their own profitability, dealers reacted negatively, although these charges could be deemed commercially reasonable. Regardless, the dealers generally viewed these added costs as unwanted incursions into their daily business lives.

The manufacturers' insistence on consistency and uniformity in dealership facilities, signage, training, and operations also grated on the dealers. Since the dealers primarily footed the bill for these items, they bristled at the manufacturers' "helpful" inputs. The dealers found such pronouncements ill-informed and thoughtless. For example, manufacturers required the same set of facility and staffing requirements for a dealer in Texas *and* a dealer in Manhattan. Since land costs (as well as the cost of just about everything else) trended substantially higher in New York than in the South, New York dealers bristled at the inequity. To substantiate their insistence, the manufacturers usually pointed to successful instances in other retail sectors. They said every kid in America knows where to get a hamburger—McDonald's. The dealers might point out that the costs of hamburgers and cars didn't compare so easily. However, the manufacturers' logic held a ring of truth. Ford might argue incessantly with dealers over the color of the parts bins in the back of the store, but the compliance and discipline paid off for everybody. Accordingly, as long as the markets held up, the cars sold, and the profits rolled in, the manufacturers and the dealers stayed locked in an effective, if uneasy, alliance.

The first major jolt to the status quo occurred in October 1973. The Arab–Israeli War tore the entire tenuous global and domestic situation to pieces. The Arab states, furious at the Israeli victory and the images of the Egyptian army starving in the Sinai, raised the price of the crude oil, resulting in a catastrophic doubling of retail gasoline prices. By December 1973, gas shot to over sixty cents per gallon throughout most of the United States. The costs of driving and car ownership became almost unmanageable. Household budgets simply couldn't handle the jolt. Correspondingly, with much less disposable income, car sales ground to a halt. Not that customers would have wanted to buy the cars the domestic manufacturers had on offer anyway; at the time of the Arab oil embargo, the US fleet of cars manufactured by GM, Ford, and Chrysler averaged about 13.5 miles per gallon in normal driving conditions. In short, owning a car was almost insanity; actually driving it was pure lunacy. Worse, the domestic manufacturers had almost no plans for smaller, more economical models. More importantly, the entire US economic model was shocked from normalcy to abject panic; since so much of what happened in the United States depended on the low, stable price of oil, everything was disrupted. So much manufacturing, aside from cars, depended on petroleum. Suddenly it cost twice as much to heat and operate a home, a school, a hospital, or a factory, even when the oil was available. On the motoring front, drivers, their faces betraying sheer panic, began to queue for gas even when their tanks were nowhere near empty.

Now fast-forward forty-five years. Adapt or change. The line seems a bit trite, but that is exactly what the American automobile industry did. The really good dealers rolled up their sleeves, put on their thinking caps, and worked through the trauma to the point where they could survive on used-car sales, coupled with aggressive service and parts marketing. They also forged new relationships with their captives and the banks and learned to play ball (better) with the manufacturers. In the almost fifty years since the shock of 1973, the American car dealer has prevailed through three more subsequent minor recessions, the 9/11 crisis, the Great Recession of 2008, and the rise of China as a rival to the United States for economic superiority. During that time, the US new-car dealer count decreased by almost a third, the price of an average new car more than quadrupled, and the number of new-vehicle nameplates available in the United States grew significantly. Technology, both in the vehicles themselves and in the processes of manufacturing and selling them, has proceeded at a mind-boggling pace. Finally, the automotive world, particularly retail, has probably changed forever with the onset of the 2019 coronavirus. Good automobile dealers, more so than any other segment of US industry except the tech-driven giants such as Google, Amazon, and others, deserve a tip of the hat for not only surviving but also thriving. Whether the current US dealer model survives for another forty or fifty years depends on how the dealers and their manufacturing partners react to the onslaught of electric technology, government regulation, Chinese competition, and a precarious global financial situation.

CHAPTER 6

THE DEALERS (PART II)

After the country and the industry had recovered somewhat from the 1991 and 1992 recessions, certain events threw a new kink into the industry and the factory-dealer relationship. Enter the public company. Around 1995 a new fat cat began to prowl the alley. Wayne Huizenga, the president of a successful waste management company, perceived an opportunity and pounced on it. As dealer profitability was recovering nicely and car sales entered the first stage of a long, successful increase, Huizenga recognized that consolidating a group of dealerships into one great big business concern could conceivably create economies of scale that would generate mountains of cash. His problem: The amount of capital required to purchase a dealership, let alone four or five or six, constituted a huge undertaking. Yet, he didn't have to look far to find other sharp cats to prowl the alley with him.

Wall Street, recovering even more splendidly than the car business from the recent recessions, was bursting with tough, talented folks on the lookout for ways to make more money quicker than by simply buying and selling common stocks of blue-chip companies. Huizenga gathered a handful of these like-minded go-getters around him, and collectively they built a model for approaching large, profitable new-car dealers who owned several prime franchises and offering to buy all their dealerships. Since Huizenga did not have that much freely available money for the venture and, like many entrepreneurs, detested using his own funds for the purpose, his army of aggressive Wall Street types and clever finance experts presented the idea of enlisting open equity markets, state and municipal pension funds, and other well-heeled individual investors for the means to make the project happen. The investors would receive stock in the holding company that would own the collection of dealerships Huizenga and his buddies would buy. The dealers would receive millions of dollars, some in cash and some in stock in the new entity, and since neither Huizenga nor his buddies had any car experience, the dealers would be induced to stay on to operate the dealerships, with a large stipend, stock options, and the ability to continue overseeing what had been their own stores.

In theory the concept thrilled all involved. The parent company would issue shares of stock and deal with all the Securities and Exchange Commission requirements—oversight, 10-K reports, earnings, and analysts calls. Huizenga planned to use his existing Waste Management, Inc. as the immediate vehicle to execute his plan. Through Huizenga's management and business acumen, the company had, over the years, lent some order to the truncated waste disposal business. From that framework, Huizenga and his partners founded Republic Industries. Overnight the new venture garnered significant attention in the automotive press, great interest from dealers, and even greater interest from Wall Street's slew of investors flush with cash, all looking for an investment vehicle that might produce a lot of dividends.

The business model appealed to a certain kind of dealer: an entrepreneur who had built a platform of profitable dealerships, reached a certain comfortable age and station in life, remained passionate about the business, but—most importantly—had no viable succession plan. This type of dealer knew that the auto business at some point would fall into another recession. This type of dealer had no heirs or, if they did, had deemed them either uninterested or unsuitable. These children may have already worked for the family business but shown no real passion. Worse, even if enthusiastic, the dealer may have found them totally inept and probably not fit to succeed.

Most manufacturers' standard dealer agreements provide for a successor addendum, which can name a successor to the business *subject to the express approval of the manufacturer*. Many grown children of successful dealers across all brands prove rather capable individuals who have been through the National Automobile Dealers Association Academy and perhaps even graduated from one of the fine colleges specific to the automotive industry, such as Northwood Institute in Midland, Michigan. In many cases, these particular potential heirs have had the advantage of working in different departments in the dealerships that comprise the family business. Even better, the dealer might have sent them to work for another dealer to learn the business.

On the other hand, some dealers have offspring who are born on third base and think they hit a home run. Even beyond the money and the chance to go through several new cars in a year, these individuals are usually coddled and not necessarily properly trained by the dealers themselves. They enter the business as a general manager with the idea that they are going to inherit a thriving business when the dealer dies. Within the manufacturer ranks, these individuals have acquired various labels of derision, such as "idiot son syndrome" and "lucky sperm club." In many cases, the dealer loves their child and probably harbors the latent hope that this individual will somehow acquire the capability to succeed them. In the best-case scenario, the dealer will employ a general manager or chief of operations who knows the dealer's business intimately and can help their heir reach some level of competency. More often than not, the dealer eventually realizes that they will never get the manufacturer's approval for their less-than-stellar child as a successor.

This type of dealer, who had seen the ups and downs of the business over the years and had amassed a respectable fortune while skillfully and strategically adding new franchises, exemplified a perfect candidate for

Huizenga's model. Since the dealer, already in his late sixties or early seventies, probably had no stomach for another recession, the idea of receiving five or six times the earnings for his business held a lot of appeal. Further, since the dealer had no immediate plans to retire, he could remain as the nominal head of the business and continue to receive stock in the new company simply by signing a noncompete agreement.

A perfect example of this arrangement arose when I served as director of dealer operations at Gulf States Toyota in Houston. Joe Myers, a strong Houston Toyota dealer who also sold Ford and Mitsubishi, had recently added Mazda when I was with that franchise in 1990. When approached by Huizenga, Myers ranked as one of the best dealers for the Gulf States distributor. All his stores made good money, and with the exception of Mitsubishi, he represented well-respected franchises, though he could claim no discernible heirs in the business. In his early seventies, he actively operated all his dealerships, and while not interested in retiring just yet, he knew the Huizenga offer might be too good not to consider.

At Gulf States Toyota, we warily viewed this development. We were not accustomed to public company ownership of a dealership. Even the most experienced among us had trouble getting our arms around the concept. Jerry Pyle, the president of Gulf States Toyota and the smartest wholesale guy I ever met, convened a meeting in his office at the distributor's headquarters. We had many issues to consider: How would the transaction be structured? Exactly who would own what portion of the Toyota store we were concerned with? Most importantly, who would ultimately be in charge, and who would be the ultimate decision-maker on day-to-day business decisions on behalf of the Toyota store?

Pyle conferenced in Bill Plourde, the general counsel of Toyota Motor Sales, USA, Inc., in Torrance, California, to address our apprehensions. Pyle detailed for Plourde all our misgivings while the rest of us furiously took notes. We did not want to squash a great opportunity for Myers, but neither did we want to see the control of one of our finest dealerships pass to a bunch of Wall Street suits with no working knowledge of the business. Further, would Huizenga stop at Myers? Gulf States Toyota could boast a number of dealers who presented the same kind of opportunity that Myers did for Huizenga: Jay Marks, Sterling McCall, and Fred Haas in Houston; Jimmy Cavender and Red McCombs in San Antonio; Steve Fox and Bob Hoy in El Paso; and Price LeBlanc in Louisiana. As Pyle went down the list, we all felt the same unease. In a manner as polished and analytical as Pyle's, Plourde noted all our concerns and asked if we had received any buy/sell notices involving Huizenga's desire to purchase any of the other dealerships Pyle had mentioned. Upon hearing that we had not, Plourde recommended that we take one step at a time, give Huizenga and Myers a chance to lay out the entire plan, and find out all we could not only about Huizenga and his group but also about their proposed business model. As it happened, Gulf States Toyota was not the only outfit with these concerns—Huizenga was approaching dozens of dealers around the country.

Pyle, quick as ever, recognized new territory. Accordingly, he enlisted a team of experts, mostly highly esteemed business school professors and economists. By this time Huizenga's model had attracted the interest and attention of some of the finest business minds in the country, so Pyle's dream team was much more aware of the business and financial implications than we were. Most of their questions to us sailed way above our heads; as day-to-day operational car guys, we did not deal with Wall Street. For over an hour, we and the experts talked at completely different levels. They wanted our ideas on how the "rollups" (their coinage for the bundling together of a number of dealerships) would affect the overall industry; we simply wanted to know their ideas on how it would influence our dealerships' operations and our current business model. The conversation became a classic example of trying to meld complicated business strategy in theory with our own narrow-minded interest in preserving the business as we knew it and how we intuitively knew it worked at that time.

About the time we made the collective decision to allow the transaction to proceed, we began getting reports from Myers and his people about how less and less attractive the entire opportunity looked to them. To start, Republic could not give Myers a clear answer on what he would receive for his platform of dealerships or how much would be in cash versus stock. Further, while Myers had been told that he would retain nominal control and decision-making in his stores, the big money decisions would actually be made by platform managers controlled by Republic. What's more, Republic irked Myers with their constant requests for all his dealerships' financial statements, the stores' tax returns, his personal tax returns, employee background checks (and not only on Myers but also on his key managers), and the very latest performance reports on all the stores.

According to those closest to Myers, Huizenga's people called him at all hours of the day and night for all these voluminous records. Since nobody can keep a lid on this type of development, Myers was also being bombarded by his own people, who were reading newspapers and trade magazines that described the business model in general and his transaction with Republic in particular. Finally, Myers and his team were getting tired of answering some of the dumber, more mundane operational questions from Huizenga's suits. As he realized that Huizenga's folks, including some of the people who had been tapped to run the Myers platform, had no earthly idea of how to run a dealership, Myers decided to chuck the whole proposition. His businesses were beginning to suffer as his employees became more anxious about the transaction and took their eyes off the day-to-day business. As Myers eventually told Pyle, the perceived payoff would not warrant the pain of enduring the process—particularly since Republic never could seem to tell him how much money he would earn or how much control he would actually retain.

Not one to dwell on a little setback, Huizenga pressed his other candidates around the country. He found plenty of takers. Dealers who had worked a lifetime building their businesses liked the idea of a substantial guaranteed final payoff. They took the cash and the stock, ceded most control to Huizenga's managers, signed noncompete agreements, and resigned themselves to staying on in their own stores in an advisory capacity for several years. Interestingly enough, many of them got right back into the ownership of dealerships once their noncompete agreements concluded.

In the end, the business model itself held an attraction many dealers couldn't resist. Sterling McCall, Gulf States Toyota's top dealer, accomplished one of the earliest sustained successes by uniting with Mike Smith in Beaumont, Texas, and Bob Howard in Oklahoma City to form Group 1 Automotive. The three dealers shrewdly recruited Ben Hollingsworth, a Houston businessman who had managed to roll up most of the profitable funeral homes in the country. They recognized Ben Hollingsworth's significant experience and deft connections to Wall Street. Group 1's acquisitions of worthy dealership platforms over the years have continued to this day under the brilliant management and direction of Earl Hesterberg, a former Ford and Nissan executive who served for a year as head of Gulf States Toyota after Pyle's retirement. Almost twenty-five years after its founding, using many of the concepts pioneered by Huizenga and his team, Group 1 Automotive remains one of the most successful public companies, if not the largest.

Not to be outdone, and mindful of the achievements of Huizenga and Group 1, other dealers backed by savvy finance types and businessmen became notable names in the ranks of public company ownership. Sid DeBoer, a Chrysler dealer in Medford, Oregon, founded Lithia, another of the leading public stock dealership groups. In Charlotte, North Carolina, Bruton Smith, already a known name in racing and a fine dealer for several brands, presided over the founding and expansion of Sonic Automotive. Luther Coggins, a major dealer presence in the southeastern US, teamed with some high-powered Wall Street types to create the United Auto Group, which eventually was acquired and brilliantly expanded by Roger Penske, one of the savviest automotive and general business entrepreneurs in the country. Asbury Automotive, one of the most visible automotive groups in the Southeast, expanded with astute acquisitions throughout the rest of the country under the keen management of several CEOs: Charles Oglesby, Craig Monaghan, and David Hult. Republic eventually became AutoNation and, through a number of highly visible acquisitions, now controls over three hundred individual dealer outlets in the United States. All told, the big players—AutoNation, Group 1, Sonic Automotive, Lithia, Penske Automotive, and Asbury—currently own and operate some one thousand retail dealerships in the United States.

Though they seemed scary at first, the public company rollups have had positive impacts on the automotive industry. Aside from the impressive economies of scale—purchasing power and the ability to negotiate very favorable terms from banks, captives, and municipal governments—the publics have had some beneficial effects on the manufacturers themselves. In many cases the publics purchased many dealers who otherwise might have presented real problems for the manufacturers. Uncooperative or nonperforming dealers, or a combination of the two, can irritate and thwart manufacturers to no end. When the publics buy a private dealer group that performs poorly but includes great brands such as Ford, Toyota, or Honda, the manufacturers rejoice. However, the current love-hate relationship of some manufacturers with their publicly owned dealerships remains complicated by the fact that the publics command considerable funds. Most manufacturers, particularly the Japanese, are overly impressed with the publics' ability to go on the open equity markets, raise $25 or $50 million in the space of a few days from institutional investors, and then, with a stroke of a pen, acquire a dealership platform of twelve to fifteen rooftops representing ten or eleven brands. In short, the publics have assumed outsize influence and power.

The larger ones actually like to think they can control individual manufacturers or entire geographic markets. The manufacturers get uncomfortable when a public company acquires too many dealerships representing their brand or brands. For example, all the public companies love the Toyota brand. The brand represents a lot of volume opportunity, the cars are reliable and sell well, and Toyota, besides being the largest import brand in the United States, has proven the most financially stable among all brands. In turn, Toyota likes being liked, but if a public company acquires too many Toyota dealerships in a certain market, or if the public's ownership of enough dealerships in a certain market entails control over a certain percentage of Toyota's total volume in that market or geography, the manufacturer might invoke a framework agreement on the public company. They intend to limit the manufacturer's exposure to any downside the public may eventually represent and to restrict the public's control over the brand's distribution channel in that geography.

The latter purpose is perfectly understandable. If a single entity controls most of the volume in a certain geography, that entity might demand a more favorable allocation of vehicles from the brand or even more favorable treatment from the brand's captive. The former reason is a little more complicated. If the public company sours on a brand while being in control of a disproportionate number of stores or the brand's volume in a certain market, the brand will feel threatened. (The concept is not that different from one person in a crowded room catching the coronavirus: If one person catches it, many others are likely to catch it as well.) This relationship "souring" occurs in actual practice, and the effect can be devastating for a brand. When Nissan took a dive in late 2018, the result on the brand's retailers in the United States was disastrous. Nissan and Infiniti dealers began dropping their Nissan and Infiniti stores en masse.

Similarly, second- and third-tier manufacturers are usually not too thrilled when a public company purchases a dealer group that has one or more of the brand's stores. Let's say, for example, that a public company is purchasing a midsize dealer platform that includes Ford, Toyota, Honda, VW, and Kia. The public company will most assuredly want Ford, Toyota, Honda, and perhaps even VW, which is notoriously difficult to deal with and almost impossible to make money with (as VW has the curious characteristic of being very successful around the rest of the world but not so much in the United States). VW, still, may have some cachet with the automotive public company because it is one of the most recognizable brands in the world, and the fixed operations opportunity could be viable.

However, the public company may not want Kia at all, which had been the case up until 2020. The selling dealer, usually quite anxious to get some value out of their second-or third-tier Asian franchise, might tell the public company that Kia's in the deal, or the whole deal is off. This stipulation creates a problem for the public, slight though it may be. The public company bites its lip and agrees to take on Kia but tells the seller that it will pay no premium for taking Kia, knowing full well that they will either terminate Kia once the overall transaction finalizes or sell the Kia franchise upon the acquisition of the selling dealer's platform. Kia then becomes a "tuck in," if for no other reason than to keep the transaction from falling apart, since Ford, Toyota, and Honda are profitable franchises in any market. No wonder lower-tier franchises such as Mitsubishi and Kia dread a transaction that involves a public company as a buyer.

Not that premier marquees are always desirable. The public company may like the prestige of a high-volume Toyota or Honda store or the foreign allure of BMW or Porsche, but the public company is always conscious of the extraordinary demands of the manufacturers for bigger and better facilities and just pure control. Nevertheless, in the end the marquee brand almost always wins out: The public company, impressed with the profitability of the marquee brand, will shake its head, grumble a lot, try to secure some concessions on branding elements or the promise of another franchise from the brand, and go to its syndicated, revolving credit arrangement and pull down $10 million for the construction.

On the manufacturer's end, the public company becomes a welcome savior if it is buying an uncooperative or poorly performing dealer. Over time, however, the manufacturer may view the public with a jaundiced eye. Some publics gain negative notoriety for revolving-door managers or stifling business rules, such as hard-and-fast strictures for price range or models of cars the local dealer-manager is allowed to order, or a prohibition against many factory programs. Worse, in the course of building or renovating a dealership to the manufacturer's specific standards and identity, the public almost always requests deviations from standards of materials, furniture, fixtures, case goods, tile, lighting, and facility layout. Invariably these irritating (from the manufacturer's standpoint) tugs-of-war filter down to inconvenient—and perhaps unfair—special treatment on order requirements, wholesale program objectives, marketing funds, and service and parts marketing programs. In the final analysis, the manufacturers seek to apply some uniformity in branding and operations, while the public companies want to have control and at the same time play off the brand's cachet. Accordingly, these small battles can often exasperate the manufacturer's regional or zone staff. Many times, manufacturer requests are referred up the chain to the public's headquarters because the local dealership managers and even the platform managers have very little decision-making power. The manufacturers will then seethe at the attempts of the public entity to fold their brand into the public's brand. Nothing will make a manufacturer's vice president of marketing more pissed off than seeing his brand folded into an AutoNation ad featuring several other brands in the same half- or full-page spot. To sum up, the public companies are specialists in having their cake and eating it too.

At the other end of the spectrum, one egregiously unfair aspect of the factory-dealer relationship has become common across public companies, as well as private dealerships: When a certain secondary brand hits the skids, that is, is no longer popular or selling well or has an overall negative perception in the industry, most dealers, public or private, are likely to give the brand much less attention and fewer resources. For what seemed like forever, low-volume brands such as VW, Kia, and Mitsubishi had a terrible time maintaining dealer support and dealer count because their volumes were so low. Any dealer, public or private, with their eye toward expense control and return on investment is likely to jam these brands together into a poorly maintained facility, in a poorly situated location, staffed by poorly trained personnel. Eventually, they will enter the wicked spiral toward oblivion. Also at play is the idea that even the lowest-ranking franchise has some value; a dealer with a bad brand, or a store that performs poorly, may hang on to it for dear life if they think they can wring some value out of it by selling it to some other operator.

However, a privately held dealership with one store of a "bad" brand may simply terminate the brand. Let's say it's one dealership in a small-to-intermediate market whose sales have been negligible. Almost any manufacturer can stomach an isolated termination; in a marginal market, the manufacturer may even welcome such streamlining. Yet with the public companies, the effect of a brand's precipitous decline has much more serious consequences. As touched on earlier, Nissan offers an illustrative example: Since the early 1990s, particularly since the inception of their Infiniti brand, Nissan has experienced more ups and downs than any other brand; to borrow from the old Jerry Reed song, "When you're hot, you're hot, and when you're not, you're not." Nissan, historically, from a volume standpoint, has usually been the second- or third-volume import in the United States. When they're on their game, they're great; when they suck, they suck really bad. When they suck really bad, their dealers tend to sell or terminate the franchise.

Accordingly, when Nissan sucks really bad, a public company, heavy into Nissan or Infiniti and aware of how Wall Street will view its next quarterly 10-K report, will also consider jettisoning the brand, either via selling it to some unsuspecting dealer or terminating the franchise altogether. At the risk of dear reader thinking that I'm picking on Nissan, be advised that this misfortune could happen to any brand. For example, if a public company has twenty or thirty rooftops of a specific brand that has hit snake-shit levels and therefore makes a sound, conscious decision to get rid of all stores of that brand, whether via sale or termination, that strategic move becomes bad news for that brand. Overall, a bad brand is a bad brand, whether held publicly or privately, though bigger-name public companies do seem to take quicker, more drastic measures to cut their losses because of a bad brand. In the final extremity, a brand making money for the dealership will be retained, while a nonperforming brand will be discarded if it commits the cardinal sin of being unprofitable.

Nevertheless, the public companies have solidified their place in the industry. Quirky operational issues aside, they simply are too big, have too much money, and possess too much scale for anyone to ignore, particularly the executive management of manufacturers under the spell of big money and the impressive number of units a public company can move when they are in sync with the brand and on their game. Private dealers, particularly those nearing retirement and thus seeking an exit strategy or looking for a big payday, like the idea of the public companies for those very reasons. The downside, however, is that soon only the public companies and another class of dealers, which I will discuss shortly, will be about the only ones left anymore who can buy anything. Although the publics have tried hard to differentiate themselves from private dealers and each other, in the end they are governed by the same state franchise laws and regulations that hold sway over a mom-and-pop dealership. An AutoNation Toyota store in an intermediate market has, under the law, no more and no fewer protections than a privately held, much smaller Toyota store in the same market. The main difference lies in economies of scale. The publicly held store is part of an organization that can negotiate with a janitorial service, office supply store, oil and grease vendor, computer company, the banks, or virtually any other vendor. Perhaps an editorial writer in the February 15, 2021, issue of *Automotive News* said it best: "Larger retail groups may have advantages of scale that align with consumers' hunger for a quick, uniform sales process. But continued and accelerated consolidation may also lead to a sea change in an industry built by entrepreneurs and their families—innovative retail competitors with deep ties to their communities."* In short, despite the

---

* Editorial, "Digital Demands Squeeze Smaller Auto Retailers," *Automotive News*, February 15, 2021, https://www.autonews.com/editorial/digital-demands-squeeze-smaller-auto-retailers/.

appeal of the publics, many in the industry still believe that customers, employees, and communities are best served by private dealers.

Finally, the public companies have had one more major, lasting effect on the industry. With their ability to obtain money in great quantities and under vastly favorable terms, the publics have unleashed a financial genie that can never be put back in the bottle. The high prices that the publics have been able to pay for desirable dealerships and platforms have totally skewed and revalued, albeit mostly inadvertently, the price tag for any dealership that might be put on the market. In other words, the stupid money syndrome has had a waterfall effect on the perceived price of any single-point, single-franchise dealership anywhere, artificially raising the price of admission for any private operator wishing to get into the new-car business. In 1979, I was able to put a Chrysler dealer into business in Louisiana for $75,000 plus the price of signs and parts. The same transaction now, even if the proposed dealer has viable property and owns a building on the land, would cost a minimum of about $4 million. This price tag includes branding the facility, stocking new inventory, purchasing an initial order of parts and special tools, and acquiring enough used cars, staff, oil and grease, computer hardware, dealer licensing, and municipal permits to be able to open the doors.

To be very frank, the automotive world has gotten itself into one hell of a shape in the United States.

CHAPTER 7

THE DEALERS (PART III)

In the never-never land between privately held, family-owned dealerships and the public companies reside a handful of players very similar to the public companies but which remain privately held. These in-between players are the private equity firms that have borrowed the acquisition playbook from the public companies but do not issue stock, which means they don't have to worry about the Securities and Exchange Commission, the Federal Trade Commission, or a host of other three-letter federal agencies that tend to make businesses nervous. Many of the acquisition and operational aspects are similar to the behavior of the publics, so much so that they present the same challenges that the publics present to the manufacturers, the selling dealers, and the public at large. The private equity firms look for highly profitable dealership platforms that include high-volume brands (usually mass-market Asian brands, esteemed European nameplates such as Mercedes, BMW, and Land Rover) and maybe GM, Ford, or Chrysler-Dodge-Jeep-Ram dealerships. (Since Chrysler sells so few cars, the lure is usually Jeep, which generates irresistible mountains of cash when the market is good.)

Like the public companies, the private equity firms like to use OPM (again, "other people's money") to roll up their acquisitions. Depending on the private equity firm, this could mean a group of large, well-heeled commercial banks. The private equity company is usually smart enough to include in its acquisition and organizational teams some experienced car guys and gals to help guide them through the process. Many times these talented individuals are retirees from Ford, GM, Chrysler, or the larger imports, and unlike the suits usually employed by the publics, these folks can read a dealership's financial statements and apply commercially reasonable values to a privately held dealership's assets (both real estate and franchise). Best of all, they know the manufacturers' approval process and can help the private equity firm maneuver through the morass of factory requirements and applicable state motor vehicle rules. Keep in mind, the suits are still there; they deal with the banks through which the private equity firm draws its funds for the acquisition and capitalization of the new enterprise. They also set up complex revolving credit arrangements, usually with large regional banks and, occasionally, with an oddball manufacturer's captive that finds the pending transaction mighty attractive. Because the private equity firm has no recognition value in the selling dealer's market, it usually retains the selling dealer's name and may even retain the selling dealer in an advisory capacity.

Technically, the private equity firm appeared on the scene about five years before the emergence of the public companies. In the early nineties, Warburg Pincus and a slick Wall Street investor named Ernie Pomerantz purchased a prominent Bay Area group called Val Stroh that represented several brands, mostly Japanese imports. Shortly after consolidating this platform, the group made a play for a highly respected Kansas City dealership group that included Chevrolet and Mazda. Since I was Mazda's regional dealer development manager at the time, I came face-to-face with Pomerantz and the other private equity representative, Robert Johnson. Pomerantz and Johnson had the good sense to bring with them their proposed operator for the Kansas City platform they were about to purchase. Charles Oglesby had a long and successful career in the car business and had been tapped by

Warburg Pincus to operate and expand the Johnson County imports platform. Seated in our conference room at Mazda's Gulf Region in Sugar Land, Texas, I asked Pomerantz point-blank why a successful Wall Street fellow like himself would leave the easy money of the New York Stock Exchange and decide to play with a car dealership. He pursed his lips and responded, slowly, "We think the returns offered by a well-run dealership group would be equal to or better than any other investment in equities we can make at this time." Johnson agreed, stating that their recent Val Stroh acquisition in the Bay Area looked very promising and that they were already looking beyond the Johnson County acquisition.

The most impressive of the three, Oglesby, grew clearly bored by the investment talk and intermittently looked askance at both Pomerantz and Johnson. However, I sensed the checked energy beneath Oglesby's nonchalant facade. In fact, the more I paid attention, the more he looked like a racehorse just dying to get out of the gate. I realized then that all Oglesby wanted to do was sell cars and make money. Although Oglesby, based on the configuration that Johnson and Pomerantz laid out for me, would have some ownership in the new platform, he couldn't have cared less. He wanted to focus on operations and expanding those operations, not on the back-end deals. From my standpoint the transaction was pretty run of the mill. One successful dealer was selling to a new group, and since Oglesby would be the on-site go-to guy, Mazda had no issue with the overall transaction.

The Johnson County and Val Stroh transactions were not the only private equity deals that Warburg Pincus made, but they were the most visible to me. Over time, however, even in the private equity configuration, the suits began to outweigh the car folks in importance. The suits were very much like the suits in the public company realm—Wall Street types who thought that a collection of dealerships could be run like a blue-chip company, when in fact dealerships are very much retail, customer-facing businesses. Oglesby didn't last long in this environment; he left soon afterward to run dealerships for a strong retail platform in Warner Robins,

Georgia. The collection of dealerships rolled up by Johnson, Pomerantz, and Warburg Pincus eventually was sold to private dealers, the most notable of whom was Rick Hendrick.

Years later, when I was the dealer development manager in Porsche's Area South, Dave Kurtz, the Area South vice president, and I were visiting with Hendrick and his chief financial officer, Ed Brown, at their headquarters in Charlotte, North Carolina. Somehow the conversation veered toward Hendrick's acquisition of the old Warburg Pincus dealerships several years before. The acquisition of these stores helped propel Hendrick to his status of the largest privately held dealer group in the United States at the time. Hendrick noted that turning these stores around mightily taxed him and his organization. Brown added that those stores had been so poorly managed over the years that, depending on the platform and the brands involved, he and Hendrick needed two to four years to rehabilitate them. Brown further noted that the pure car guys and gals in the private equity groups were solid citizens. He said, "The Wall Street suit guys and the bankers really screwed 'em up," which was a bold comment coming from a guy like Brown, who had held a high position at Bank of America in Charlotte before joining Hendrick Automotive Group.

As tough a time as the private equity groups had in the market, the concept still held a lot of luster for some operators. For example, after Group 1 Automotive purchased the dealerships of Ira Rosenberg in Boston, Ira's son, David Rosenberg, waited out his noncompete agreement until he could dive back into the retail auto business. While David had made out quite well on Group 1's purchase of his family's dealerships, he was a car guy and not content to sit around and count his money. Also, as a car guy, he was not going to jump back in using only his money. Accordingly, David Rosenberg formed Prime Automotive Group with GPB Capital Holdings, LLC, a New York–based self-styled alternative asset management firm specializing in acquiring income-producing private companies. The most visible of these companies were new-car dealerships. David Rosenberg supplied the car-guy knowledge, and GPB provided the bulk of the private equity. For over a year, Prime Automotive Group ran like a top, fueled by David's know-how and GPB's financial connections. By the end of 2019, Prime had over fifty dealerships representing over two dozen brands with five regional platforms spread across the northeastern US generating almost $3.2 billion in revenue, according to a September 17, 2019, article in *Automotive News* by Melissa Burden.

Something this good, growing this fast, and making so much money is bound to get a lot of attention, but the attention that Prime and GPB received was not the kind of attention either of them sought. By 2020 GPB had ousted David Rosenberg and had become the subject of several investigations, including by the Federal Bureau of Investigation, the Securities and Exchange Commission, and the Secretary of State of the Commonwealth of Massachusetts, who alleged that GPB had misled Massachusetts investors. Massachusetts also alleged that GPB had failed to disclose its ties to a shady broker/dealer who pitched GPB funds to other brokers and retail investors. GPB denied the allegations, but by that time it was too late; David Rosenberg had already sued GPB over his concern with GPB's investment practices but primarily to protect his stake in Prime Automotive Group. The whole mess was further complicated by Rosenberg's request for an injunction to ensure that GPB set aside enough money to buy out his share in Prime.

To muddy the water even more, Toyota and at least one other brand moved to strip Prime of its portfolio of Toyota dealerships, maintaining that Rosenberg's ouster by GPB violated Prime's dealer agreement with Toyota. As 2020 drew to a close, the suits and countersuits involving Rosenberg, Prime, the brands it represented, the federal government, the Secretary of State of Massachusetts, and regulators in the eight states where Prime had dealership platforms were still playing out in a number of local, state, and federal courts, even as Prime sought to divest itself of some of its most recent dealership acquisitions. Overall, the case marked a precipitous fall from grace for an automotive group that had ranked fifteenth in the top 150 automotive groups in the United States at the end of 2018.*

However, such is the allure of potential big money that dealers will look into any vehicle that can offer them a substantial return or provide a lucrative exit from the business. Accordingly, on March 1, 2021, *Automotive News* included an article by Melissa Burden, "In SPACs, dealers see a viable option to go public", concerning special-purpose acquisition companies (SPACs). Not surprisingly, the SPACs seem to have originated more among accountants and consultants than from private equity firms as we know them or even from the dealer acquisition and merger firms, of which there seems to be no end. Ms. Burden's article also proclaimed that going public with a SPAC could not only provide quicker access to capital for a dealership group to buy more platforms or pay down debt but also shorten the process of going public by months.†

At the time of this writing, we can't predict how many dealership groups would want to avail themselves of a SPAC; however, with dealerships just coming off a record year of profitability for 2020 and with the amount of money successful car platforms command, some accountants believe the potential is there. The SPACs emerged in late 2019 as a number of businesses, such as electric vehicle manufacturers and used-vehicle start-ups, appeared and went public. Some accountants surmise the SPACs are specifically interested in dealership groups because of the 2020 financial results. Indeed, the high stock prices of some of the public groups and Wall Street's interest in the big six public entities (Lithia, AutoNation, Group 1, Asbury, Penske, and Sonic), as well as in public used-vehicle disrupters, have the market stirred up. Most of us in the industry believe that a dealership group would need a couple of dozen stores to provide the scale necessary to make going public via a SPAC make sense. Moreover, some consultants assert that

---

* Melissa Burden, "GPB Capital Names Westfall Interim CEO of Prime Automotive, Removes Rosenberg," *Automotive News*, September 17, 2019, https://www.autonews.com/dealers/gpb-capital-names-westfall-interim-ceo-prime-automotive-removes-rosenberg/.

† Melissa Burden, "In SPACs, dealers see viable option to go public," *Automotive News*, March 1, 2021, https://www.autonews.com/dealers/spacs-dealers-see-viable-option-go-public/.

SPACs, particularly those attracted to platforms strong in digital retailing, could make a future wave of consolidation possible. In any case the big six public groups could soon be joined by a host of upstarts.

SPACs generally must acquire a platform or merge with a company going public within two years, but with dealers flush with cash after strong 2020 and 2021 performances, many available targets abound. Yet some dealership groups are wary. While the accountants and consultants could be absolutely giddy over the prospects (since they stand to make a big payday for a successful acquisition), privately held dealer groups still face the prospect of working with the "suits." Also, the issue of approvability by the manufacturers looms. Manufacturers, some of whom privately grumble about working with less-transparent public entities, want to know where every investment nickel is coming from, and they're deeply interested in who will have operational control of the individual stores representing their brands. Another possible negative would involve answering to a board of directors, shareholders, regulators, and a whole phalanx of accounting specialists and auditors. Few dedicated private dealers relish the thought of adding that kind of complexity to their lives. Some advisors caution that SPACs may not be the right choice for some dealerships, but they could be a perfect option for private equity firms looking to invest in the retail business by partnering with good dealers who have good relationships with strong manufacturers.

Some entities trying to enter the auto business are just plain mysterious. In October 2020, when I was the senior dealer development manager for Kia's East Region, one of my colleagues in the California Retail Development Department asked me what I thought about a company called LMP. Since I pride myself in keeping up with industry events and trends, I was totally embarrassed when I had to tell him that I had no knowledge of any LMP. This staffer, a great colleague who runs Kia's Retail Development Department at headquarters, was trying to get information on LMP because, through its counsel, LMP had entered into an asset purchase agreement for two of Kia's largest stores in the East: Billy Fuccillo Kia in Cape Coral, Florida, at one time the largest Kia dealer in the country, and Billy Fuccillo Kia in Port Charlotte, Florida. My antennae immediately went up because the Fuccillo organization also owned and operated three high-volume Kia stores in Kia's East Region in upstate New York. Curious, I started doing my homework. LMP, I discovered, was a vehicle subscription service company that also retailed used cars and had gone public in December 2019 with the idea of rolling up several dozen new-car dealerships. Beyond a very cursory description of the company itself and a list of the officers, none of whom I knew, I could find out little more about LMP.

A few days later, I received a call from my Kia dealer development colleague in Kia's Southeast Region office in Atlanta. Since the Fuccillo stores in play were in Florida, and he was now facing the prospect of these two high-volume stores going to new owners he knew nothing about, he was justifiably concerned and was gigging me for the same information my California colleague had asked for the previous week. I couldn't tell him much beyond the meager facts I'd found. However, he was doubly concerned because not only was LMP attempting to buy the Fuccillo stores, but it was also looking to purchase 85 percent stakes in two Kia dealerships in West Virginia. Based on the respective asset purchase agreements, the Florida transaction with both stores merged together was for \$68.5 million, while the West Virginia transactions were to be purchased by LMP for \$24.6 million.

Wow, I thought, *surely these guys aren't serious*. Not many people in the car business run around with \$90 million in their pocket. I asked my colleague in Atlanta where LMP was getting the money, and he said, "They say they're paying cash," to which I replied, "Bullshit." Then I asked him, in the course of his conversations with LMP to date, if the three Fuccillo stores in New York had been similarly targeted by LMP. He answered no but said that the rumor was LMP intended to roll up as many as a couple of dozen dealerships around the country.

The following week I learned that LMP had entered into an asset purchase agreement with the Atlantic Auto Group for at least sixteen of that group's dealerships. My alarm bells went off for a couple of reasons. First, John Staluppi, the owner of the Atlantic Auto Group, is one of the most successful and best-known automobile dealers in the United States. Second, Staluppi owns a Kia dealership in Huntington, New York, and at the time this news broke, my boss and I were in negotiations with Staluppi to award him a new Kia dealership in Bay Shore, New York. Finally, to add more complexity to the picture, the total deal was said to be worth over $700 million. I drank heavily that night.

The next day, a Sunday, I received a panicked text from my boss asking what I knew about LMP and whether the Huntington store and the Bay Shore Open Point were included in the Atlantic Auto Group-LMP deal. When I got hold of my contact in Staluppi's organization, he emphatically declared that neither Huntington nor Bay Shore was involved in the deal. Further, he claimed that while LMP would be in financial control, Staluppi and his management group would retain operational control of the stores involved.

In my experience, whenever a large transaction is proposed in the automobile business, it attracts a lot of attention. When a large deal involving three quarters of a billion dollars appears, it gets *all* the attention. Never mind that the West Virginia deals and the price related thereto included a Hyundai dealership, a Subaru dealership, and two used-car stores. In the Kia world, we began asking ourselves, (1) Where is the money really coming from? and (2) Who is actually going to be in charge of these stores? My boss and I were pretty much off the hook as Staluppi had indicated to us that the Long Island stores were not part of the Atlantic Auto Group-LMP deal. But my colleague in Atlanta, whom I'd hired at Mazda and had known for thirty-five years, still had lots of questions and much work to do. Repeatedly he asked LMP for the sources of the funds. Beyond telling him that the money was there, he got nothing in the way of hard data.

Moreover, in a press release on Friday, October 9, 2020, LMP indicated that the organization would be holding a conference call at 8:30 a.m. Eastern

Time on Monday, October 12, 2020. LMP had informed all the manufacturers involved in the proposed Atlantic Auto Group acquisition that they were moving forward with Atlantic Auto Group and Staluppi on a $688 million deal and that all the manufacturers involved were agreeable to the transaction. This news sounded decidedly odd to me, so I telephoned my counterpart at Hyundai, Dave O'Brien, and asked him what he knew about LMP's proposal since Atlantic Auto Group owned and operated four or five Hyundai stores on Long Island. O'Brien's reaction was much like mine when I heard about the LMP purchase of the Florida Kia stores. "We haven't heard anything from these guys," he said. "Not a call, not a text, not an email, and we sure as hell haven't seen a buy-sell agreement." I reread the LMP press release, which included some curious and interesting bullet points. Primarily, LMP claimed to be adding all kinds of value to the Atlantic Auto Group. After that, the message was all about LMP and how much the company's share price and standing in the financial markets would skyrocket based on the Staluppi transaction.

The LMP chief operating officer mentioned the advantage of Atlantic joining the LMP fold. He gave the Atlantic team a couple of great "attaboys" and, in a patronizing tone, stated that LMP was absolutely giddy at the prospect of taking the already premier retail organization on Long Island to the next level by accelerating their (and, by extension, LMP's) growth and earnings. In true Wall Street fashion, the chief operating officer adamantly declared that LMP believed the acquisition would produce continued revenue and earnings growth for LMP and its shareholders. But the release had nothing—absolutely nothing—about how and why this transaction was good for the manufacturers involved. And the only mention of customers referred to subscription leasing options that LMP would offer. In short, the entire press release read like a nightly business report.*

Accordingly, at 8:29 a.m. Eastern Daylight Time on Monday, October 12, 2020, I dialed into the LMP conference call. Interestingly enough I got a recorded message designating another number to dial into for the actual conference call. To make matters more puzzling, a recorded message on the second line stated that the call would actually be at 8:45 a.m. and offered up a third number from which to join the call. I dialed this third number at 8:45 a.m. and, at 8:46 a.m., finally found myself in the call. The call began with opening comments from the chief financial officer, Evan Bernstein, who basically parroted the press release of the previous Friday. The chief operating officer, Richard Aldahan, did the same. Then ensued several minutes of obligatory Wall Street "fluff" from LMP's chairman and chief executive officer, Sam Tawfik. The group eventually opened the call for questions from any analysts and investors on the line. The first questioner asked LMP how they proposed to pay for all these acquisitions; LMP could not get the least bit specific on how they were paying for *any* of their acquisitions. The second analyst asked the same question; he got pretty much the same answer. The third analyst, with a sharper tone and more exasperation, asked the very same question and received the very same answer. At that point LMP ended the call; I imagine they thought they'd better sign off to avoid further embarrassment.

Again, even though Staluppi had assured us that none of the Kia stores that Atlantic Auto Group was involved with on Long Island were included in the LMP transaction, I still had more than a little interest in this transaction—LMP was actively attempting to acquire two of the largest Kia stores in the Southeast, which were owned by the same guy (our guy) who owned three of the biggest Kia stores in the Northeast. I couldn't discount the fact

---

* Press release, "LMP Automotive Holdings, Inc. Revises Atlantic Automotive Groups Acquisition Agreements to a Combination of Cash and LMPX Stock and Excludes Certain Dealerships in a Deal Valued at $330 Million," LMP Automotive Holdings, Inc. via Yahoo!, January 13, 2021, https://finance.yahoo.com/news/lmp-automotive-holdings-inc-revises-120000946.html?fr=yhssrp_catchall&guccounter=1.

that if LMP was as big a badass as it claimed, it wouldn't hesitate to make a play for those three stores.

On Wednesday, October 14, a colleague at Kia headquarters in California sent me a copy of the asset purchase agreement through which LMP was acquiring the Fuccillo Kia Florida stores. Both stores were lumped into the same buy-sell document, which was unusual but not unheard of. The document read much like any other asset purchase agreement except that it was much longer and dealt with much more money. But it contained absolutely nothing about how LMP proposed to pay for the Fuccillo acquisition.

October bled into November and November into December, and I got so busy with dealer development activities in my own Kia East Region that I didn't have much time to pay attention to LMP anymore. Then on January 13, 2021, I received an email from my Kia colleague from the Southeast Region asking me to take a look at a "credit agreement" between LMP and several well-known banks, the largest of which was Truist Bank. Basically, LMP was putting together a revolving credit facility to finance the transaction. The document was remarkable in its complexity and length (123 pages). Even more remarkable, it began with thirty-seven pages of definitions. I read the entire dossier, though I generally can only scan such tripe. When I finished, I had to come to the conclusion that LMP apparently was investing none of its own money. I emailed my colleague, "Looks like a big, revolving, syndicated bank arrangement similar to what Sonic or Group 1 would work up with a range of banks (to spread the 'risk'), except that at this point Truist is the only bank." Incredibly, in the end, Kia headquarters approved the Florida and West Virginia transactions. The Staluppi transaction in New York, however, died a very abrupt and quiet death. We never knew for certain why, but the nine-figure price tag and LMP's inability to come up with the real money almost certainly had a lot to do with it. By August 2022, LMP was in the process of liquidation.

As the story of LMP suggests, the lure of the incredible amount of money an automobile dealership can generate has proved almost irresistible for entrepreneurs, from businesspeople with Wall Street connections to dealership employees with big dreams of owning and running their own show. The travails of LMP, GPB Capital, and others attest to the difficulties encountered along the way.

CHAPTER 8

THE DEALERS (PART IV)

Privately owned automotive dealerships have been the backbone of the retail automotive world almost since the inception of the business. At their best such dealerships have strong leadership teams; excellent business ethics; outstanding expense, inventory, and operational controls; great factory-dealer relationships; and positive ties to their communities. The most highly perceived of these dealers in the United States generally runs platforms of seven to twenty rooftops representing a couple of dozen brands. They far outclass the aforementioned public companies and, in their own way, are far more successful at driving positive business results and making customers happy.

For example, as noted in a previous chapter, the most successful private dealer is Rick Hendrick, whose Hendrick Automotive Group consists of ninety-four dealerships generating about $13 billion worth of revenue on the sale of about 195,000 new cars a year.* Although skewed toward Honda on the import end and Chevrolet on the domestic side, Hendrick's group represents just about every brand sold in the United States. While his locations are concentrated heavily in the Southeastern United States, particularly

---

* "Corporate History," Hendrik Cars, https://www.hendrickcars.com/corporate-history.htm.

North Carolina and Georgia, Hendrick is one of the few dealers who has managed to profitably operate dealerships throughout most of the country.

Out West, two other dealer groups, although smaller than Hendrick's concerns, also rank highly among private dealers because of their success across most brands. Ken Garff Automotive Group in Salt Lake City consists of over fifty dealerships selling over seventy thousand new cars a year. Sadly, Chairman Bob Garff succumbed to the coronavirus relatively early in the pandemic. Such was his succession plan, however, that his wife and children have been able to maintain the group's momentum and standards. Also headquartered in Utah is the Larry H. Miller Dealership Group with over sixty dealerships spread mostly over Utah, Colorado, and Arizona. Although Miller died several years ago, his successors have continued to expand the group.

In the Northeast, a particularly difficult geography in which to do business, John Staluppi manages a group of about forty dealerships, mostly import and mostly in the New York metro area. Such is Staluppi's performance with brands ranging from Honda, Hyundai, and Chevrolet to Nissan and Infiniti that he can practically name the desired location for his next automotive enterprise. At over seventy-five years old, Staluppi shows no signs of slowing down. He is also blessed with two of the sharpest operational managers in the business, John Gentile and Rick Alessi.

Terry Taylor of West Palm Beach, Florida, owns over one hundred dealerships through his acquisition and management company, AMSI. Taylor's organization has expanded so rapidly that he rivals Hendrick.

Indeed, Hendrick, Garff, Miller, Taylor, and Staluppi are the best known of the privately held dealer groups, though mostly because of their size and scale. My reference to these dealers is a tip of the hat to their phenomenal success and their ability to influence manufacturers and markets. However, smaller privately held dealers fill out the list of the top 150 dealers in the United States, ranked each year by *Automotive News* based on unit sales of new vehicles. Family owned and operated, these dealers sell a lot of vehicles, keep both their customers and employees happy, and make a lot of money in the process. What makes these dealers successful? From what I can tell, five particular qualities set them apart.

First, almost all dealers either grew up in the business or started at a very young age at the bottom of the dealership hierarchy. Jimmy Ellis in Atlanta, for example, worked in his father's VW and Mazda dealerships as a boy. Though both Jimmy and his father have passed on, his family-run stores are now the most recognized and respected in the Atlanta area. Ben Keating, who owns an enormously profitable platform of seventeen dealerships in Southeast Texas, gravitated toward the new-car business early in his racing career. Jeronimo Esteve is the son of a Cuban immigrant who became the first Honda dealer in Puerto Rico and thus worked in his father's Honda store before running the successful Headquarter Automotive Group in South Florida.

Second, the most successful private dealers remain heavily involved in every aspect of their businesses. Their systems of reporting, accountability, and controls remain robust and translate well across all brands and markets in which they are represented. These dealers still make the major hiring decisions for their dealerships, and they continue to make all the major financial decisions as well. They personally negotiate major real estate acquisitions, and they remain the face of the dealership group to the manufacturers—a big difference from the publicly owned dealerships that employ a platform manager to hire and fire and deal with the manufacturers.

Third, privately held dealership groups attract, retain, and promote exceptionally strong managers. Keen judges of talent surround themselves with like-minded managers who reflect the values that great dealers espouse. The marching orders for general managers at, say, Carter Myers Automotive Group may come from Carter Myers himself or his daughter, Liza Borches. But as dealer owners, they have been shrewd enough to hire only the best managers, technicians, and parts people.

Fourth, the best private dealers enjoy tremendous loyalty from both their employees and customers simply by "doing the right thing," a well-known mantra in the auto industry. They pay their employees well, and in most cases they make the effort to offer and maintain competitive benefit packages, including insurance and profit sharing. Word-of-mouth advertising is worth its weight in gold, and these dealers also treat their customers so well that not only do the customers keep coming back, but they tell their friends about their experiences as well. Great dealers make sure that their customers remain the focus of their organizations. For instance, Rick Case, the great Honda, Kia, and VW dealer in South Florida, wrote a book with his wife, Rita, about their lifelong relationship with their customers. Before his death in 2020, Case was renowned in the industry as one of the best exemplars of total customer satisfaction.

Finally, the best private dealers maintain good relationships with their lenders, their local governments and communities, and most of all, their manufacturers. Manufacturers value a dealer who is cooperative, meets sales and service objectives, makes money, and treats customers well. Dealers who cultivate good relationships with their manufacturers get issues such as order requests for parts and vehicles resolved quickly. A manufacturer will treat a tireless advocate for their brand with respect, and a level of trust develops between a dealer who aggressively promotes the brand and a manufacturer who recognizes a great retail partner.

Thus far in this book, we've covered the overall car-buying process and a bit of the history of the industry. In the last four chapters, we've also studied the dealers who are the heart of automotive retailing in the United States, through whom new vehicles get from the assembly plant to customers' driveways. In the next chapter, we'll look at some of the features of new cars over the years that have popularized certain makes, models, and manufacturers.

CHAPTER 9

IT'S NICE TO HAVE OPTIONS

Since the the Industrial Age, American entrepreneurs ranging from garage tinkerers to mechanical geniuses have built America's industrial complex into one of the finest in the world. Eli Whitney's cotton gin went from a simple box and crank in 1792 to multifunction buildings in the 1950s. The flintlock musket evolved to high-powered assault rifles. The television, which began as a small screen in a brown box, became a giant flat screen, and many American homes have several.

The automobile, since its inception as little more than a motorized bicycle with three or four wheels in the 1890s, represents the pinnacle of industrial mass production. By December 2018 just shy of eighteen million automobiles were sold in the United States alone. Just as television's *The Six Million Dollar Man* represented the epitome of something that could be made faster, stronger, and better, each generation of the automobile grew progressively faster, stronger, and better (not to mention, more expensive).

Henry Ford gets a lot of credit in the annals of automobile lore. His real genius was figuring out how to produce cars on a monumental scale. This preoccupation with the process as opposed to the product itself led to his famous monolithic approach to choice: in his own words, "People can have 'em in any color they want, as long as they're all black.'"* Accordingly, the Model T was enormously successful for years in the one color and one engine configuration. Not surprisingly, however, the competition caught up with Ford. By 1928, Chevrolet, Chrysler, and other manufacturers offered more choices in colors, engines, and configurations. Eventually, Henry's engineers, product people, and his son, Edsel, forced him into producing the Model A.

Akin to the parallel development of the airplane, the automobile industry over the years has provided Americans more choice, more thrills, more frills, more satisfaction, and correspondingly, more ways to part with their hard-earned dollars. Some of the most classic cars ever produced were the result of automakers' ability and willingness to cater to Americans' increasingly insatiable tastes. Some of the grandest classic automobiles ever produced were the eight-cylinder behemoths assembled by Studebaker, Ford, Mercedes, DeSoto, Cadillac, and others in the late 1920s and early 1930s. As the mass production capabilities of the manufacturers increased, so did the choices in colors, engines, interiors, seating, and suspensions. This proliferation reached a pinnacle in the early 1980s; by 1980, Chrysler Corporation could build a Plymouth Volaré in any one of about sixty thousand configurations.

Most of the improvements in the automobile in the early days involved a desire for more power, more speed, more comfort, flashier exterior colors, and more opulent interiors. By the late 1940s, American preoccupation with styling induced American manufacturers to slap wood on the exteriors of some of their flashy wagons. One look at the 1948 Chrysler Town & Country Wagon gives one an idea of the extent to which this syndrome took hold. Since mileage was not a consideration in those days, the power-to-weight ratio calculation in automobile design and production was not taken terribly seriously; with gas at about $0.20 per gallon, fuel economy was largely an

---

* Ronnie Schreiber, "How Cars Went from 'Any Color, as Long as It's Black' to a Rainbow of Hues," Hagerty, October 11, 2022, https://www.hagerty.com/media/automotive-history/how-cars-went-from-any-color-as-long-as-its-black-to-a-rainbow-of-hues/.

afterthought. The general thinking among the manufacturers, the dealers, and the motoring public became simply more, more, more.

By the 1950s, sustained by cheap gasoline and some inspiration from the space program, speed and power became two of the most dominant drivers in automobile design, with size a close third. This influence can readily be seen in some of the surviving cars from the late 1950s. The long, sleek exterior body panels; the futuristic tail fins; the raked back glass; and even the names all evoked references to the space race; Oldsmobile even named one of their cars the "Rocket 88." Similarly, Chrysler adopted for its DeSoto marque such astronomical descriptors as "Starflight" and "Starfire."

The 1950s also saw the advent of considerable option-loading in most models: upgraded suspensions, more powerful engines, a plethora of new colors, power brakes, power steering, and that new essential for driving in the increasingly congested American cities, the automatic transmission. These features exemplify some of the most notable mechanical accoutrements. The motoring public demanded such improvements, and the automotive manufacturers gladly obliged.

The motoring public had also developed an oversize preoccupation with quality sound and other creature comforts. Already by the time AM radios were being installed in most midline US car models, air-conditioning had also made significant inroads into automotive design and installation rates. In the American South, up until the early 1950s, the standard joke in motoring comfort had been, "I have a four-forty air conditioner in my car—four windows down at forty miles per hour." Anyone who had ever taken a motor trip from Memphis to New Orleans in August could not have failed to be impressed by a newfangled contraption that could lower the interior temperature of their car from a sweltering one hundred degrees to a cool seventy with the push of a button. Of all the convenience features devised by the manufacturers for installation in their product offerings, air-conditioning became a favorite.

As the decade of the 1950s churned into the 1960s, manufacturers built most vehicles with at least an AM radio, an air-conditioning unit, and an automatic transmission. By about 1960, the automatic transmission had become so all-pervasive that the manufacturers began to toy with sly innovations on the ever-popular PRNDL—the little insignia on the steering column that indicated the various functions of the automatic transmission. Before the late 1950s, most cars were afflicted with two nagging reminders of the essentials of locomotion: the infamous third pedal or clutch to the left of the brake pedal and the annoying shift lever on the right-hand side of the steering column. The manufacturers' answer for the actuation of the new automatic transmission was, in fact, a different lever on the steering column to put the vehicle into whatever mode was necessary—park, reverse, neutral, drive, and, depending on the model, D1 or D2. A couple of manufacturers, namely Chrysler and American Motors mainly through its Rambler division, came up with an ingenious configuration to eliminate what some still viewed as the annoying lever on the right-hand side of the steering column. They put buttons on the dashboard to activate the desired transmission mode.

I remember, for example, the pride with which my father demonstrated the automatic transmission functions of our newly purchased Rambler American Wagon. Put your foot on the brake, press *R* for reverse, gradually decrease the pressure on the brake, and lo, the car began to roll backward out of the driveway and onto the asphalt road. Increasing pressure on the brake brought the car to a complete stop, whereupon my father would gleefully engage the button prominently labeled *D*, and lo, the vehicle was propelled forward to the astonishment of my mother, my three siblings, and me. In all truth, this variation of the PRNDL proved an enormously successful development, but at a premium somewhat above the lever configuration, it did not have a long shelf life. The old habit, borne by long experience of shifting a vehicle via the "three on the tree" and the automatic transmission lever, proved too powerful for the push-button configuration to overcome over time. By the mid-1960s, the automatic transmission lever on the right-hand side of the column and the inception of the console on the floor in the center of the front seat led to the early demise of the push-button automatic transmission.

Thus far in this chapter we've discussed mostly mechanical advances that improved cars and trucks over the years. However, strides in electronics made vehicles much more enjoyable to drive. Car sound systems evolved from AM radio only to include AM-FM as the technology became available. By the late 1960s, audio engineers learned how to coax stereo sound out of dash-mounted units, and the eight-track tape deck provided an even more exciting option. Though derided today as an antiquarian blip on the automobile timeline, eight-track units provided a really cool addition that allowed the music of the 1960s to proliferate. A hotshot teen in his first new car no longer had to wait until a radio station's playlist rolled around to their favorite tunes. By 1970, cassette tapes became widely available, and the manufacturers obliged customers by replacing the clunky eight-track decks with better-sounding cassette players. The citizens band radio craze, which burst upon the country in 1976 after the release of the song "Convoy" and the film *Smokey and the Bandit*, led to the widespread factory installation of combination AM-FM CB units in new vehicles. By the early 1980s, the development of high-quality compact discs further enhanced the customers' audio experience. With the inception of the internet, auto sound systems began to include MP3 players. Today manufacturers produce mostly vehicles with sophisticated systems for wireless connections with music services and cellular phones. And customers know that as quickly as technology advances, the system in the vehicle they purchase today will be obsolete in a year or two.

But even more important than the effect of technology on auto sound systems, the manufacturers, egged on by more demanding customers and more readily available gadgetry, have advanced the art of "infotainment" to new heights. Bluetooth communication, navigation systems, and remote-start accommodations have made today's ubiquitous cell phones actual extensions of the driving experience. Best of all, technology has made cars fun again—and maybe even more fun than cars used to be, which we'll touch on in the next chapter.

CHAPTER 10

THIS USED TO BE FUN, AND EVERYBODY WAS HAPPY

Anyone above the age of fifty will remember that the purchase of a new car and the anticipation of visiting the dealership was, if not a joy, something actually fun. Never mind the fact that the reasons for visiting the dealership in the first place may have been more out of necessity than joy: an accident in which the previous car had been totaled; the fact that one's current car had, pardon the pun, "reached the end of the road"; or on a more pleasant note, a new addition to the family now necessitated more room, more comfort, more car. For a kid in the 1960s, a new car meant more gadgets and doodads, an air conditioner where before one might have been at the mercy of the facetious four-forty, and the sheer joy of luxuriating in the spacious back seat and breathing in that new-car smell. Gone was the vile stench of Dad's cigars, which not only had been absorbed by the cloth seats but had also imbued itself into the cloth headliner. Gone also were the tidbits and detritus of daily commuter life—discarded apple cores, bits of paper ranging from cigarette packages to fast-food receipts, and the odd melted M&M that encrusted the carpet. In short, a new car meant renewal in every sense of the word.

Dad and Mom probably didn't look on the episode with such aspiring eyes and thoughts. Almost invariably a new car meant higher monthly payments, perhaps even a hefty down payment in addition to the old vehicle trade-in, and higher insurance rates. All these increased costs became valid concerns and considerations that were amplified as cars got bigger and more expensive. But still, the new-car experience was pretty neat if you were a kid. Every four or five years, you got to go to a dealership and see all the nifty new models. One could sit in the driver's seat and pretend to be a big person and never want to leave the store while a nervous salesperson or dealership receptionist kept an eagle eye out lest you stick your gum in the door panel or fart in the seat. And hey, in the corner of the showroom, there might even be a popcorn machine. In the South, especially in the summer, if you were lucky enough to get to the dealership on a Saturday, there might even be cold Cokes on ice in a number 3 washtub outside or a table full of sliced watermelons. Never mind the fact that as soon as the car was driven off the lot, its value dropped 30 percent. The newly purchased car was sure to gather a few kernels of popcorn or errant watermelon seeds that missed the mouth.

At the end of the day, the family drove away with a shiny new car, and the dealer put another four grand into the till. The salesmen involved in the transaction could look forward to surviving another week and celebrating with a six-pack that night. At the end of the day, everybody was happy. Throughout most of the 1960s, everybody became happy. The Big Three delighted their customers with their domestic offerings. In turn, increasing sales delighted dealers with ever-increasing profits, and the higher volumes also meant more and more lucrative fixed-operations opportunities. These newer models required maintenance, which also entailed more part sales. Manufacturers became exuberant. Nothing lit the candle of the auto executive in the 1960s more than year-over-year sales increases, especially when each of those sales represented ever-higher transaction prices. The assembly line employees became perhaps the happiest of all because steadily increasing sales meant steady work, job security, and bigger and more lucrative union contracts. The manufacturers, wishing to see the cycle perpetuated, and with their coffers already filled to the brim, made even bigger bargains with the union, confident that their actions engendered by a great economy, great sales, and a steady revenue stream would more than make up for what they had to pay the workers to avoid a strike.

Parts suppliers reveled in the moment for the same reasons; ever-increasing sales spurred an ever-increasing demand for components. Almost all vendors remained relatively healthy throughout this time. Advertisers were happy too. With more money to spend and ever-newer, bigger, and more powerful cars to hawk, more manufacturers upped their advertising and marketing budgets, confident that these expenses, too, would pay off handsomely. Bonuses at the executive levels at GM, Ford, and Chrysler in some years matched or exceeded base salaries; the bonuses in turn kept status venues from the Detroit Athletic Club to the Grosse Pointe Country Club nice and prosperous.

Even through an insidious war, when student demonstrations and gnawing civil rights issues induced a nagging backdrop, everybody's pockets remained full. As long as the economy hummed along, the American public could stomach isolated civil unrest and a low-intensity foreign conflict. Back in 1953 "Engine Charlie" Wilson had uttered a much-misquoted phrase that was interpreted as, "What's good for General Motors is good for the country." Fifteen years later the maxim still held largely true. People were spending money; most municipalities remained flush with tax revenue, and everybody was happy.

The first cracks in this veneer of paradise did not appear until 1970. That summer GM workers went out on a general strike that lasted most of the season and had a discernible negative impact not only on GM's earnings but also on the American economy in general. Moreover, the strike illustrated that the workers, emboldened by years of prosperity, were proving the old adage, "The more you have, the more you want." The entire episode marked a substantial breach in the previous cozy relationship between the manufacturers and the union.

At the same time, Chrysler and Ford viewed the GM work stoppage with great interest and greater concern. Short strikes had occurred occasionally at all the manufacturers. A strike of over one hundred days brought home to American manufacturing what could and would happen during a prolonged work stoppage. Far from taking advantage of the GM strike, the other manufacturers experienced flat or declining sales. Aside from the decline in the GDP, the nation was experiencing doubts about the Nixon administration's handling of the economy in general and its prosecution of the war in Southeast Asia. American incursions into Cambodia and the related ensuing unrest on college campuses proved tragic. On May 4, 1970, four Kent State University students were killed when jittery National Guardsmen fired upon an organized student protest. Outrage over the war continued to create great unease across the country.

President Nixon's decision to institute price controls in 1971 hardly helped the situation. The late 1970 run-up in inflation, while nowhere near the level of the crisis nine years later, was significant enough to cause the acerbic Nixon to take this action. The economists howled, the manufacturers choked, and the consumers puked. In short, the 1970s became a miserable time for business, the economy, and the country. Although the country, the economy, and consumers' attitudes recovered enough to allow Nixon a second term (George McGovern's brand of liberalism was just a little too far out for what was still a rather staid America in 1972), the fissure in the delicate, complex relationship involving manufacturing, the economy, politics, and consumers proved irrevocable.

Suddenly nobody was happy anymore.

What happened next has been covered in a previous chapter. The year 1973 brought one of the biggest upheavals in American manufacturing business and politics and changed life in the United States forever. The year 1979 and the recession that accompanied it cemented a curious yet barely concealed dissatisfaction with the way things were—and are. And although the industry, American society, and the economy recovered somewhat and the US car industry generally grew steadily, the year 2008 and the Great Recession constituted an unhealthy jolt that reminded Americans, and particularly American businesses, how truly vulnerable we remain.

In 2018 the US car industry logged more than 16.5 million retail sales. Dealer profits seemed still relatively healthy. Unemployment had reached one of its postwar lows. The stock market, despite a blip at the end of 2018, was still strong . . . and practically nobody was happy. Not to sound like a broken record, but clearly, "The more you have, the more you want." Despite Democratic and Liberal pronouncements of how bad things had become, despite a general dissatisfaction with the US government, despite increased social upheaval, snippiness, and general sense of malaise, Americans were (and are) relatively *more* pessimistic than they've ever been.

Why?

This just isn't as much fun anymore.

When it was fun, there was a solid certainty in the way things were and the way we all thought they would be. I'll digress to a personal point of view. When I entered the automobile business in 1979, things were as bad as they possibly could be or had ever been before. For a young Chrysler trainee with a newly minted graduate degree, the times were as exciting, confusing, and promising as they could be. Chrysler had just gone to Congress for a $1.2 billion bailout. Paul Volcker, the embattled chair of the Federal Reserve, appeared before a panicked Congress to try to explain why 20 percent interest rates could eventually defeat 13.4 percent inflation and bring the US economy to a sense of equilibrium. Chrysler was laying off people every day, shutting plants, canceling production, and praying for the stroke of luck that would enable its survival. My own narrow field of vision stayed focused on the $14,921 per year that I was earning, the 1980 Dodge Mirada I was driving for free (even with free gas and free insurance), and an expense account that enabled me to stay at Holiday Inns at $12 per night while merrily driving from Dodge to Chrysler dealers who were staring insolvency in the face.

Nobody was happy, except me.

In time, however, everybody got happy, including me—I just got happier. By late 1982, we all could see flickers of hope for the economy and the country. Chrysler's introduction of the K-car began slowly turning the company around. Paul Volker's sustained assault on inflation began to bear fruit. President Reagan's unbridled optimism, hard stance against communism, and irrepressible attitude proved infectious. All of a sudden, in April 1983, the business, the country, and the economy seemed to turn on a dime. As a young district sales manager for Chrysler in New Orleans, I went from begging dealers to take cars they didn't want to having those same dealers beg me for cars I couldn't provide. The automobile business took off like a rocket. As interest rates declined and new products hit the market, consumers screamed for new vehicles of every size, shape, and color. If a rising tide lifts all boats, Chrysler was raised to a level that seemingly surpassed all others. The demands for Chrysler's new minivan exceeded anyone's wildest expectations. Customers, who in the depths of the recession had delayed any and all major purchases, snapped up all the offerings of all the manufacturers in numbers nobody expected. Car dealers, who a year before had been ready to fold their tents and go home, were suddenly faced with customers, products, and profits they could scarcely have comprehended a year before.

Chrysler was so successful throughout the first part of 1983 that by the time of Chrysler's annual dealer meeting in Las Vegas that August, it gleefully announced that it had paid off its loan guarantee obligations. Lee Iacocca jubilantly showed the assembled Chrysler, Dodge, and Plymouth dealers a large facsimile of the check to the US Treasury, in excess of the final $800 million. A star-studded lineup of Tony Bennett, Joe Namath, Jim McKay, and Iacocca himself joyfully led the celebration of Chrysler's resurrection from near demise. In a show of opulence not enjoyed by Chrysler field people in years, the company regaled its field force in a bacchanalian celebration featuring premium wines, untold top-shelf whiskeys, lobster, crab, and assorted other delicacies combined with a show by the diminutive and deep-throated Spanish entertainer, Charo. Heady stuff for a totally unsophisticated district sales manager who, four years before, had been lucky enough to be hired by a totally insolvent, down-at-its-heels car company. Charo herself left the stage, microphone in hand, to entice audience participation in a rousing rendition of song and story while generously rubbing her ample cleavage into the bespectacled face of this writer. "Cuchi-cuchi" had never sounded (nor felt) so good.

Only a couple of hours later, with four thousand dealer people and their spouses, as well as the Chrysler factory folks and vendors who had survived the crucible, Tony Bennett crooned "Because of You," as Iacocca entered stage left. The crowd went wild! The *Wall Street Journal*, which, along with other business and automotive publications, had gleefully predicted Chrysler's early demise, must have cringed when Iacocca pronounced, "Screw the *Wall Street Journal*."

And everybody was happy.

CHAPTER 11

THIS JUST ISN'T FUN ANYMORE, AND EVERYBODY IS UNHAPPY (PART I)

Fast-forward forty years. The automobile business has seen more change than even the tumultuous period from 1979 to 1983. Dealers, manufacturers, suppliers, and icons of industry have come and gone. Even before the 2008 Great Recession, GM had added a brand, Saturn, which for one brief shining decade seemed to change the retail experience. Oldsmobile, one of the industry's iconic brands, was shed by GM, even though five years before, the division was retailing almost a million cars per year. The Japanese, who had built their business for years on quality, fuel economy, and price (largely due to currency advantages), recognized that another way to profitability was to move upscale, thus introducing their own luxury offerings. Honda's Acura, Toyota's Lexus, and Nissan's Infiniti received great initial reception among wealthy American consumers and eventually supplanted the traditional US standards of luxury such as Cadillac, Lincoln, and Continental. Except for one brief but powerful downtick in 1992, the industry rebounded quite well. From 1993 to 2001, the industry, the economy, and the country, with astonishing advances in technology, production, and efficiency, chalked up ever-increasing gains in employment, profitability, and general well-being.

The Great Recession then, in a sense, reflected the paradox of living in the greatest country in the world in a period of its greatest distress. The greater social upheaval of that period has been dealt with in other publications quite well. My particular goal here is to recount what the Great Recession did to the automobile industry and to illustrate how it helped shape why most everyone in the industry feels "this just isn't fun anymore." The billions expended by the government to save GM and Chrysler pale in comparison with the $1.2 billion offered up in loan guarantees to Chrysler just thirty years earlier. The debate over whether those billions were well spent will continue for decades. GM shed a chairman, thousands of workers, hundreds of dealers, and several brands (Pontiac, Saturn, Hummer, and Saab), while Chrysler lost hundreds of dealers, thousands of workers, its chairman, its owners, and its identity. The brands that survived, chastened by the ordeal, adopted a new attitude steeped in an ever-greater need for profitability and the need to survive.

Accordingly, the dealers who survived the ordeal adopted much the same mindset. Dealers and manufacturers, always contentious, had nonetheless heretofore acknowledged that each needed the other. Subsequent to the Great Recession, each side, acknowledging the obvious lack of "fun," adopted an every-man-for-himself type of philosophy. As we have seen, the manufacturers keenly understood that volume was the name of the game. The dealers, more than ever, understood that, absent profitability, they had no future. The two concepts collided: The manufacturers had to drive volume, and the dealers had to make money. As we have seen, incentives driven by the dark, desperate days of the 1979–1983 recession were here to stay. As the industry limped out of the Great Recession, incentives took on a new form that presented grim challenges for the surviving dealers.

During the earlier recessions, incentives had actually made everybody happy. In those days incentives were usually a flat amount per car with occasional accruing bonuses for additional sales. The manufacturers were satisfied because sales jumped, the plants stayed open, cars rolled off the line, and dealers, flush with the incentive money, were largely able to make long-range strategic plans. The manufacturers, recognizing that the dealers were profitable again, slowly became emboldened to tie lucrative incentives to volume objectives. Specifically, the manufacturers' incentives grew "hooks" that tied dealer payments to volume objectives. Through the period of 2010–2014, a dealer could earn tens of thousands of dollars per month from the manufacturers if they achieved certain volume objectives. Most manufacturers tied dealer payments to tiered objective levels. The avaricious nature of dealers naturally kicked in; they chased the money.

The nature of the retail transaction changed completely; more than ever, dealers began to "deal." To hit the lucrative volume objectives, the dealers had to skin all the fat out of the deal to get the car over the curb, knowing that they wouldn't be paid the volume objective unless they hit the manufacturers' prescribed number. From 2010 to 2014, the dealers grumbled all the way to the bank. During that period, the objectives remained achievable, though difficult, for the most part. Many dealers were able to hit the objectives, and the money went straight to their bottom line.

However, the dynamics of the business changed. All of a sudden, dealers were pushing cars out the door without much regard to the efficacy of the transaction, the satisfaction of the customer, or the effects on service operations and their own sales employees' livelihoods or morale. Since the incentive payments went directly to the dealers in most instances, individual salespeople were cut out of the gravy. Most salespeople work on commission, and since most dealers had not revised their pay plans, dealers found themselves richer but with a showroom full of disgruntled salespeople (because they were making much less money). More importantly the dealers faced dissatisfied customers (because the retail experience had been replaced by the need to simply drive volume).

By 2019 the situation was such that dealers were actively deploring the ever-present stair-step incentive programs. Moreover, for everyone, this volume game just wasn't fun anymore. The objectives got higher and higher. As manufacturers needing the volume slowly began to raise the objectives, the dealers on the hamster wheel, recognizing the corrosive effects that such programs caused, began to push back. An article by Melissa Burden and Amy Wilson in the February 18, 2019, issue of *Automotive News* addressed the problem of the emblematic challenges caused by stair-step targets: "The programs are brand destroyers that confuse and anger customers," said Steve Kalafer, a New Jersey dealer quoted in the article.*

More and more dealers began to give up on chasing the money. Whereas in the first few years after the Great Recession, stair-step targets were often achievable and even preferred by some dealers while the industry was booming, other dealers grumbled that they worked too hard each month chasing the targets. Dealers had to decide whether to chase an ever-increasing objective or try to survive by structuring each car deal individually and relying on fixed operations to drive gross. It was not until April 2021, as also reported in *Automotive News*, that Nissan junked its reviled stair-step sales incentive process that pushed for sales volume and replaced it with a program that focused on value.

The debate over facilities offers another reason why this just isn't fun anymore. The manufacturers increasingly demand that dealers build newer, bigger, and more grandiose facilities. These demands come at a time when technology is enabling customers to shop online and, in some cases, even consummate the car deal electronically. While this online trend has been increasing for several years, it gained momentum with the onset of car-buying services. Oblivious to the trend, the manufacturers continue to insist that the dealers not only ascribe to the manufacturers' facility and branding standards but that the dealers also use mandated design firms, materials, and equipment vendors. In many cases these services are much

---

* Melissa Burden and Amy Wilson, "Growing Backlash Against Stair-Steps," *Automotive News*, February 18, 2019, https://www.autonews.com/retail/growing-backlash-against-stair-steps/.

more expensive than a dealer could obtain on his own volition in the open market. Invariably, such factory demands fall disproportionately on the dealer's showrooms and sales departments, but curiously so, as the size of cars sold in America has decreased, the size of the actual showrooms that the manufacturers demand have actually increased. (The exception here is pickup trucks, vans, and SUVs, which have grown tremendously in size since the early 1980s.) The effect of these mandates not only manifests itself in more expensive materials but also in higher costs for heating and cooling a larger indoor space. Ask a dealer in New York how pleased they are about heating their expanded showroom; by the same token, ask a dealer in South Texas what fun it is to write a check to their utility company for air-conditioning for a west-facing showroom in July.

Some manufacturers are so determined to exert their control over the retail process and attain a uniformity of brand identity throughout the country that they offer dealers financial assistance to build or renovate facilities to the manufacturers' specific designs and configurations. In many cases this assistance also comes with "hooks." For example, a dealer might be offered $1 million to renovate his facility to the manufacturer's look, down to the last floor tile or brochure rack, but here's the thing: The dealer may be paid a portion of this assistance up front, say $500,000, but the balance will not be paid until a manufacturer "walk-through" and punch list are complete, to make sure the dealer is compliant with every scintilla of a manufacturer's published requirements. Not surprisingly, many of the successful brands are able to get compliance out of their dealers; after all, the manufacturers hold most of the cards, primarily the supply of new-vehicle inventory. For example, by the time this writer left Porsche, a typical Porsche renovation or new construction cost almost $500 per square foot. The Porsche dealers and sales staff grumbled loudly but then grumbled less loudly when they remembered that they grossed as much as $15,000 on each individual Porsche sale. Woe betide the Kia dealer who is tasked with the same facility requirements with no financial assistance whatsoever.

Aside from the facility requirements, the factories also control warranty reimbursements, vehicle production, and in most cases, vehicle financing, mortgages, and capital loans—all in addition to incentive payments, as we have seen. Warranty reimbursement has come in for some special and persistent complaints by dealers. Almost invariably dealers complain that the warranty reimbursement rates offered by the factories do not cover their costs adequately. Years ago there was some truth to this complaint. Before the late 1970s, most vehicles sold were domestics, built in aging plants with materials and processes that did not entail adequate quality control and built by workers who were tired, drugged, hungover, or otherwise just plain disgruntled. The old adage, "Never buy a car built on a Monday or a Friday," actually held some truth. Ever the opportunists, dealers have now turned that argument on its head by exclaiming loudly that the cars are so well put together that they cannot make money on warranty. The claim sounds ridiculous, but it's actually true. As in the matter of stair-step incentives, the dealer's dependence on factory warranty reimbursement has many dealers more concerned about making money off the factory than making money on each individual customer transaction.

To further emphasize how and why "this just isn't fun anymore," the factories have always deployed teams of auditors to check dealer warranty claims for out-of-line conditions or, in some cases, outright fraud. Hell hath no fury like a warranty auditor on a mission from the factory; these propeller-headed, Coke-bottle glasses-wearing, pencil-whipping, pseudo accountants are some of the most despised factory employees a dealer encounters. They are also very good at what they do. Not that they have to be very good; generally speaking, the people involved in warranty claims submissions at dealerships are among the most poorly paid and poorly trained in the dealer's employ.

Advances in computer technology have enabled the auditors to review massive amounts of data in a short period, and the tightening of the factory's warranty policies and procedures has greatly enhanced its "gotcha" capabilities. Nobody has any fun during a warranty audit exit meeting: The dealer comes out of it usually many thousands of dollars less wealthy, and the service manager comes out of it knowing that they will get a royal ass-chewing from the dealer (as well as the attending factory representatives) for their lack of leadership and poor adherence to warranty policies and procedures. The poor warranty administrator almost always fears for their job for simply doing what the dealer or the service manager tells them to do. Similarly, the factory representatives at a warranty audit exit meeting have no desire to be there either; nobody likes to be the bearer of bad news, and informing a dealer that they are about to be charged back $30,000 or $40,000 is nobody's favorite chore.

Aside from the concerns of sales pressure, warranty audits, product recalls, service issues, administrative buffoonery, and the rising costs of doing business, I can offer yet another reason this just isn't fun anymore. Advances in technology, the overriding pressure to perform, and a general loss of the thread of collaboration and cooperation that used to exist between the manufacturers and the dealers make the car business nowadays more drudgery than anything else. One could argue that the speed of today's supercomputers, with their ability to deal effectively with so much data at once, has simply surpassed the ability of many people to deal with the problems that the advances in technology have been developed to solve. Even thirty years ago, many functions in a dealership, from accounting to sales to service diagnosis, were done by hand or by sheer gut instinct. Now computers can handle everything from diagnosing a service problem to managing dealership payroll, to planning thousands of units' worth of production, to tracking how many pencils a dealer needs to order. Adding to the industry angst is the legion of computer specialists necessary to hold everything together. Since the late 1980s, one of the fastest-rising expense items on a dealer's financial statement has been outside and data-processing services. Similarly, one of the most powerful departments in the factory's entire organization is its information technology component. The ever-increasing complexity of the technology used in the automobile business can baffle even seasoned executives. One of the great ironies of the technological age is that the very people charged with the execution of policy and the attainment of objectives are now subservient to technology-spouting twits with no real comprehension of critical business objectives.

To illustrate more specifically, the need to get better faster has led to the development of programs ostensibly designed to accomplish just about anything. On the manufacturers' side, computers have been used for over forty years to assist with production orders, plant fill, supply chain maintenance, employee benefits/human resources, and warranty and recall issues. The result is that a district sales manager for a manufacturer today spends more time in front of his laptop computer screen than in front of a dealer or general manager developing relationships and building bridges toward collaborative behaviors that would truly help everybody whenever the shit does hit the fan. Forty years ago a district sales manager and a dealer could hammer out a monthly order allocation on a cocktail napkin while drinking after a round of golf and an afternoon of hail-fellow-well-met conviviality and good humor. Now the same function is usually completed in less than half the time with the run of an Excel program and a fifteen-minute phone call between the general manager and the district sales manager. Sure, the task gets done, but in the process the human touch—the literal and figurative feel and grasp of the transaction—is all but lost.

From a regulatory standpoint, nobody's had any fun for over forty-five years. Not that the Clean Air Act was a bad move, but anytime the government gets involved, costs, angst, and tempers rise accordingly. This rule holds true in every area of the automobile business, from safety to emissions to the regulation of finance, insurance, plant safety, and government requirements of dealerships. A dealer not only has to build a new dealership according to the specifications of the manufacturer but must also abide by building codes and the Americans with Disabilities Act (which, in itself, was also not a bad move). All government oversight is done without ill will, but its intrusion has nonetheless vastly increased operating costs and eroded everyone's good humor. One might argue that the industry's cars are cleaner, safer, more efficient, and overall better. But . . . the cars are also much more expensive to build, store, sell, and purchase, and that expense is probably the main reason why this just isn't fun anymore.

CHAPTER 12

"THE FACTORY"

For years dealers have colloquially referred to their manufacturer partners as "the factory." Actually "the factory" is a catchall term not only for the structure where the cars are built but also for everything that emanates from the manufacturer. For the general public, the factory refers specifically to that building where the cars are assembled. The factory is the most tangible and visible symbol of the automobile manufacturer. In the Upper Midwest and the Northeast, entire communities and regions became defined by the manufacturing facilities in their areas. For instance, most everyone has heard of manufacturers such as Bethlehem Steel in Bethlehem, Pennsylvania, and Corning in Corning, New York. The automobile manufacturers, by virtue of their far-flung network of component and assembly plants, signified the very manifestation of the concept that the industry defined and sustained the community. Detroit, Michigan, may no longer be the capital of the automotive world, but in many people's minds, when somebody mentions the automobile business, they almost automatically think of Detroit. In the early 1920s, when the manufacturers began to plant facilities throughout the Rust Belt and the Northeast, "Detroit" was, in effect, transplanted to dozens of new communities.

Manufacturers first built the new plants relatively close to the original action. Flint, Lansing, and Dearborn, Michigan; Kenosha, Wisconsin; and South Bend, Indiana, all made for locations easily accessible by truck or rail. Later, to shorten shipment times and take advantage of the proximity of the Great Lakes, Chicago, Illinois; Toledo and Cleveland, Ohio; and Buffalo, New York, became prime sites for new factories. The oar boats that plied the Great Lakes from Duluth, Minnesota, across Lakes Superior, Huron, and Erie could bring iron ore and coal as easily to Lorraine, Ohio, as they could to Detroit. To feed the thunderous maw of the assembly plants, the industry established smaller, more specialized component plants in proximity to the assembly plants. As a result, even the smaller communities began to be identified by their factory affiliations. For example, the New Process Gear plant for Chrysler became the mainstay of Syracuse, New York. The GM plant in Linden, New Jersey, became the town's economic lifeblood. For years "Dodge Main" was synonymous with the old Dodge Brothers plant in Hamtramck, in the Poletown East neighborhood of Detroit.

After World War II and throughout the 1950s and early 1960s, the concept of the factory even further solidified automobile production in dozens of northern communities. The fortunes of entire regions rose and fell with the production quotas of contiguous auto plants. There was not a community where GM was represented that did not feel the sting of GM's 1970 strike. Similarly, every manufacturing plant and its adjacent community were walloped hard by the recession triggered by the 1973 Arab–Israeli War, which led to the Arab oil embargo. After each calamity, though, the factory recovered and once again sustained the community. By and large this trend continued until 1979. When the shah left town in the spring of that year, however, his departure created a monumental shift that changed the concept of the factory completely. For the most part, the plants that had built cars or components for cars for years now geared up either for utilitarian pickup trucks or large-engine behemoths that still got lousy gas mileage. Similarly, the component plants built pieces for these very cars. Further, many of these plants had been running almost continuously for over seventy years. (For example, Chrysler's Hamtramck plant, which by 1979 built Aspens and Volarés, and AMC's Jeep plant in Toledo both dated from the first decade of the twentieth century.) None of the plants and therefore none of the manufacturers were ready for the seismic events of 1979 and the three years that followed.

The recession of 1979 to 1982 jolted the factories into reality. Practically the entire manufacturing base had to be reworked. In some cases existing manufacturing plants could be gutted and redesigned to house the new equipment needed for a new generation of cars. However, many component plants that built parts for rear-wheel-drive cars became casualties of the new order. Chrysler's Huber plant in Detroit was one of the first to close; Chrysler, knowing that rear-wheel drive would play a much smaller part in its future production plans, simply just didn't need Huber anymore. Similarly, two other Detroit-area plants geared strictly for rear-wheel-drive cars—Chrysler's Lynch Road plant and the aforementioned Hamtramck plant—both closed. All across the industry in communities large and small, the same phenomenon was happening in Rust Belt towns heretofore sustained by Ford, GM, and AMC.

Suddenly "the factory" wasn't viewed as kindly anymore. Towns that had risen on the fortunes of the automobile business suddenly had no place to turn. Whole communities shrank as work of all kinds dried up. The new popular cars bore strange names such as Subaru, Toyota, Mazda, Isuzu, Honda, and Datsun. They came from far away, on huge boats, and rolled off those huge boats into American lives. They were small and cute, got incredible gas mileage, and seemed to run forever with very little maintenance. Moreover, they were one-half to two-thirds the price of the cars that Americans were already driving. Not only did the American factories have no current models to compare with these strange little cars, but they also had no plans or even the capability to build such vehicles.

That the American factories recovered at all could be credited to sheer grit, painful decisions to close many plants, perseverance in the face of Fed policies that drove up interest rates that by 1980 had reached over 20 percent, and eventually the willingness and foresight of the Japanese to institute voluntary restraints on their exports to the United States. The Japanese realized that the 1979 jolt to the American economy had presented them a once-in-a-lifetime opportunity. For years the Japanese had been making painstakingly slow progress in the United States. They knew their cars were better built, more fuel efficient, and, because of the value of the yen, less expensive than American cars. They also knew that America was the largest market for automobiles at that time. Finally, they realized that the combination of high interest rates, high inflation, rising gasoline prices, and Americans' increasing hostility toward the Japanese (whom many blamed not only for the troubles of the American auto industry but also for the American economy in general) might result in political action that would legislate the Japanese out of business in America. Sensing that an embargo could be slapped on their suddenly wildly popular products, by 1980, the Japanese officially agreed to limit shipments of Japanese cars to the United States.

As we have seen in a previous chapter, the voluntary restraint agreement actually carried advantages for the factories: With the supply of popular Japanese cars curtailed, the American manufacturers felt free to raise prices on their vehicles once the recession ended in early 1983. Only when the Japanese established manufacturing plants in the United States did the supply of their vehicles reach a point where pricing pressure eased. Japanese cars were still highly popular, but the Japanese had also learned that the key to keeping something hot was to keep it scarce. Accordingly, Honda, Nissan, Mazda, and Toyota plants in Ohio, Michigan, Tennessee, and California respectively produced at less than full capacity. As far as the Japanese were concerned, this strategy entailed only two failures.

The first involved Mazda's factory in Flat Rock, Michigan, which was announced with much fanfare in 1984 and then opened in August 1987 to much acclaim. The planning and production of this plant were done with Mazda's knowledge that, despite their modest but notable success in the

United States, Mazda did not have the market share, advertising dollars, or dealer network to support full-scale production at Flat Rock. Accordingly, Mazda partnered with Ford in an arrangement that called for production of Mazda's popular MX-6 coupe alongside a new iteration of the Ford Probe. The resulting company called Mazda Motor Manufacturing (USA) Corporation (MMUC) never quite got enough traction to make it as viable an enterprise as the Japanese originally envisioned. The joint production of the MX-6 and the Probe never enabled MMUC to attain enough critical mass to make the enterprise completely profitable. Accordingly, in 1992 Mazda completed its quality research building and an inland support facility directly across I-75 from the Flat Rock plant. MMUC became a joint venture between Ford and Mazda named Auto Alliance International Incorporated. Even the introduction of Mazda's 626 sedan at Flat Rock was not enough to make the plant truly viable. Eventually, as Mazda was beset with low volume, declining dealer quality, and other problems, Ford took over the operation of the plant completely. In 2012 Mazda discontinued production in the United States, and Ford Motor Company retook full management control of the plant, making a half-billion-dollar investment for production of the Ford Fusion.

The second failure occurred in 1985, when Mitsubishi formed a joint venture with Chrysler for American-built cars in Normal, Illinois. The new company, Diamond-Star Motors, was formed along the same premise as Flat Rock: American-built cars would not be subject to the same import restrictions as vehicles from Japan. However, like Mazda, Mitsubishi, as a second-tier Japanese import company, just didn't have the product lineup, the finances, or the strong dealer base needed to make the plant viable. By 2003, as Mitsubishi's large-scale fleet sales, a recall cover-up scandal, and disastrous, expensive finance programs began to eat away at the company, Mitsubishi tried to take advantage of the unused capacity in Normal to produce small sedans for the export market. Despite a streak of almost two years of year-over-year sales increases, Mitsubishi decided in July 2015 to close its Normal operation. In 2016 electric truck maker Rivian Automotive, Inc. bought the facility from a liquidator.

The stories of Mazda and Mitsubishi offered stark lessons for future attempts by second-tier manufacturers wanting to begin production in North America. For the most part, the lessons were well taken. For example, VW waited until 2008, when its corporate finances, worldwide sales and standing, and US base of over seven hundred retailers made the establishment of its Chattanooga, Tennessee, plant a more viable proposition. By 2010 VW's totally redesigned Passat sedan began to roll off the Chattanooga assembly line. The Passat represented VW's first successful production effort in the United States.

Likewise, Volvo, long a niche player in the American near-luxury market, established a manufacturing plant near Charleston, South Carolina. Volvo's action showed shrewd planning, valuable insights, and a bold strategy: The plant's location at the Port of Charleston meant easy access to export markets hungry for Volvo's high-quality, increasingly popular luxury offerings. Volvo's half-billion-dollar investment was offset by over $100 million in state and local incentives. In addition, the plant's location near Interstate 95 made US transport of Volvo's popular products to the high-dollar markets along the Eastern Seaboard much easier. In summary, Volvo's keen takeaways from the Mazda and Mitsubishi failures positioned it as a serious rival to Audi, Jaguar, Land Rover, and BMW, which, by the way, had already established a production facility two hours away in Greenville, South Carolina.

We can discern a pattern here. Most US auto plants that have opened within the past three decades have been in the South, where costs are lower and where unions hardly existed until a few years ago. Nor are the Japanese alone in this pattern. Mercedes built a huge plant in Vance, Alabama. Hyundai and Kia also constructed plants in Alabama and Georgia, respectively. Conversely, in 2019 GM closed several of its plants in the Rust Belt, including Lordstown, Ohio. Seeking ever-cheaper venues for business,

German, Japanese, Korean, and US domestic manufacturers all established presences in Mexico, where labor costs are so much less than in Canada and the United States.

Since I have mentioned labor specifically at this juncture, I should now note that the union retains a most important place in any discussion about "the factory." For the United Auto Workers (UAW), the term "the factory" meant not only the place where they spent most of their time but also the institution that held the power to regulate schedules, overtime, and wages. With the establishment of Japanese plants in the United States, the UAW saw an opportunity to replenish its ranks, which had been decimated considerably in the 1979–1982 recession. However, only in Toyota's Fremont, California, plant did the UAW make any significant inroads. Furthermore, many years later, as other manufacturers established plants on these shores, the union's efforts became even less successful. Workers at VW in Chattanooga, Tennessee, and Mercedes in Vance, Alabama, at Hyundai and Kia in West Point, Georgia, and Subaru in Lafayette, Indiana, figured they had a good deal already and consistently rejected advances by the union to establish in those plants. Their reasoning proved simple: In most of the areas where these facilities were established, the factories represented plum jobs, full employment, above-average wages for the market, and economic stability after the nightmare recessions of 1991, 1992, and 2001, not to mention the Great Recession of 2008. Even more importantly, workers in these newly established plants had seen with their own eyes what had happened to union plants in the North when their demands became too egregious. Toyota, Nissan, Hyundai, Kia, Mercedes, and VW surprised no one when they set up shop in the largely right-to-work South. Costs were low, workers were eager and plentiful (and with none of the bad habits of the union workers), and by comparison, the infrastructure, utility costs, and rail and highway systems were more favorable than in the North.

As previously noted, when the automobile business boomed after the war and throughout the 1960s, the unions became beneficiaries of the factory mindset of doing almost anything to avoid any interruption in production. Idled plants meant no cars built and no revenue, so to keep the union at bay, the factories acquiesced to progressively more lucrative contracts. The unions, knowing they had a good thing going, always made a pretext of dissatisfaction. However, since most union members liked the idea of steady work, above-average wages, and a second home on one of the lakes in Northern Michigan, nobody in the union complained too loudly. The lone exception, as we have seen, was the sixty-seven-day strike against GM in the summer of 1970. The relationship between the factories and the union had always been a little contentious; the unions never forgot the high-handed tactics of Henry Ford or the 1937 shenanigans of GM in Flint. For a number of years, however, both the factories and the union gritted their teeth and accepted the status quo: The union contracts meant continued production and corresponding cash flow for the factories; they also meant golden-egg circumstances for the workers.

The 1979–1982 recession inserted a new wrinkle in this dynamic. With the economy and especially the automobile market crashing in flames, the factories were forced to lay off workers and close plants. The union, scared to death, finally realized that the factories were actually their livelihood, not Big Brother hovering to lord over their lives. In December 1979, Chrysler secured the support of its UAW section as part of the Chrysler Corporation Loan Guarantee Act of 1979, knowing that if Chrysler went down, its members would have no work; therefore, the union agreed to significant concessions in its contract in exchange for a seat on Chrysler's board, an event heretofore never contemplated.

To the great relief of the workers, the manufacturers, the dealers, and the government, Chrysler emerged from the crisis much stronger. Battered but intact, the unions in particular made it a point of honor to emphasize their contribution to the success of the company in future contract negotiations. Overall, the cooperation of Chrysler and the UAW in the recession of 1979–1982 represented a positive turn in factory-labor relations. For years both entities had periodically maligned each other until they got to the precipice, looked over the edge, and saw their doom unless they could come together to help save each other. In the process they wrote a chapter in business school textbooks that will stand as a good case study for as long as the American auto industry survives.

In this chapter on "the factory," I have summarized the most common perceptions most customers have of the manufacturers, ending with a brief discussion of the laborers—the men and women who actually build the vehicles. Next, we'll focus on some lesser-known aspects of the factory that will probably surprise most customers.

CHAPTER 13

THE GAMES PEOPLE PLAY

A lot of consumers believe that an automobile assembly plant simply spits out the cars and delivers them to dealers for display and sale. Before my own hiring by Chrysler in the 1970s, I thought very much the same. However, another aspect of "the factory"—one that many people know nothing about—immensely influences the customer's buying and ownership experience. Between the factory and the dealer/manufacturer resides a layer of brilliance, bureaucracy, efficiency, incompetence, administrative awe, blatant buffoonery, technocratic turbidity, and outright abject automotive ineptitude. This huge layer includes several substrata, and these entities, taken as a whole, also are termed "the factory" because they are paid by, take their orders from, and are subservient to the automobile manufacturers. The most fascinating and important of these in-between entities are the staffed headquarters, where policy and strategy are formulated, and the regional offices, whose employees are charged with implementing those policies and strategies, thereby maintaining a modicum of tactical control over the dealers and the sales and service experience. Both the headquarters and the regional offices are critical to the operation of a manufacturer, and both, sadly, have come to cultivate a deep, visceral loathing for each other over the years.

A manufacturer's headquarters building and its resident corporate leadership team are the most tangible symbols of the organization aside from the actual factories. As the automobile business grew after the war years and as production and sales increased, putting more cars on the road that need more service and repair, car companies realized that they required a strong central organization to manage the business and provide feedback and information to the manufacturers' decision-makers. Accordingly, the headquarters of every automobile manufacturer houses some of the most energetic, disciplined, competent, and successful people in the world. This assertion proves especially true as the technological revolution switches to higher gear, and brilliant people gravitate toward the opportunities that the transportation industry offers. Some of the finest engineers, designers, marketers, financiers, technicians, and salespeople work in automotive headquarters. Throughout the last half of the twentieth century, the most talented of these people became either household names or icons of the industry.

Nearly every kid who was in high school in the 1980s believes, quite rightly, that Lee Iacocca saved Chrysler. He did, but he had a lot of help from guys such as Tom Pappert, Steve Sharf, Steve Miller, and Dick Vining, all of whom, while not as well known as Iacocca himself, nonetheless went on to become highly respected professionals within their disciplines in the industry. Henry Ford II may have been the face of Ford Motor Company in the 1960s and 1970s, but he couldn't have done it without Lee Iacocca, Phil Caldwell, Don Petersen, and a funny-looking little guy named J. Edward Lundy, who controlled Ford finances for over thirty years.

On the other hand, GM muddled through for over one hundred years mostly on sheer size, since most of its upper echelon were mediocre morons. GM managed to drive away one of the most capable minds in the business, John DeLorean, but they had enough solid engineers, finance people, and production managers to survive. The main point: The headquarters of an automobile manufacturing company (generally) attracts and keeps exceptional personnel. However, a headquarters also is home to well-intentioned idiocy. Some folks just don't get it, and these people can appear in any department: engineering, parts, service, finance, sales, logistics, and, of course, HR and IT. Since many staffers in an automobile company's headquarters have never worked in an automobile dealership or an assembly plant, they just don't have the conceptual framework for communicating with dealers or their end users—the customers who buy their products from the dealers.

Accordingly, in between the headquarters and the dealers is yet another layer of smart, (mostly) well-experienced professionals who inhabit what is called the regional office. Aside from salespeople in the dealership, the people in a regional office have, arguably, the toughest job in the automobile business. The regional office exists ostensibly to support the dealer network, enhance the brand experience, and project the brand into the local market. In reality, the headquarters depends on the region to curtail dealer and customer complaints, minimize warranty expense, hammer the dealers for orders to keep the production line going, wholesale parts to the dealers, and finally, ensure, to the greatest extent possible, that the dealers follow the factory's established policies and procedures. In short, the regional office runs interference for the headquarters.

Positioned as it is, the regional office is the car dealer's main contact with the factory. If a dealer wants a particular car, they will usually call their sales representative, who works out of the regional office. Similarly, if a dealer has a problem with a warranty claim, they will call a service representative, again, who works out of the regional office. Occasionally, if a dealer has a car in a service department for which they desperately need a part to complete the repair, they will call the regional office's parts representative to expedite the delivery of the part. All these are normal functions and common transactions in the factory-dealer relationship.

However, other individuals within the regional office also rely on direct contact with the dealer. These field technical specialists are trained to help with technical issues on vehicles. Nearly every regional office has a distribution department to balance out dealer inventories and, more importantly, at least from the factory's point of view, to make sure that the plants have an acceptable mix of orders from the dealers to enhance factory profitability. Similarly, the sales, service, and parts representatives I just mentioned drive the regional organizations. Among the major manufacturers, the regional office may also have a marketing department, whose main function is to ensure that any marketing assistance the factory doles out to the dealers is spent within very strict guidelines and closely follows the factory's marketing message. On some occasions a regional office may also have a training department, whose purpose is to educate a dealer's fixed operations personnel but in reality is there to minimize repair times and act as the dealer's ombudsman for customer handling issues. The training department also now assumes responsibility for electric vehicle (EV) training and, as such, gets a lot of flak from some dealers for the costs of EVs and their components, particularly the heavy expensive batteries that power the EVs. The training department does not produce EVs, but since they train for their sale and maintenance, some dealers insist on the association, much to the chagrin of the trainers.

At the top of the regional office hierarchy sits a general manager or regional director—a tenured manager with both headquarters and regional staff experience, who has operational responsibility for the region. Almost invariably, a regional director can prove the most essential, versatile, and important manager in the factory hierarchy. Their job is also the most difficult. The regional director represents the last line of defense in any disagreement that arises between a dealer and the factory. For this reason, in most factory organizations, the regional director has enormous power and authority. The last thing a headquarters vice president or manager of distribution or logistics wants to hear is a low-volume dealer complaining about the lack of a very desirable model. Similarly, woe betide the regional director whose dealer reaches a vice president of service and parts with a complaint about a vehicle on repair for want of a hard-to-get part or a borderline warranty claim from a large, powerful dealer whose service representative denied the claim.

Over the course of my career, I worked in both headquarters and regional positions. I am frequently asked about the differences between these two entities of "the factory" and in which I preferred to work. The biggest difference is in the entities' approach to the dealers. Almost without exception, a headquarters, with little practical knowledge of the business world and even less knowledge of the morass of customer complaints, regulatory obstacles, and market factors the dealers must maneuver, delights in the games of incentives, pricing and allocation imbalances, and shifting policies and procedures that make proper planning so difficult for dealers. The regional office must try very hard to temper the more difficult policy directives of the headquarters and make life more tolerable for the dealers. Personnel in a regional office talk with dealers every day. Staffers in a headquarters do not, and for many the prospect of speaking with a dealer is terrifying since a dealer is where the action occurs and few headquarters people have visited a dealership, much less worked there. Throughout my career my strength was close-point dealer contact and assisting dealer people through problems, some of them brought on by the games the factory people play. My preference? I'd work in a regional office any day.

In either case the car professional of today deals with something that didn't even exist when I entered the business. Our next chapter details working with ever-changing information technology.

CHAPTER 14

IT—CAN'T WORK WITH IT, CAN'T WORK WITHOUT IT

Forty years ago the primary (almost sole) communications medium for the car professional was the landline telephone. When I needed to report into the headquarters or regional office, I had to find a phone booth or a hotel and use a phone credit card to dial in and complete a report or transmit an order. (Now cell phones are ubiquitous, of course.) By 1990, the fax machine made communication between the office and a dealership a bit more convenient. The arrival of the personal computer was a major milestone as well. Email messages became practically instantaneous, as with the included attachments. In short, the rapid advances in technology have influenced the car business just as much as the rest of society. In fact, the pace of technology since the wider use of the internet represents one of the stress points between the dealers and "the factory," which I just discussed at the end of the last chapter.

In many cases the advances in software development and the sheer speed at which information travels have far surpassed the ability of a lot of people to fully deploy the vast resources available to them. For example, I can remember several instances in the 1970s wherein a month's allocation for a dealer was worked out on the back of an envelope. On considerably more occasions, the same task was accomplished on a couple of whiskey-soaked cocktail napkins. For as primitive as this method seems now, it worked. Both dealer and factory representative knew what they had concocted and were agreeable to the results. Now the same mundane task can be accomplished within a few seconds and several dozen keystrokes.

It's not just sales; currently, most dealership functions are performed by computer. Both manufacturers and dealers have invested billions in the development and installation of dealer management systems (DMS), from which almost unlimited information can be pulled from dealership ledgers, reports, payroll records, and other key performance indices. A thriving business has developed over the last forty years in information technology specific to car dealerships. Once the province of three or four large vendors, the DMS world is now occupied by dozens of vendors with varying capabilities and values. Some of the best of these outfits are fewer than ten years old and can calculate data as mundane as how much bulk oil a dealership uses to the amount of tax due on a transaction involving the sale of a mud flap.

From a dealership controller's point of view, the explosion of DMS firms has given dealers a great measure of choice. The increase in information technology that gave birth to such firms means that dealership controllers, payables clerks, inventory management personnel, parts personnel, service personnel, and finance and insurance managers, if they are properly trained, have the opportunity to perform in minutes tasks that sometimes took two or three days. For example, before the mid-1980s, a dealership controller could take three or four days closing the books on a month's activities by processing the information from a general ledger, service repair orders, dealership checking records, sales records, and parts/sales invoices and receipts. Nowadays an assistant controller can push a button on a desktop and generate a dealership financial statement or at least a trial balance within seconds. Such is the speed at which information travels today that a dealer, a region staffer, and the headquarters can have a fairly accurate snapshot of a dealer's monthly performance within a few hours of the end of the month. Similarly, vendors such as tire distributors and shop equipment firms, who sell to the dealers and the manufacturers, have the ability—within certain confidentiality constraints—to receive as complete a picture of a dealership's financial performance for the previous month as the dealer themselves. Information is power, so these vendors and the dealership's manufacturers maintain their own IT staffs to disseminate, analyze, and make what they will out of all this information. The result is information overload, which the manufacturers and vendors delight in dumping on despondent dealers for their own selfish means.

Let me explain. If information is power, many low-level manufacturer and vendor staffers can create great cottage industries for themselves by pointing out the most mundane inconsistencies in a dealer's data. These range from the sublime to the ridiculous to the asinine. A dealer whose incentive claims are well above those of the dealers in his comparison group will automatically find himself in the crosshairs of a manufacturer's audit group. On a more pertinent and reasonable level, analysis of the dealer data can reveal important trends, such as dealer gross profits across model lines, the number of repair orders a dealer writes, or blips on the radar screen as significant as the number of warranty claims on a specific service job, always an item of interest to headquarters auditors. In all fairness, such attention to detail has its place. Quick and thorough analysis can be very useful to a manufacturer in determining how many cars in certain numbers and colors to build. Manufacturing executives need and value such certainty.

Now we get to the eight-hundred-pound gorilla in the room. That room could be a cube farm on an entire floor in headquarters or an innocuous IT intern in a third-party vendor office. The sheer amount of information generated by the flood of new technology dictates that the manufacturers and even some vendors employ legions of IT specialists to help maintain the voluminous reporting systems, apply Band-Aid patches when necessary, or walk tech dinosaurs at the dealerships, vendors, or regional offices through the maze of buttons, bits, and bytes. To be sure, the heads of these specific legions of contract employees often are employed by the manufacturers or the vendors directly. The worker bees themselves almost always have no knowledge of the retail automobile business or the manufacturers' own policies and procedures. These people are absolutely brilliant in their specific field. Some may even have had a role in the development of the systems with which they work.

However, a deeper dive reveals the shortcomings of the way the entire system works. The IT specialist often has no frame of reference for the retail car world or a manufacturing environment. You know where this is leading. These people have the indignity of being stuck on a call line and having to deal with a frustrated US dealership or manufacturer employee who, however well intentioned, cannot put an IT problem into language intelligible enough for the IT specialist to help. Bernadette Boudreaux, the payables clerk for Napoleon Arseneaux Motors in Breaux Bridge, Louisiana, has a hard enough time deciphering the helpful instructions crackling down a phone line from Havrati Srinavasan at the manufacturer's call center in Trincomalee. Now look at it from Srinavasan's point of view: He is trying his level best to help an obviously flustered dealership employee, but he can only pick up every third word because it is delivered in Cajun-inflected Southern vernacular slang. All Bernadette wants to do is get the answer to a question, however poorly phrased, so she can get her software to perform and get home to her six-pack and étouffée. After what seems like eons of unintelligible enunciations, all Srinavasan wants is to get the problem handled and Bernadette back in her bunker.

Similarly, at the factory level, the scenario is much the same, just bigger. Even the smaller manufacturers doing business in the United States rely heavily on advanced computer systems to conduct their business. Since so much of the information that a manufacturer needs is tied up in a half-dozen computer systems, the failure of one or more of those systems causes enormous inconvenience for manufacturers and, by extension, their vendors and dealers, to say nothing of customers. Despite the redundancy built into these systems, things can, and will, go wrong.

I recall one instance when I was taking some time off and was 1,500 miles away from the office. I tried to log in on my company-issued laptop. (Unless one is in the hospital and near death, there is really no such thing as a "vacation" anymore; particularly in the auto business, one is expected, at a minimum, to keep up with email, and in this day and age, that requires a computer or cell phone with good connectivity.) In most automotive companies, working remotely requires invoking a virtual private network (VPN) to access the necessary systems for conducting business. On this occasion a pop-up box informed me that my access to VPN was denied. Like a good soldier, I tried again while pouring myself a cup of coffee and lighting a fresh cigar, only to receive the same message. This time I set aside the coffee and my smoke to concentrate on inputting the correct user ID and password. No dice.

At this point I had two choices: Since I was on paid time off (the modern euphemism for "vacation" in today's work world), I could say the hell with it and hopefully enjoy my time off. On the other hand, if I were really diligent, I could call my company's help line and get to the bottom of my technical problem. I chose the former, took a sip of coffee, and relit the cigar. It was eight o'clock in the morning, and I really had no desire or inclination to spend my time off working through a computer issue, particularly since there was no special assignment or heat case pending. Fortunately, my cell phone was still getting email, so I could keep up that way. Still, it bugged me because most computer problems I have are usually easily fixed by getting on the phone with a help desk technician and being embarrassed by the ease with which they pointed out my operator error. This worm of unease continued until my cell phone received an email from my region coordinator, which read, "I am hearing that some people are actually locked out of their computers due to the IT issues we are having." So much for my operator error. It looked like nobody was getting anything done.

The whole point is that IT, for all its magic, miracles, and convenience, has basically outpaced the ability of scores of people in the industry to handle it—like I intimated in this chapter's title: can't live with IT, can't function without IT. And the march of technology will only gather momentum. Too many billions, too much effort, and too much time have already been expended. All any of us can do, whether at the manufacturer, vendor, dealer, or customer level, is get as technically adept as we can as quickly as possible. It's a tall order, but at every level we'll all realize that time, money, and a lot more effort will be needed for training, retraining, and recertification. All this needs to happen sooner rather than later: From advances in EVs, audio technology, and infotainment systems to manufacturing, it's all going to affect the auto business mightily.

We've seen the onset of a generation that eschews getting their license at age sixteen in favor of transportation services, which, by the end of the current decade, will entail driverless vehicles. Who needs a license when you don't need to, can't, or don't want to drive? One of the last commercial bus services in North America had an advertising tagline in the 1960s that went, "Go Greyhound and Leave the Driving to Us." Fifty years later the idea remains even more appropriate for Lyft, Uber, Tesla, or even the car-buying services. In summary, driverless transportation will be here quicker than anyone realizes—all courtesy of information technology.

CHAPTER 15

BASTARDS, BANDITS, AND BOZOS (PART II)

In the previous chapter, we examined, at a very high level, how technology has influenced and continues to influence every facet of the automobile business. For anyone who has been in the business fewer than, say, ten years, the industry at every level has always involved bits and bytes, laptops and cell phones, web-based training, computer-aided design and manufacturing, and an untoward preoccupation with alternative fuels. Because the technological advances move so quickly, the people who have come into the industry in the last ten years and those who will come into for the next half century will think quicker with more focus and, by necessity, more energy and cerebral capacity than those who had entered the industry in the previous fifty years.

I do not mean to disparage mine or other previous generations. In fact, those generations made the current and future viability of the industry possible. Anyone who started in the business forty or more years ago has a treasure trove of automotive anecdotes to look upon fondly. These anecdotes archive a history of how we got to where we are during the postwar boom, the oil-related recessions of the seventies, and the booms and busts that accompanied the roller-coaster tech ride of the early years of this century. All these stories, and the casts of characters who survived the industry's trials, provide rich entertainment—but more importantly, vital lessons in sheer determination, ingenuity, pure gut feeling, and, unfortunately, abject automotive idiocy too.

When I arrived at Chrysler in the late 1970s as an administrative trainee with a newly minted liberal arts graduate degree, with no business education or knowledge of the automotive industry, I was fascinated by the stories my superiors told of the bigger-than-life automotive executives, wildly successful car dealers, over-the-top new-car announcement shows, ridiculously opulent ads, and equally ridiculous cars that they had been compelled to sell over the years. At the time Chrysler was, by far, the weakest of the domestic manufacturers. (AMC did such little volume, labored on such a small scale, and frankly was such a mess that it created or represented no threat to the other three and was hardly an afterthought in the minds of everyone except its employees and dealers.) A recession that had kicked off in February 1979 continued to worsen throughout the year to the point where interest rates rose to 20 percent and inflation to 13.4 percent.

Over cigarettes and coffee in the office (you could still smoke at work in those days) and cigars and whiskey in the bars at night, these guys whose worlds were being turned upside down would recall fondly their best memories from the halcyon days of the late fifties and sixties. Because getting orders to build product was the main focus then, some of the earliest stories I remember involved district sales managers who actually could get dealers to buy cars. In the business environment of the time, dealers were not buying many cars, so the stories from the days of yore when dealers would buy cars became of great interest to me, as odd as that might seem. One district sales manager in Louisiana, for example, was called Four-Acre Ray. In the sixties and seventies, when Chrysler cranked out hundreds of thousands of cars to no particular dealer order, Ray somehow had the ability to sell several dozen cars with the strength of a phone call alone. Throughout the decade of the 1960s and well into the 1970s, Chrysler would park these unsold, mostly unwanted vehicles in open spaces the company was lucky enough to acquire. Since at the time Chrysler was renting space all over the Detroit metropolitan area from the Michigan state fairgrounds to the parking lot at the Pontiac Silverdome, it was easy to make the connection to make the moniker—four acres of cars. (In those days, since the cars were bigger, you could park about forty-eight of them on an acre.) Accordingly, Ray's exploits became the stuff of legend.

Ray wasn't the only one with the magic touch. One guy in particular could be such a nuisance in trying to sell cars that a dealer would buy just to get him to shut up. And understandably—when you heard him on the phone, all you had to do was close your eyes and you would swear you were listening to a highly trained country auctioneer. Sometimes particular dealers would be the stars of the conversations. In Houma, Louisiana, dealer Joe Teuton could smell a bargain from five hundred miles away. All the dealers in those days were crafty and knew when the district sales manager and the zone office were getting desperate. Teuton made bargain shopping an art form—he knew when to deal and when to disappear. Almost invariably, the factory would offer up money to dealers who ordered cars. The best dealers such as Teuton knew exactly when to spring the trap.

In late 1979, while business throughout the rest of the country was absolutely deplorable, the South Louisiana area was still ginning. The oil field, for a time anyway, seemed impervious to the violent recession that ravaged the rest of the county. Teuton waited throughout October and November without ordering a car. Chrysler had not only built tens of thousands of cars in the third quarter, all unsold, but the company had also bought back tens of thousands of cars from unfortunate dealers who had been forced out of business because of the current conditions. In early December 1979, Chrysler offered $2,000 per car, regardless of model, to any dealer willing to buy them. Teuton, knowing this moment was coming, had assiduously avoided ordering any unnecessary cars and had a healthy account of open-inventory financing. He could take almost as many cars as he wanted, knowing that at $2,000 off each, he was in a superior position versus other dealers. Joe Teuton was not the only dealer gaming the industry this way, but he was the best at it. Most dealers of any brand, if they survived the recession, were just as adept but maybe not quite as successful.

Ford and GM, for most of 1981 and 1982, were in the same shape as Chrysler, so their dealers became just as ingenious as the Chrysler guys. For example, Ronnie Lamarque was a high-volume Ford dealer in Kenner, Louisiana, well regarded by Ford, and a master at playing the game. Since vans were hot sellers in the New Orleans area in the early 1980s, Lamarque would somehow always play the factory for what he could sell easily, and he was as good at cutting a wholesale deal as any dealer in Ford's network. Lamarque could get vans when nobody else could. The same scenario applied to pickup trucks, which, in the early 1980s, were one bright spot in an otherwise dismal sales picture. According to legend, Lamarque could get an entire order for some goofy program in vans and pickup trucks. Meanwhile, surrounding dealers would have to stumble through the order requirements, which usually entailed dozens more difficult-to-sell sedans than they possibly needed.

Throughout the country the really crafty and slick dealers, regardless of brand, played these programs for all they were worth. Out West mega-dealer Cal Worthington made a name for himself by eagerly subscribing to such programs, having hundreds of cars shipped to his locations. Then Worthington would resort to some of the most outrageous advertising to get that same inventory pushed out the door. Some of these ads blew the limits of propriety and credulity. The image of a sixty-year-old dealer riding an elephant around his new-car lot or walking the wing of a single-engine plane at four thousand feet at least got everybody's attention. In his heyday, Worthington had more business than he could handle.

Nor were the domestic dealers alone in their wholesale and retail gamesmanship. Dallas Mazda dealer Big Billy Barrett was famous for putting the squeeze on factory representatives whenever the wholesale push came along. In the late 1980s, when Mazda cars were not quite as popular as they had been in the first part of the decade, Barrett would put the screws to the factory by saying that he would order the requisite number of cars required by the wholesale program, but he would get to choose what models, colors, and price classes. Of course, this tactic was vastly unfair to the other dealers and, for all we knew, probably illegal, but because Barrett sold upward of three hundred cars per month, the factory didn't have the budget (or the balls) to refuse him.

Such practices left the smaller, more remote dealers far behind in competitiveness and, more importantly, profitability. Raymond Hunter, a very mediocre VW and Mazda dealer in Tupelo, Mississippi, found himself a typical victim of such stunts, and he took every opportunity, quite rightly, to bitch up a storm when he knew some Dallas-area schmuck such as Barrett was working the factory. Hunter's phone calls on this item, as well as other points of concern, also became the stuff of legend. His Mazda district sales manager, who to this day remains one of my best friends, loves to recount one 1985 call from Hunter as one for the ages. In those days all of us Mazda district sales managers worked from home the first couple of days a month to telephone all the dealers with the details of the wholesale programs and the corresponding wholesale allocations. My friend was in the middle of disseminating the allocation for the month when Hunter launched into an unsolicited soliloquy, criticizing my friend, Mazda, and Japanese high-handedness in particular, ranting about our region management's mistreatment of the smaller ham-bone dealers. Ten minutes into the tirade, my friend put the receiver down since Hunter was dominating the conversation and wouldn't let him get a word in edgewise, walked from his home office into his kitchen to get a beer, and smoked a cigarette just as a way to get a small break. When he walked back into his home office eight minutes later and picked up the receiver, Hunter was still in full throttle. "Damn!" said my friend as he recounted the episode. "That's the first time I got nailed on a program and allocation before I had the chance to complete either. Shit, even Castro took a break! Didn't he?"

The dealers can be colorful and entertaining, but sometimes their employees steal the spotlight. Among the bona fide bastards, bandits, and bozos in the industry are the sales managers, general managers, service managers, finance managers, parts people, and used-car personnel who bring the business to life. Given that most of these people work on commission, as I have stated before, and somebody above them—the dealer, the manager, or controller—invariably will want to pimp their pay, dealership managers are ever attentive to any opportunity to fatten their wallets. First, let's take the sales end. Let's say a young couple comes into the dealership with their eye on a certain vehicle. Let's say they've done their preliminary research, have their financing in place, and really have their heart set on a particular model. At the same time, the dealer, general manager, or sales manager might have put a spiff or sales bonus on a particular model. Let's say that this particular model is not the car that the young couple desires to buy. Depending on the bonus that has been placed on the car that the dealer or the general manager really wants sold, the sales manager and the salesperson will naturally do anything within their power to persuade a customer with cash on the ready and financing arranged to turn their attention to the bonused vehicle. Indeed, many a sure sale has been lost by a sales manager or a salesperson too stupid to fulfill a customer's wish. Granted, money is a big motivator, but a bird in hand is worth two in the bush. Chasing the dough can lead to woe for a sales manager or salesperson and make them look like a bozo to boot.

Of course, I've written previously about finance managers and their skill at packing hundreds of dollars' worth of items into the price of a car—after a customer has supposedly settled on a "deal." However, I can cite other ways in which a dealership can royally screw up a customer. Let's take another example. Since the inception of leasing, a customer has had the option to buy his leased vehicle after the termination of the lease. In recent years, though, finance managers, increasingly commonly, and sometimes with the full knowledge and complicity of senior management, will "forget" to pay off the lease with the finance company, roll the same vehicle into a used-vehicle purchase contract, and simply steal away into the night with the money. I personally can recall several dozen instances such as this one involving an import dealer in North Jersey. Even more egregious is the dealership that fails to properly ground a lease when a customer turns in a closed-end leased vehicle at lease termination.

To explain, a customer brings the car back to the selling dealer at the expiration of a closed-end, thirty-six-month lease. At that time a customer can simply turn in the car and walk away from the lease, less any wear and tear or fee for excess mileage, or purchase the vehicle as a used car. If the customer chooses to just walk away at the end of the lease, the dealer should notify the finance company, which often is the dealer's captive finance source. Yet in recent years, as dealership finance managers have become less experienced, sloppy, or just plain lazy, this step is increasingly being skipped. Or, worse still, the dealership or the finance company entices a customer, via direct mail, for an early lease turn-in. In this situation, at about month thirty of a thirty-six-month lease, a customer will get a promotional piece from the finance company or the dealer, or sometimes both, to come into the store and lease or buy another shiny new car.

The unscrupulous finance manager could, if the customer chooses to buy or lease a new car, "forget" about resolving the unexpired lease turn-in. Several weeks later the unsuspecting, innocent customer could get a notice from the finance company that he is delinquent on the last four payments (or more) of his thirty-six-month lease. This "mistake" happens more often than the dealers, the finance companies, or the manufacturers will admit, and it causes enormous problems for the customer. At this point the unsuspecting, innocent customer is now on the hook, not only for the new car they just purchased but also for the payments remaining on the early lease turn-in sitting (hopefully) at the dealership. I say "hopefully" because in recent times some dealerships would sell an early lease turn-in to another unsuspecting customer, financing through a different finance company. "Moving the metal" rings the cash register.

Speaking of ringing the register reminds me of the first and most important lesson I learned in the retail car business: nothing happens until somebody sells a car. During the recessions of the early 1980s, the manufacturers had to keep the plants open, but knowing that sales were still tough, they had to devise a way to get their dealers to accept cars, as well as the incentives used to push the cars out from dealers to the customers. Thus, the push-pull programs were perfected. When the plant fill (that is, the number of orders necessary to keep the plant operating and avoid a shutdown) became too small, the manufacturers would go to the dealers with a program to pay the dealers for ordering cars on the front end, coupled with a separate program of incentives to make the inventory disappear.

All the manufacturers used this procedure with varying degrees of success. For their part, the best dealers of all brands played the manufacturers like a dinner fork. For example, for the first couple of weeks of every month, all the manufacturers' district sales managers were hammering highways—driving from dealer to dealer trying to get the dealers to order cars in a prescribed mix and quantity within that mix. Most of the time, the dealers had as much need for more cars as the man in the moon. The dealer, knowing that he had to play ball to some extent, would order several cars just to fill the few holes he had in the inventory or to get rid of the district sales manager and get on with his workday. Almost always a huge shortage of orders remained at the end of the two weeks. As if not having enough hot cars to satisfy the dealers isn't scary enough, real fear for an auto executive was not having enough orders to keep the plant running. So about midmonth a panic call would go out from the regional office to the district sales managers; sometimes this call would come in the middle of a meeting with a general manager or dealer and would be an order to get to the regional office as quickly as possible or to get to a large dealer, then camp near a phone to await a subsequent call. Almost invariably, the first eventuality, to get to the regional office, would come when the district sales manager was six hundred driving miles from the office or nowhere near an airport to get back to the headquarters city. In the case of the latter, it meant a ten- or twelve-hour drive back, usually through the night, to get the program in person.

Invariably, the program looked like this: It ran for thirty days; any small car ordered means $300 for the dealer and then $300 when it is retailed, for a total of $600 per car. For a medium-sized car, $400 when it is ordered and $400 when it is sold, for a total of $800 per car. A large car—say, a Chevy Caprice, Chevy Impala, Ford Crown Victoria, Mercury Grand Marquis, or Chrysler New Yorker or Newport—earned $500 when ordered and $500 when retailed, for a total of $1,000 per car. Across all brands and models, the dollar amounts might vary, but the concept was the same—the manufacturers were just pushing production to the plants on the front end and pulling them out of the dealerships on the other. The program was usually christened with a goofy name such as "Spring Order Run" or "Race to the Record" (nobody could ever tell us what the record was—for all we knew, it was Vic Damone's latest LP) or "Build-Out Bash." We would receive copies of the programs (email had not been invented yet), call all our dealers, pitch the program with as much enthusiasm as we could muster, and start writing car orders.

In the course of our phone conversations, the dealers would pick out all the warts in the program. The most typical questions are as follows: "What about the cars already in my inventory? Are they eligible for the sales incentive?" "The program is thirty days long. Can you build these cars and get them shipped within thirty days? And if you can't, will they still be eligible for the sales incentive? If not, what happens then? Will you have a new program to help me sell the crap that ships late? When will I get paid for the cars that I order? When will I get paid for the cars I sell?" Now if you're thinking that this scenario sounds ridiculous, you're right!

Usually these push-pull programs were ill and hastily conceived, hardly ever thought through completely, and announced without a full understanding of the dealer's current inventory, the availability of components to build the cars in the first place, and no set mechanism at headquarters to monitor the programs in a systematic way.

In truth, the manufacturers almost always did not know how much money these programs would generate, how many costs they incurred on the incentive end, or, on the logistical end, how quickly the cars could reach the dealers, be prepped and front-lined, and delivered to customers. The main idea remained to get the plants filled and stave off a shutdown. Second, the programs had to generate some excitement at retail and get sales reported. In those days manufacturers reported sales every ten days. The companies lived and died off those reports. The automotive press and business publications, in turn, eagerly reported the numbers. Everybody from the Federal Reserve to the Council of Economic Advisers studied the figures and trends and used them to set and adjust economic policy. Chrysler, in particular, hoped for an uptick in sales to keep from getting killed in publications from *Automotive News* to the *Wall Street Journal* to *Car and Driver*.

Consequently, the manufacturers often revised the programs on the fly. The howls of protest from a dealer who had ordered a ton of cars before the program was announced (which cars technically would be ineligible for the wholesale incentive) would have to be taken into consideration. Dealers with inventory imbalances would scream that they just couldn't stomach another fifteen Malibus or twenty Granadas, no matter how much the factory offered to pay the dealer to order and sell them. Similarly, the captive finance sources would groan and grumble that many of the dealers they floor-planned would be imperiled, particularly if the wholesale part of the programs entailed egregious order objectives by model, which they almost always did.

To a certain extent, the same problems exist today, over thirty years after the heyday of the push-pull programs. Since the bean counters still run the manufacturers, the cars built almost never match the cars consumers want. For all the manufacturers' platitudes of having the right car, at the right time, and at the right price, what gets built is almost always what the accounting and finance staff want built. That is, the most profitable units for the factory. For all the dealer council minutes professing the need to incorporate dealer preferences in production, manufacturers build cars to generate the most revenue when wholesaled to the dealer.

I offer a couple of prime examples of this dynamic of factory idiocy. The first involves an allocation/production run for, say, a particular month. As an area executive for VW at the early part of this century, I can remember many instances wherein I was given an electronic guide of what to order—by model, by trim level, by engine, by transmission, by option package, and even sometimes by exterior color. Since by this time the technology enabled even a low-level field representative to input orders on his laptop, I would spend perhaps a day keypunching orders for as many as several hundred to a thousand cars (a couple of months' production for my area) and, within the guidelines provided by the distribution department, would feel pretty good about getting as many salable models to my dealers as possible. However, several days later I would get an electronic message from my distribution or production contact stating that the entire order had to be canceled and resubmitted. Usually, the resulting order guide would bear no resemblance to the production order I had submitted a few days prior. Calling around to my fellow area executives, I would not be surprised at all that this message went to everybody. Although nobody would ever confirm it, we would all know that everyone's production orders had probably been reviewed by some finance pricks who would determine that the order mix wasn't "rich" enough.

Faced with a choice of losing what in those days proved pretty good jobs, or building what we recognized as difficult-to-sell merchandise, we all turned chickenshit and complied. Besides being sick to our stomachs of being part of the charade, we were pissed as hell because we had wasted perhaps an entire day for nothing. Or we might get a message indicating that some other country needed the plant capacity our previous production orders had entailed. Since in those days VW built cars for sale in many countries, the production slots meant for our dealers might be shifted to Moldova, or some other Eastern Bloc country, or worse yet, China. Never mind that the United States at the time was still the biggest and most important automotive market in the world; if some German accountant figured VW could make more money shipping a 2003 Touareg to China instead of Gilroy, California, that's what would happen. Currency fluctuations and logistics figured as much into production as free-market factors.

A second factor also figures into the equation of what gets built. Over the last dozen years, many manufacturers have opened up preference and order capability to retail dealers. The idea is that, given a template of order requirements by model, engine, transmission, and trim level, the orders will simply flow in from the dealers, the appropriate trim level will achieve the plant fill necessary, and everybody—from the factory managers to the accountants, the dealers, sales managers, salespeople, and customers—will go swinging down the lane like Frank Sinatra and Doris Day. Not surprisingly, dealer personnel, except in the rarest of cases, are simply not trained well enough to follow such guidelines as strictly as needed. Generally speaking, turnover at the dealership level remains extraordinarily high, and the individuals charged with such ordering responsibility might also have the same task for the dealer's other stores. A sales manager for a VW store might also have the responsibility for a dealer's Honda, Toyota, Mazda, Ford, or GM store. Further, a sales manager's true responsibility is to oversee the *sale* of the dealer's cars, and he can't do that effectively if he is doing what should be the factory's job by building cars.

So guess what happens next.

The factory representative, whether they are called a district sales manager, an area executive, a car coordinator, a truck specialist, or something else, has to get involved. This already overworked, overwrought individual has to go into the computer system or contact the responsible individual at the dealership and "fix" all the orders. Dealers, their managers, and the manufacturers waste a lot of time in such instances. In short, the factories would do better, make more money, and have better dealer relations if they simply listened earnestly to the dealer input and simply built what the market demands. That way the dealers could concentrate on what they do best, retailing cars, and the factories could concentrate on what they do best, building them.

CHAPTER 16

LEADERS BEING LEADERS AND DEALERS BEING DEALERS

Any organization—a country, an army, a business—survives and thrives on leadership. The concept of leadership is particularly important in business, and more specifically it is crucial in the automobile business. The overworked cliché on the sign on Harry Truman's desk, which said, "The Buck Stops Here," remains appropriate in the American car business. Similarly, the old navy adage, "The speed of the skipper is the speed of the ship," speaks volumes at every level of the automobile business.

The entrepreneurs who put America on wheels possessed more than ideas, energy, and vision; they also had focus. The early titans of the business, such as Henry Ford and his contemporaries, as well as the generation that came after them, mostly seemed to have led by sheer force of will. As founders of their respective companies, they instinctively nurtured their drive to succeed. They tolerated little delay and even less dissent. Clearly, Henry Ford's treatment of workers at River Rouge and other plants seemed severe at the time and is considered reprehensible today, but in the end his clarity of vision, perseverance, and single-minded determination practically created the modern age.

The Ford plant managers who supervised the workers who actually assembled the cars appeared no less stern and strong. The discipline they meted out seems excessive today, but production schedules demanded by Ford entailed nothing less. By the 1940s, when the auto industry was practically taken over by the government for war production, leadership, while it had become a little more enlightened, proved no less important. Bombers and tanks still needed to be built. The endless line of two-and-a-half-ton trucks still needed to be cranked out to keep Russia from knuckling under to the Germans.

When Henry Ford II left the navy to take over his grandfather's company, he realized that while he might have the leadership skills to head America's leading industrial concern, he still needed the technical expertise of a group of Army Air Corps statisticians and a couple of seasoned GM executives to lend some credibility to his leadership. The years 1945–1953 were important in the industry; during this period, smart, tough, charismatic leaders were assisted by equally smart, visionary supporting characters. These men had conceived, built, and run the logistical machine that had won the war for America in Europe and the Pacific. Since most of them had been in the military, they were also steeped in the concepts of leadership: obedience, discipline, adherence to doctrine, and compliance with the new order.

As the business became more complex, bigger, and increasingly in need of capital not only to churn out the cars and trucks America wanted but also to expand the physical wherewithal to produce these products, the finance men began to emerge. It is doubtful whether we would know Ford Motor Company in its current form had Henry Ford II's finance men not been able to convince Ford to go public in 1955. The result was a company that was poised to greatly capitalize on America's insatiable desire for cars and trucks. Ford's sensational performance as a company throughout the 1950s and 1960s cemented the reputation of Henry Ford II and his leadership team, particularly Lee Iacocca, who had become Ford's general manager of sales in 1960, as the premier leaders in their field. The same phenomenon was happening at GM. Guys such as Bunkie Knudsen and Pete Estes, bolstered by a supporting cast of no-nonsense, seasoned, tough-as-nails finance, engineering, and production teams, eventually overtook Ford and skyrocketed to an almost sixty percent share of the automotive market in the United States.

The more enlightened leadership style of the 1960s was a far cry from the days of Henry Ford's security staff and GM's internal security beating striking workers over the head with billy clubs in 1937. If leadership begets success, the opposite is also true—Lee Iacocca's launch of the Mustang in April 1964 proved a great catapult to his career. Such was his style, charisma, and capability as a manager that he was able to recruit, develop, and retain a loyal team well into the 1970s. This cadre of adherents became critical to Iacocca's resurrection of Chrysler in the 1980s.

Leadership of employees is one matter, but only a special kind of guy can pull off what Iacocca did during the Chrysler loan guarantee crisis. In that instance, first, Iacocca had to also motivate a quarrelsome covey of some 2,500 scared dealers. Second, he had to convince a multiplicity of suppliers to keep shipping parts, sometimes not knowing when they'd be paid. Third, he had to convince literally hundreds of banks, financiers, saving and loans, and just plain old mom-and-pop investors to ascribe to a plan that none of them liked and seemed extremely likely to bankrupt some of them. Fourth, he alternately used cajoling, begging, pleading, and sheer force of will to get the Chrysler section of the United Auto Workers (UAW) to sign on. The union agreed, but their price was high; one of their demands entailed a seat on Chrysler's board of directors for Douglas Fraser, the head of the UAW bargaining section for Chrysler. Finally, Iacocca spent the entire fourth quarter of 1979 convincing a reluctant Congress and President Jimmy Carter to support the Chrysler Corporation Loan Guarantee Act of 1979.

It almost didn't happen. Any one of the groups of major stakeholders—the vendors, the banks, the union, or the government—could have torpedoed the deal. That it succeeded is a testament to strength of character, depth of conviction, a keen vision of what life would be like once the storm had passed, and a great deal of motivation to show Henry Ford II what a real grassroots leader could do. Never mind that Chrysler has lurched from one crisis to the next over the last thirty years—that Chrysler is still around at all is Lee Iacocca's enduring legacy.

On a less grand scale, other talented guys, not as well known as Iacocca but no less important, had their own impacts on their companies and the industry. Yutaka Katayama spent most of the 1960s and 1970s building Nissan's structure in the United States. Though he had help from experienced American managers, the vision and the result were purely Katayama's. As such, Katayama endures as a symbol of Japanese determination. His work paved the way for the success of all the Japanese car companies that held a tenuous toehold in the American market throughout the early 1970s.

By the late 1970s, the Japanese still lagged behind GM, Ford, Chrysler, and even AMC in profitability, dealer success, and brand recognition. The cars had improved to the point where quality had surpassed that of the American's, and the price points were much more favorable. Despite these advantages, the Japanese still struggled with a brand image problem and a lingering cultural stigma in the American mindset—an idea that Japan simply couldn't compete in the tough US market. Japanese management was determined, ambitious, patient, and optimistic. Most importantly, however, the Japanese understood that they needed experienced Americans to help take them to the next level in the US market. Bob McCurry, a longtime employee of Chrysler's Dodge division, became the head American at Toyota in 1978. Frank Girard and Rod Hayden, also longtime, highly experienced Chrysler hands, joined Mazda at the same time. Similar events occurred, almost simultaneously, at Nissan, Honda, and Subaru. The Japanese gave enormous leeway to their newly installed American managers, although product development, design, and manufacture remained firmly within the hands of the Japanese.

However, the American managers became the sorely needed face of the Japanese imports in the United States. Guys such as Bob McCurry and Rod Hayden and, somewhat later, Mitsubishi's Dick Recchia, possessed experience and levels of gravitas that made them instantly credible to dealers and salespeople. These guys could talk to the dealers in their own language, and dealers being dealers, they could translate the dealer concerns back to Japanese management without anybody losing "street cred" or face. Further, the American managers were able to guide the Japanese through the maze of regulatory and political landmines that made doing business in the United States such a terrifying experience to the Japanese. Having worked mostly through distributors in Asia, the Pacific, the Middle East, and Europe, the Japanese were woefully unfamiliar with the US dealer network and the American pastime for lawsuits. Particularly after the 1979 Iranian Crisis helped Japanese car popularity skyrocket, the American managers deftly maneuvered their Japanese colleagues through their newfound success.

For almost twenty years, the Japanese had been trying with intermittent success to establish themselves in the American market. They were well aware of the story of VW, who managed a modicum of success in the late 1950s but gained incredible momentum in a small section of the car-buying public with the Beetle. By 1972, VW was retailing half a million cars in the United States with a loyal dealer body represented by several regional distributors. The Japanese did not fully capitalize on the VW model or even its modest success. The much more powerful domestic brands—GM, Chrysler, and particularly Ford—were the real targets the Japanese wanted to emulate. Theirs was a tough sell: GM and its dealers held a 60 percent share of the American market, and Chrysler was the smallest of the three, but its dealers were loyal to the brand. Even more loyal were the Ford dealers, some of whom had been with the company since its inception, and all of whom were very profitable selling Ford products.

The only guys the Japanese seemed to be able to interest in their offerings were used-car dealers who wanted an opportunity to be new-car dealers. Many of these used-car dealers had sales and service experience but never enough money to become a dealer for any one of the Big Three. Further, most of these dealers, in addition to having the stigma, if you will, of being "used-car dealers," operated in small, inefficient facilities in undesirable locations. For the most part, the Japanese recognized these men as their best opportunity at the time. The new-car dealers that they had were GM, Ford, Chrysler, and Jeep dealers who took on the Japanese brand but paid them little attention, relegating their Toyota, Datsun, or Honda franchises to small showrooms in the least effective locations on their lots. They were okay with their Japanese franchises as long as they didn't lose money.

Then an odd event occurred. As we have seen, when sales of domestic land yachts ground to a halt, the domestic dealers, suddenly mindful of the overnight success of Japanese brands, began flooding Japanese headquarters and local and regional offices, begging for a chance to become Datsun, Honda, or Toyota dealers. This shift was the point at which the domestic dealers' cozy relationships with their manufacturers retreated before the business imperative of selling inexpensive cars and making more money.

Now the senior American managers at the Japanese companies really shone. Because of their experience in the previous decades with the domestics, these managers could tell the Japanese who the best dealer candidates were. Bob McCurry at Toyota had an encyclopedic knowledge of Chrysler's dealer organization. The group of ex-Ford managers at Nissan guided their Japanese colleagues to the best-performing, well-financed Ford dealer hand-raisers. Since Rod Hayden, Frank Girard, and Dick Colliver at Mazda had spent decades with Chrysler between them, they were able to ferret out for the Japanese the best Chrysler and Dodge candidates for Mazda dealerships. At the same time, for the same reasons, these American managers were easily able to strike deals with eager domestic dealers hungry for the chance to sell these strange, small cars with funny names and subsequently carry the profits to the bank with wheelbarrows.

As more domestic dealers gravitated toward the imports, the role of the

American managers became even more important. As popular as the Japanese cars had suddenly become in the spring of 1979, the senior American managers at all the import companies were keenly aware of three important factors. First, the Japanese companies simply did not have the availability, as hot as the import market was, to satisfy the dealer demand. Second, because the Japanese pipeline was long and cars took months instead of days to ship from Japan, even to the West Coast of the United States, the American managers had to readjust dealer expectations—a customer ordering a Mazda RX-7 could expect a significantly longer wait for his car than a Buick customer ordering a LeSabre. Third, because of the first two factors listed here, the Japanese simply could not unilaterally demand that their American dealers build exclusive facilities for their brands.

This last point remained a sore subject for American dealers for several years, and its significance was particularly heightened after the institution of Japanese voluntary restraints in 1981. The Japanese, though grateful to have the sales outlets to market their cars, were still highly irked that their Datsun, Honda, Toyota, and Isuzu facilities were so much smaller, less well kept, and less well staffed than a typical dual dealer's domestic operation. Worse, in many instances, to be able to get the dealer to take on the Japanese franchise in the first place, the Japanese often allowed a domestic dealer to dual the Japanese franchise in the same showroom and service department with the dealer's Chrysler, Ford, or GM lines. The domestic manufacturers were just as irked as the Japanese; they all hated the idea of their Pontiac, Lincoln, or Plymouth customer walking into what they thought was *their* showroom and have *their* customer buy a Datsun 510, Honda Prelude, or Toyota Corolla. The domestic manufacturers could do little; state statutes protected dealers from such manufacturer demands. Additionally, business for the domestics was still too bad for them to come down hard on a dealer who also had Accords, GLCs, or Isuzu I-Marks in the showrooms. Manufacturers bristled that often the import brand outsold the domestic brand even with limited availability.

Thanks to the leadership, savvy, and keen sense of business relationships of the American managers at the Japanese companies, the land mines were maneuvered through, and major incidents were avoided. On the domestic end, the manufacturers wanted no pissing contests over a funny little foreign brand that they thought they could push out of their dealer showrooms once the recession ended. On the Japanese end, no one wanted to kill the golden goose of their newfound popularity, even if the Japanese resented the domestic dealer's prior relationship with their domestic partner. As the American managers more than adequately explained to their Japanese supervisors, opportunities abounded for making more money, exploiting more segments, and earning new customers.

An uneasy truce continued to hold even after the recession ended. The voluntary restraint, which had been intended as a temporary expedient to allow the domestic manufacturers and their dealers some breathing room, soon was openly flaunted by the domestics themselves, who raised prices to recoup their terrible losses of 1979–1982. Noting this development and also knowing that their products were as popular as ever, the Japanese longed to impose demands on their dealers for larger and better facilities and improved customer treatment. Again, the American managers stepped in and deftly counseled the Japanese. Too heavy a hand, they said, would result in a mutiny by dealers who could get only a limited number of import cars, while the domestic factory order pipelines were flush with Dodges, Pontiacs, Fords, and Jeeps, which, with the end of the recession, were now selling briskly again.

Aside from the allocation, governmental, legal, manufacturer relations, and cultural land mines, the American managers of Japanese companies also helped bring the Japanese into the big leagues of finance. By the late 1970s, the domestics had had their own captive finance companies for years. As detailed previously, most domestic brand dealers had a relationship with their captive—Chevrolet, Buick, GMC, and other GM dealers could not have made it through the 1973–1974 recession without the General Motors

Acceptance Corporation (GMAC). The same was true for Ford and Lincoln-Mercury dealers regarding Ford Motor Credit. Chrysler Credit was practically the sole source of financing for many Chrysler dealers, as the banks were nervous about Chrysler's historical ups and downs. The senior American managers for Toyota, Datsun, Honda, Mazda, and Subaru understood too well that for their brands to grow, their dealer bodies had to have access to capital beyond the banks and the motley of array of diversified financial institutions (ITT, Borg-Warner, Debis, and others who loved to get into the automotive finance business when sales soared but exited the business quickly when times were bad).

The road to captive finance companies for the Japanese was long and took time. Since the Japanese became anxious about laying out the capital for floor planning and retail business (including capital loans, mortgages, and wholesale finance lines for used cars), the American managers took it slow, deftly arranging agreements with the diversified lenders and the best commercial banks well suited for the automotive lending business. The arrangements were far from ideal. The diversified institutions and most of the banks trailed the captives in familiarity with the market and did not truly understand the dealer mindset. Mazda's relationship with Marine Midland Bank became an exception, but the dealers still chafed at the terms and conditions, as well as the poor level of service at not only the buyer level but also the field level.

Neither the banks nor the diversified institutions measured up to the task, particularly regarding capital loans and mortgages, but after several years of dazzling profits for the Japanese, the American managers convinced them to establish their own captive finance companies. To be fair, the American managers had help. Some import dealers, who also had Ford, GM, or Chrysler franchises, had managed to get GMAC, Ford Motor Credit, or Chrysler Credit to floor their Japanese brands. When the US auto recession hit its low in the fall of 1982, domestic captives let these dealers know that they wanted nothing to do with the imports. The captives informed their

Ford, Chrysler, and General Motors dealers, who also had import franchises, that not only would they refuse to finance retail deals for import sales, but in many cases they would also stop floor-planning their import lines. Curiously enough, about the same time, many banks and the diversified institutions exited auto financing. The American managers had known for some time that this event was coming, and since many of the American managers had worked in the captive credit arms of their former domestic employers, they had been doing some brilliant behind-the-scenes work on the creation of Toyota Motor Credit Corporation, American Honda Finance Corporation, and Nissan Motor Acceptance Company. The foregoing is a little-known aspect of the history of the Japanese imports in the United States, but it's also a testament to the business acumen and leadership of the senior American executives of the Japanese companies. Like the voluntary import restraint agreements of the previous year, the domestic captive decision to kick the import business to the curb actually had the opposite effect of what was intended.

Factory executives at the second tier of American managers in the Japanese companies performed just as brilliantly in the shaky days of the last year of that recession. The supply of Japanese cars was extremely short, the domestic business had not yet recovered, and financial markets were still jittery enough to have dealers, domestics, and the Japanese all scared out of their wits. Almost without exception these skilled regional managers and staff managers (they were still all men in those days) had started their careers with the domestics. They worked long enough to have seen the good and the bad of the business with the domestics, they had dealt with the best and the worst of business and dealers, and they knew how to handle these uncharted waters. Particularly among the ex-Chrysler executives, nearly all of whom had spent their entire careers lurching from crisis to crisis with short bursts of prosperity in between, these men recognized opportunity. They knew that with commodities as desirable as Japanese cars, they could get their dealers to go to extraordinary lengths to support their brands—particularly when those dealers, many of whom already had a GM, Ford, or Chrysler franchise, were down in the mouth over their domestic franchises and business in general. The regional managers and district sales managers told their dealers, in their own language, how important it was to build new facilities or, at the very least, renovate the facilities in which they had stashed the Japanese imports. This level of managers also deftly communicated to the dealers the importance of properly marketing and advertising their import cars.

The effort to improve facilities continued for several years until the Japanese established plants in the United States, and the acute vehicle supply shortages eased somewhat. Moreover, these regional managers and the district managers who worked for them had to convince the dealers not to mark up the prices on these popular, hot-selling cars to the point where they totally alienated customers. This last point cannot be stressed enough: Dealers who had lost hundreds of thousands of dollars, or even millions in the previous three years, were acutely aware of the value of their import commodities, and dealers being dealers, the greed factor almost always kicked in. All the American managers at the national, regional, and district levels knew that at some point the recession would end, and the domestics would come roaring back. And come back they did, although these managers got stupid and raised prices since the Japanese were still under voluntary import restraints.

Once the recession had ended and everybody was making money again, the American managers at the import companies steered the Japanese executives carefully toward increased customer satisfaction, knowing that the domestics were making great strides in quality and customer handling. At the same time, the American managers acted as something of a buffer between their Japanese bosses and their dealers over the institution of brand standards that would require discipline on the part of the dealers to upgrade operations, personnel, and facilities. By this time, the late 1980s, the Japanese understood how outgunned they were in terms of both the size and appearance of their brands' facilities. Not wanting to be outdone, they demanded that dealers upgrade immediately. The American managers tamped down expectations, understanding that the dealers couldn't or wouldn't make the required investment when cars were in such short supply. Another way in which the American managers brought order and discipline to their organizations was by hiring, training, and retaining good managers to work with the dealers and tamp down *their* expectations. Every import dealer at this time wanted more cars than the import companies could provide. The responsibility fell to regional, distribution, and district sales managers to talk the dealers off the ledge and give them operational goals to aspire to instead of just looking out the showroom windows for the transports to show up.

Since most of the import managers at the national, district, and regional levels had come from the domestics and had lived through the agonizing days of vehicle oversupply, they warned the dealers to be careful what they wished for. Too much of a good thing is not a good thing at all, as the imports found out when they established assembly plants in the United States and vehicle shortages became much less acute. Enlightened leadership at all levels of the wholesale organizations struck a healthy balance between dealer expectations and reality. That the imports mostly maintain this balance today is a credit to several hundred now unknown and unsung former domestic car guys who were smart enough or fortunate enough to experience firsthand how the Japanese and, to a lesser extent, the Koreans, took control of the American car market.

To be sure, the American executives at the import car companies are much less powerful now than they were thirty or twenty or even fifteen years ago. As the Japanese spent more time on these shores, lived and worked through a few recessions themselves, and saw the business become more complicated, they wrested more and more control over their operations. There will never be guys such as Bob McCurry or Dick Colliver or Rod Hayden in the business anymore—the Japanese, as well as the Koreans, feel much safer either having control themselves or spreading control among more technical middle managers. An old Japanese saying goes, "The nail that sticks up gets hammered down." Never again will an import executive have the power that these men had when the Japanese were establishing themselves in the American market. Not that the Japanese are alone in this mindset. For a number of years throughout the late 1970s and 1980s, Jim Fuller was the face of VW to its dealers. A big, in-your-face type of American, Fuller was the perfect man for VW at a time when the brand was struggling mightily in the United States. In typical Teutonic hardheadedness, the Germans allowed VW to fritter away from over half a million cars sold in 1972 to less than fifty thousand retailed in 1993. That VW survived the 1980s at all is a credit to Fuller, who died tragically in the explosion of Pan Am Flight 103 over Lockerbie, Scotland, in December 1988. Fuller and a blunt South African named Clive Warrilow managed to hold VW together until the new Beetle took hold and resurrected the company.

Today the American manager in any car company who wields any influence or power is almost extinct. Americans, by nature, and American car folks, in particular, are so brutally honest, confident, and outspoken that none of the imports wants to put one in charge of their US operations. Yale Gieszl and Jim Lentz at Toyota were titular heads of the organization, but almost all the calls concerning product development, investment, advertising, and incentives were made by the Japanese. Scott Keogh at VW had more power, influence, and decision-making authority than any American since Fuller, but he still had to answer to Wolfsburg. For the most part, however, nowadays the head auditor round eye at any Japanese company has less authority than a vice president of finance or a head auditor. Finally, and sadly, the head American at an Asian car company has less longevity than a postwar Italian government.

Even more sadly, the leadership is gone—the best American managers of the seventies, eighties, and nineties were leaders in every sense of the word. They encouraged the dealers and led them to profitability through hard work and discipline. They led their field forces at their respective companies by speaking plainly, rolling up their sleeves, and getting a little dirt under their fingernails. Most importantly, they led their Japanese superiors by acting as the important layer between the Japanese and the dealers. Take a look around at the major players in the US automotive market by volume, quality, profitability, and reputation: Honda, Toyota, Nissan, and Subaru thrive, thanks to the efforts of their courageous American managers of thirty years ago. These men inspired their companies' efforts, which surpassed GM, Ford, and Chrysler. Aside from Lee Iacocca, I challenge anyone to name a manager from one of the Big Three in the last ten years who has truly made a difference.

The executive vice presidents and presidents of the Japanese companies have ultimate power and are relatively well known. However, just below the headquarters level are the region and zone managers, who are charged with implementing national policy, getting the dealers to retail the volumes that keep everything clicking, and keeping the more vocal dealers off the backs of headquarters personnel. These men and women have the toughest job in the automobile business. They get none of the acclaim when sales records are broken. They certainly don't get their name in lights at new-car introductions, and they have very little say in product development cycles, production schedules, ship arrivals, or the factory programs (some of which are really dumb and simply border on intrusions into the dealer's daily business). A regional manager, however, can and will be called on the carpet or fired if the zone or region habitually misses objectives. The zone or regional manager is the first person an irate dealer calls when a dumb program is announced or an allocation of hot cars doesn't meet dealer expectations. The regional manager is the first person to feel the brunt of vehicle price increases, parts shortages, and recalls.

Ironically, a good, solid regional or zone manager is in this unenviable position because, up until their appointment, they usually had an enviable career. Most of them start out in sales. (Some of the really good ones start out in parts and service and switch to sales relatively early in their career.) They might make two- or three-year stops in progressively important sales districts before being promoted into the office as an advertising manager, distribution manager, or, if they'd been fortunate enough to have fixed operation experience on the way, a regional parts and service manager. A person marked for a better future (or a person who has a highly placed, influential mentor within the company or industry) is usually able to bypass rotating through the chairs in the office and go straight from being a district sales manager to being a regional or zone manager in six or seven years. A good, well-rounded, seasoned zone or regional manager not only will have rotated through at least three departments in a region or zone office but will also have a couple of tours overseas or in headquarters assignments. These roles—district manager, department manager, headquarters staffer—are the ones that really develop a good future region or zone manager and give them an opportunity for real success. More importantly these roles provide these folks critical leadership training. Departmental roles in a regional office, and even more so staff jobs at a national headquarters, involve supervising others, working under pressure to meet deadlines, and coordinating with outside vendors. Invariably, these roles also involve budgeting, long-range planning, and hiring and firing decisions—all critical skills that a good zone or regional manager must have.

As mentioned earlier, what a good zone or regional manager experiences often has little to do with selling cars. Most of the time, their work involves deescalating confrontation such as warranty disputes or dealer gripes over sales objectives or mediating a spat between a district sales manager and a dealer. Further, a region or zone manager's time is disproportionately spent talking with headquarters over such issues as dealer sales objectives, regional production issues, advertising, and incentives. Not surprisingly these individuals are fairly well compensated at the salary level, as well as the bonus level. They have to be—their work entails some of the toughest relationship building or relationship rebuilding that can be imagined.

Interestingly, in the years before the arrival of computers, cell phones, and other technologies that add to today's data dumps, even before the arrival of the Japanese imports, a Chrysler, Ford, or Chevrolet zone manager was a highly honorable, almost cushy job. Since they had fewer reports to ponder, less information to sift through, and fewer headquarters personnel to respond to, a zone manager could actually meet dealers for lunch or dinner, travel with district sales managers on dealer calls, and talk civilly with the few headquarters representatives who had a direct bearing on the zone's or region's business. With more quality time on their hands, zone and regional managers could effectively conduct important business on the golf course with a couple of dealers and settle crucial issues regarding allocations, advertising spending, and facility improvements.

One of the most important aspects of a zone or regional manager's role in those days was the level of decision-making authority in financial matters. Back then they could make decisions at the local level and authorize the expenditure of fifty thousand or one hundred thousand dollars. Such capability made them very important in the life of the dealers and the success of the zone or region. These folks, by virtue of their experience and their ability to communicate face-to-face, enjoyed true respect, if not actual affection, from their dealers and their subordinates. Most important of all, they personified leadership for the company, rousing and motivating their dealers and their teams. The best ones remain prominent in the minds of their region employees and dealers long after they leave their role. In retirement, if they are willing, they remain trusted advisors and consultants to dealers they once partnered with to produce sales results and are almost always sought out by manufacturers (their own and even their rival's) for their experience and insights. Accordingly, and sadly, great zone and regional managers are never fully appreciated until they're gone.

Fast-forward to today. A day still remains twenty-four hours long, but the amount of crap that a zone manager has to deal with, much of it with nothing to do with business, has multiplied exponentially. Cell phones mean that a zone and regional manager has to be available on his own time and office time. The ever-present computer means that a zone or regional manager, as well as his staff and district sales managers, spend more time looking at a computer screen than talking with a dealer face-to-face or meeting with several dealers to talk about sales, incentives, and advertising. Since the cars are so much more expensive, the cost of doing business ever higher, and headquarters' desire for control of every matter at every level greater, the typical zone or regional manager has very little decision-making authority. What's worse, they have very little budget and therefore can spend very little money. To show you how quickly things have deteriorated, as an area executive with VW in 2003, I had a discretionary budget of half a million dollars. I had remarkable leeway in what I could spend that money on. A half a million dollars could settle numerous customer complaints, fix many incentive disputes, and administer some pretty nifty sales contests. Nowadays, a regional manager is lucky to have ten thousand dollars to run a sales challenge.

With these restrictions it's a wonder that anyone would want to be a zone or regional manager. The good ones make the best of a bad situation, achieving their regional objectives almost in spite of the limitations placed upon them. They more than adequately interpret company policy, procedures, and programs to their dealers and shield their staff from the more asinine edicts and make-work tasks that come down from headquarters. The best ones sacrifice their health, families, and minds for the company. Really good regional managers can serve about six or seven years before the demands of the job make it almost impossible to continue. More often, though, a change at the executive level of the company means some hotshot executive with a string of three-year terms running previous companies decides to make a change at the regional level. Sadly, I have seen more than one very competent regional manager forced into early retirement because some prima donna wanted to bring along his own manager to a new position.

As long as we're talking about leadership, the best, most successful dealers, not surprisingly, are almost always the best and most successful leaders. In an industry sorely lacking people of character and integrity, a successful dealer is usually a great leader, not only for their retail organization but also for their brand and community. The role of the dealer, as far as the manufacturer is concerned, involves aggressively and successfully marketing the brand in their assigned sales territory.

In every dealer sales and service agreement I have seen, aggressive sales and marketing leadership remains the first and foremost responsibility of the dealer. More importantly, by extension, the dealer is the exemplary face of the brand in the community. This role includes leadership among local car dealers in terms of sales volume, profitability, and customer satisfaction. Additionally, the dealer is often a leader in the general business community. The very good dealers take on leadership roles in local business associations, government, and civic and philanthropic pursuits. Such dealers are held up by their manufacturers as "bell cows," individuals whom other dealers will follow in philosophy and business practice. These dealers take leadership roles in their factory organizations, such as chairman of a brand's dealer advisory council or dealer ad group. Many dealers assume leadership roles within their state dealer associations and become the face of the brand to their constituents and local business.

I have had the good fortune to know and work with several such dealers. George M. Roy was the president of the oldest dealership in Louisiana when I met him. Successful, profitable, and highly visible, he was already a legend among Chrysler dealers in the South and a treasured businessman in South Central Louisiana. His advocacy of the automobile business inspired not only rival car dealers but also other general business leaders throughout the region, and his promotion of the Chrysler brand made him a leader among Chrysler, Dodge, and Plymouth dealers in his area of the Memphis zone. His sales leadership engendered true respect, but his endorsement of factory products, positions, and policies made him a valued ally of Chrysler executives in the zone and in Detroit. In my opinion, what truly made Roy a leader was his treatment of his customers and the extent to which he valued his employees, many of whom had been with the dealership all their adult lives. Such was his standing among customers and employees that they gladly followed his lead in supporting the Chrysler Corporation Loan Guarantee Act of 1979, whose passage helped ensure Chrysler's survival during the worst time in the industry. Dealership employees told me often of how enthusiastic and persuasive Roy could be. "I never voted for Russel Long [senior senator from Louisiana during that time] in my life, and Senator Long knew it," one dealership employee told me. But such was Roy's passion for the brand and for his employees that this particular salesperson was inspired to go to Washington and meet with Senator Long personally to ask for his vote for the Chrysler Corporation Loan Guarantee Act.

As long as we're talking about Chrysler, which throughout most of its modern history had lurched from crisis to crisis, two of the brand's dealers assumed important (if ultimately unsuccessful) roles nearly thirty years after Chrysler's 1979 ordeal. At the depths of the Great Recession, Chrysler, as a condition of its 2009 government bailout, was forced to shed 789 of its dealers. The way Chrysler went about choosing the dealers who were to be terminated did not sit well with Tammy Darvish, at the time the leader of her father's well-known dealership group in suburban Washington, DC. The move also rankled longtime Baltimore-area dealer (with stores in Washington and Annapolis as well) Jack Fitzgerald. Both Darvish and Fitzgerald had Chrysler dealerships slated for demise, and both had had more than their share of arguments with the brand over many years. As outspoken dealers, they had also had arguments with all the manufacturers they represented. Over the years they had almost as many arguments with their fellow dealers. Both could be as reviled among manufacturer lawyers and the Maryland and Virginia state dealer associations as any dealers in the country, but their buttons had been pushed. The arbitrary decisions by the government and Chrysler over who stayed and who went ignited a spark.

They tirelessly campaigned in Washington and Auburn Hills, Michigan, about the shoddy treatment, advocating relentlessly and tirelessly for the reinstatement of the demised Chrysler dealers. They portrayed leadership seldom seen in an industry fraught with cynicism and selfishness. Although very few Chrysler, Jeep, and Dodge dealers were reinstated as a result of their actions, the leadership of Darvish and Fitzgerald stands in stark contrast to the abdication of leadership by GM and Chrysler executives at the time. Love them (and few did) or hate them (and many did and still do), Darvish and Fitzgerald deserve a lot of credit for the principled stand they took. Their courage and tenacity in the face of overwhelming odds bear witness to their character and sense of integrity.

The real leaders of the industry, however, are dealers, large and small, who have painstakingly built up their businesses, taken care of their customers, and supported countless families by employing the people in their communities. These dealers go to work every day, roll up their sleeves, and take care of business. The best ones take the time to walk through the dealership and greet every employee, complimenting the office staff, energizing the sales force, and shaking the oil-stained hands of their technicians. Many of them even take the time to walk through the customer lounge, glad-handing, slapping backs, and bragging on customers' kids. They don't need to see their names in *Automotive News*—they are satisfied selling cars, making their customers happy, taking care of their employees, and earning a comfortable living for themselves and their families.

CHAPTER 17

THE GOOD, THE BAD, THE UGLY—AND THE JUST PLAIN DUMB

In over forty years in the automobile business, I met all kinds of people and developed relationships with many of them through the best and the worst of times. For all the desires of the manufacturers to compress the business into meaningless numbers spit out by equally abhorrent information systems, the automobile business still remains very much a people business. The memories that remain with the greatest clarity are those of good people putting forth their best efforts. However, equally notable are the colleagues, cads, curmudgeons, curs, clowns, characters, bozos, bumblers, buffoons, bastards, wimps, wafflers, scoundrels, scalawags, scum, and sons of bitches who have their honored place in automotive lore as prime exemplars of the depths of depravity to which otherwise decent men and women descend. All—the good, the bad, the ugly, and the just plain dumb—can be found at every level of the automobile business. Fortunately, the good always triumphs. The good people in the business, even those forced by circumstance to occasionally and unintentionally perform some pretty dumb stunts, shine through the fog of the automotive wars. In my career I believe I saw it all.

Among the best in my recollection, five women who administrated for the Chrysler Memphis zone office rank the highest. In this instance I'll use their real names because their integrity, work ethic, dedication to the company, and plain common sense helped me develop some skills that guided me through my first critical years in the business. Agnes Kearney seemed to me to have been at Chrysler since Walter P. founded the company. Kearney essentially ran the office, which was a medium-sized office as Chrysler zones went. Kearney knew every dealer in the zone. She had an opinion about every Chrysler, Plymouth, and Dodge vehicle the company offered. Many Chrysler managers, reminiscing years later, recalled their association with Kearney as a key memory. Kearney rode herd on four other administrators—all women, all in their fifties, all Chrysler lifers, and all with a dedication to the brand that equaled or surpassed her own. Similarly, every manager in the office, and even every field manager visiting dealers, trembled in their boots lest they say, do, or think something with which Kearney violently disagreed. At five feet even, about 160 pounds, with pince-nez glasses, Kearney remained a force to be reckoned with. Well into her sixties, she portrayed energy, efficiency, and command. She didn't suffer fools, and although a Southern lady all her years, she was not beyond telling a manager how a cow ate the cabbage. One day a new trainee, whose job was to buy doughnuts for the office staff, arrived fresh from Krispy Kreme with a selection that definitely did not sweeten Kearney's disposition. Since he had been given no instructions on what to buy or in what quantities, he was justifiably befuddled at her assessment of his purchases and began making effusive apologies, to which Kearney replied, "Don't fuck with me today, sonny—I'm not in the mood." Future purchases were vetted beforehand with the indomitable Kearney.

On the other hand, Kearney was both comforter and confidante. After one particularly unsavory afternoon trying to sell a bunch of cars to a bunch of dealers who very clearly did not want them, I was feeling particularly low. Kearney took the time not only to console me but also to offer up some helpful hints. One dealer had been especially abusive to me, and I related the episode to Kearney: "Screw that guy," she intoned. "When he bellows, just bellow back." When I was promoted to the New Orleans zone several years later, I finally realized how much Kearney had done for my early development. Short, gruff, and sometimes pointedly acerbic, she knew what she was talking about. None of the new admins or secretaries in my new billet had the great no-nonsense demeanor or bearing of Kearney.

Betty Slack, like Agnes Kearney, was a Chrysler lifer. I think she had joined Chrysler in the late forties when business boomed. Chrysler treated her very well, and as a result, it became her life. Slack died a millionaire because she took advantage of every Chrysler stock offering that came along. When I was working in the Memphis zone, she still drove the same 1966 Chrysler Newport Custom that she had bought new under the employee purchase program. (This in itself was an accomplishment given the quality of the behemoths that Chrysler churned out of its Lynch Road plant in the 1960s.) Slack epitomized the fifties' ideal of the perfect secretary. Quiet, thoughtful, attractive, she remained ever attentive to the needs of the zone manager and assistant zone manager to whom she reported.

In December 1979, as tensions in the company rose because of the loan guarantee activities, Slack, of her own free will and accord, organized a zone office Christmas tree–trimming party. This party became her baby. She set up a large Christmas tree in the corner of the office. Slack herself supervised the application of twinkling multicolored lights, ostentatious ornamentation, and tinsel. The finished product would have been the pride and joy of Mel Tormé, Burl Ives, Dickens, and Currier and Ives. Her adulation was short lived, however. As I was carrying the ten-foot ladder that had been used to adorn Slack's tree with the requisite Star of David, the ladder tapped the heavily laden Christmas tree just so. Down went the tree in a crescendo of busted glass, sizzling sparks, torrential tinsel, and alternating hues and cries of "Oh my god!" and "Holy shit!" As with the Agnes Kearney doughnut episode, I was, once again, the office goat. (Yeah, that doughnut guy was me.) The remarkable thing, though, was that while I caught holy hell from everyone in the office until we broke for Christmas, Slack alone took me aside and said, "Look, don't let those guys get you down. It was so much fun. We'd love to do it again."

Like Kearney and Slack, Doris Porter had worked at Chrysler all her adult life. Also like Kearney and Slack, the company was her life. Though not as efficient as the other two, she was thorough in a plodding kind of way and friendly. Porter was curious, observant, and altogether a busybody. Porter's claim to fame was her legendary ferreting out of a salacious tryst between the assistant zone manager and one of the other office secretaries. As best buds, Kearney, Slack, and Porter lunched together every day. Most of the time, lunch consisted of crackers, tuna fish salad, and pitchers of iced tea at the desk of one of the three. But there came a time in the late sixties when they decided apparently to splurge a little, taking Porter's old Plymouth Fury out to lunch.

At least that was what we thought they were doing. Much later the junior managers in the office became curious about why the ladies were leaving for lunch as opposed to dining in. This curiosity got stronger when the junior managers learned that the Plymouth, full of inquisitive office personnel, was not dining out at all but rather engaged in a not-so-covert surveillance. Porter had discerned that the assistant zone manager and one of the young, newer secretaries happened to leave for lunch at exactly the same time every day. Sometimes the assistant zone manager and the young secretary left in their own separate cars. Sometimes they went in the zone manager's car. For three single, lonely women in their late forties, this information proved heady stuff. Immediately after the departure of the supposed clandestine lovers, the office sleuths piled precipitously into Ms. Porter's Plymouth in hot pursuit. Sure enough, the ladies tracked them to a midrange motel not far from the office. They quite naturally came to the conclusion that hanky-panky *definitely* ensued.

Arriving back at the office, usually shortly before the now-confirmed clandestine lovers, they would nod to one another in triumph as they took their seats and resumed work. It didn't take long—only a few weeks after the inception of the spectacle of the assistant zone manager returning to his office with his tie somewhat loosened and socks on backward, and the sight of the secretary with a little too much rouge on her cheek and a bead or two of perspiration adorning her forehead—for the junior managers to suspect some salacious activity. But the even richer entertainment was the observation of Kearney, Slack, and Porter returning slightly ahead of the sexual afterglow. Some months later, after the assistant zone manager and the secretary had both been dismissed, Porter recounted her successful spy-craft to an assembly of wide-eyed, gape-mouthed junior managers. The entire episode was assiduously recounted, even ten years later while I was in the Memphis zone. These are the kinds of activities that make the humdrum zone office environment tolerable, if not invigorating. As they say, you can't make this up.

Not all the professional administrative staff's time was expended in such observations. Carolyn Gobert was just a few years younger than Kearney, Slack, and Porter, but she was no less experienced or dedicated to her work and the company. As the distribution secretary, she spent a lot of time talking with dealers, sales managers, salespeople, traffic coordinators at Chrysler Credit and other finance sources, and district sales managers. Hers was probably the most demanding job in the office, yet she performed it with the ease of one who has done repetitive yet important tasks for years. As a distribution trainee, I found her an invaluable source of information, solace, and good old practical wisdom. Since she spent so much time talking to rough-hewn dealer people, truckers who conveyed vehicles from the railheads to the dealerships, and a bunch of junior managers whose language at that time was just that notch above an army barracks, and since her husband, Dick Gobert, was the fleet manager at nearby Liberty Chrysler Plymouth, she retained and maintained a vast storehouse of ribald car jokes and other acidic automotive arcana. As cars were being ordered and shipped constantly, Carolyn Gobert was always very busy, yet she always found the time to explain order discrepancies, dealer language, and other issues to me patiently. From her I learned why you didn't order a New Yorker with a slant-six engine and why dealers preferred short wheelbase, four-speed overdrive pickup trucks to the more expensive models that Detroit wanted to push. "Times are tough now," she told me one gray afternoon in January 1980. "If a dealer wants anything on his lot when interest on inventory financing is 21 percent, he wants something inexpensive, something that will sell quickly." As always, she was right. I learned quickly from Mrs. Gobert how to configure cars to dealer acceptance and ultimate retail sale to customers. Her lessons carried me through the next ten years as a sales manager.

When I left distribution to become the business management trainee, I worked closely with the business management coordinator, a worldly, sophisticated fifty-five-year-old divorcée named Nell Pewitt. Pewitt openly disdained the office gossip and surveillance shenanigans of the other office staffers. She not only relished her role in business management and dealer development, but she also knew everything about putting a dealer in business, analyzing financial statements, and arriving at solid conclusions from the study of data, which was a real trick in the days before desktop or laptop computers. She became so adept that from time to time the senior staff spoke of giving her a company car and sending her out into dealer-land as a business management analyst. However, in those days, before movement toward equality, her candor, age, and physique mitigated against the initiative. (Interestingly enough, forty years hence, such smart, experienced women abound in regional and zone offices throughout the industry. Similarly, these types of individuals are quickly snapped up by consulting firms.) Pewitt became a great instructor to me. Sometime during the winter of my first year in Memphis, Pewitt had to have her car repaired. We lived relatively close, so I would pick her up and drive her to work in my newly purchased Plymouth Volaré Special. During these long commutes, Pewitt taught me the basics of dealer development and business management, the disciplines in which I later spent most of my career. Like Carolyn Gobert, Nell Pewitt took her work very seriously, and she remained a valuable resource for me until Chrysler's massive August 1980 layoffs. Her mandated departure constituted not only a tremendous loss for me but also a sad commentary on the tendency of companies to let great experience walk out the door.

As memorable as the ladies in the Memphis zone office became, the men, back then, still dominated the environment. Charles Schuette also became instrumental in my early development. Fifty-three years old when I first encountered him, Schuette had started with Chrysler in 1957, a year in which the country, as well as the car business, slid into its first serious postwar recession. You knew business was bad when Schuette, a cigarette dangling from his mouth, put down his phone in the middle of sales bank calls and started talking about business being worse than it was when he started. At one time or another, Schuette had held just about every job in the office except zone manager and was fond of recounting some of the stories of his wilder days. By the time I met him, Schuette was satisfied with the occasional beer or glass of wine, but in his heyday in the 1960s, he was famous for the Jack Daniel's stains he left on his contact reports written at night in his hotel room, usually somewhere in Louisiana or Mississippi. He recalled being chewed out by the zone manager who was having trouble reading the contact report material through the brown stains. Schuette often recounted the story of the Mississippi dealership where salesmen were changing out the cars in the showroom one day. While the showroom doors were wide open, a bird flew into the showroom and began flapping around. A phalanx of salespeople, porters, and other staffers began waving their arms and brandishing brooms to shoo the panicked bird out the door. Business, however, had been so bad that the sales manager yelled at the assembled people, "Wait a minute! That's the first customer we've had in here for days!"

One of Charlie Schuette's other good stories was about wobbling into a Dodge dealership in South Louisiana in the midst of a sleet and snowstorm, very rare for that part of the country at any time. The building was an old store with a cracked concrete floor and a few ratty chairs and sofas around the perimeter, and on that morning, five or six folding chairs were occupied by older gentlemen surrounding a Folgers two-pound coffee can with a charcoal fire going in it. No other activity was occurring in the store. Since it was only Schuette's second trip to this dealership and he did not recognize any of the gents around the fire, he thought he'd break the ice a little bit. "Wow," he said, "when was the last time it did this in Abbeville?" Nobody answered for about five seconds until a deep, hoarse voice croaked, "1863." Schuette let it go at that—he figured anybody that old and that sure about the date had to have been there.

Yet for all his tobacco-laced stories and seeming failure to take himself or anybody else very seriously, Schuette became deadly serious when it came to his job at Chrysler. Over the years he had seen ceaseless downturns and recessions, had sold more poorly built cars, and had gotten into more arguments with Chrysler superiors and dealers than anyone I knew at the time. His long experience gave him a grasp of reality unsurpassed by anybody else I met before or since. Because he also took advantage of every opportunity to buy Chrysler stock, he was exceedingly well-off and probably could have retired comfortably instead of powering through during Chrysler's loan guarantee travails. "Shit!" said Schuette. "I'd rather be doing this! My wife is mean, she doesn't play golf, and she probably would have long since kicked me out of the house."

However, not everybody in the Memphis zone office proved so helpful. A supervisor whom we'll call Jim Wise had a needle about a foot long and wouldn't hesitate to jab it into anyone who presented a ready and appropriate target. Wise, too, had made a career out of Chrysler, and at fifty he had held a host of jobs in several different zones. But the fact that he had never been a zone manager clearly rankled him. The resulting bitterness led to bleak sarcasm and caustic jibes directed at just about everybody. Business was terrible at that time—cars were not selling and plants were closing—so everybody was on edge, and none more so than Wise. One talented young sales manager, Peter Fortier, received one of Wise's snippy expostulations, even though he had had a good day wholesaling cars in a terrible environment. "That bastard," said Fortier, "dispenses compliments like a pissed-off ex-wife." Another colleague, having heard that Wise had been taken to the hospital with a suspected mild heart attack, exploded, "That's friggin' impossible! You have to have a heart to have a heart attack." All of us delighted, however, whenever a Chrysler superior, like a vice president or a regional director, would show up. Wise would stand as close as he could to the visitor, nod pontifically at all the positive pronouncements, and repeat the last four or five words the visitor had said. The practice unnerved all our visitors but provided great fun for the rest of us. Schuette, standing at the back of the sales bank room with me after a speech by US Vice President of Sales Tom Pappert, who was obviously annoyed at Wise's antics during the speech, said, "Well, Randy, that's how old Jimmy-boy got his nickname." Not having heard that crack before, I said, "Really? What's Wise's nickname?" Schuette, trying his best not to let loose with a belly laugh, said, "Little Sir Echo."

Moments like the one above helped relieve the stress of recession, a terrible business environment, and the loan guarantee travails. I soldiered on, frankly because I didn't know that the car business consisted of anything else, and at twenty-three years old, I needed the work and relished the challenges. Very new in the car business, I did not know what good business conditions looked like. I got up every Monday, drove to the airport, flew down to New Orleans, picked up a car, and spent the week bouncing from dealership to dealership, begging people to order cars. On Friday, I would drive back to Moisant Airport, board a Delta plane with my meager take of the week's paper orders (we didn't have laptops in those days), and spend the weekend doing what unmarried car guys did on weekends: washing underwear and socks, picking up shirts and dry cleaning left there the previous Saturday, and trying to get in a Sunday of golfing or fishing before flying out again on Monday morning.

Zone management preferred that we stay on the road, hammering dealers in person for car orders. Yet, sometimes the previous week's order count was so poor that management would panic and decide to keep us all off the road and instead sequestered in the "sales bank" room, a large space in the bowels of the zone office building with long tables with LAN line phones, overflowing ashtrays, and the requisite chalkboard, which was nicknamed the "Lita Board," a bitter double entendre on the golf term "Leader Board." "Lita" meant "Light in the Ass," and the unfortunate guys who were having a tough time wrangling orders out of dealerships on the telephone saw their names on that board every day. The dreaded term "sales bank" itself referred to the cache of unsold cars, and thus the exercise of trying to sell them took on the same moniker.

During sales bank, every day was boiler room blasphemy. Picture fifteen grown men in white shirts, colorful ties, and expensive suits; phones in their ears; cigarettes or cigars stuffed in their mouths; and their right hands scribbling *X*'s next to three-digit codes and two-word descriptions on the paper order blanks. The visual is only part of the fun—the verbal chicanery and cajolery used by most of us to try to squeeze orders out of the dealers was the stuff of snake-oil legend: "Ralph, come on, somebody as handsome and successful as you couldn't help but sell this Cordoba with green seats and red carpet. Come on, Ralph, this thing is prettier than a show dog." Which, of course, it wasn't, but in those instances wherein we were peddling cars that had already been built, as well as simply trying to get orders, the hard sell was work that had to be done.

In fact, throughout 1980, we always faced two tasks: (1) getting enough orders to enable the plants to keep running and (2) selling the garbage that had been built to no specific dealer order, nearly all of which was parked against a fence somewhere in Southeast Michigan. In many cases the cars we were selling in the sales bank had been repurchased from dealers who had gone out of business in the really rotten days, right before the loan guarantee act was passed. Nothing entailed more difficulty than selling a non-air-conditioned "new" car that was already two years old to a dealer in the South. By mid-1981, we pretty much had gotten rid of the sales bank, but we still had the problem of slow sales driven by the ongoing recession and the specter of working for a failing car company. Shortly after Ronald Regan took office, life began to change. Interest rates came down; the economy got better; we introduced a new minivan, the first vehicle in its class; and everybody got happy. Dealers who hadn't answered my calls for months all of a sudden were calling *me*, begging for cars. Dealers who wouldn't see me in 1979 and 1980 because they just *knew* I was going to try to sell them something were all of a sudden buying me lunch and telling me how pretty I was. I had more company than a female cat in heat.

In September 1983, I took the opportunity to join Mazda as district sales manager in New Orleans. I did so with some trepidation. Chrysler was my first job out of university. For all the travails I endured with Chrysler throughout my four years at the company, I survived, built many strong and lasting relationships, and earned the satisfaction of having assisted the company through a rough patch. I was known and respected by my dealers and peers, and at twenty-seven years old, I had a bright future with the company. On the other hand, Mazda was about one-tenth the size of Chrysler and had a much more limited product range. But I should not have worried. I was about to enter the best period of my entire car career.

CHAPTER 18

STORIES FROM THE ROAD (PART I)

Business remained strong after I left Chrysler and through most of my time at Mazda. Because the American car industry in the early 1980s had stayed so on its ass, the Japanese agreed to the aforementioned voluntary restraint pact that limited the number of imported Japanese cars any Japanese company could ship into the United States. The regulators believed that the curtailed Japanese deliveries would free up the market for domestic companies to catch up, as it were. With Ford, GM, and Chrysler writing red ink by the tanker truckload and President Reagan, knowing that he had to do something to assuage the domestic industry until Fed Chairman Paul Volker's tight money policy kicked in, the voluntary restraint agreement (VRA) was adopted without much opposition. The smaller imports (Mazda, Isuzu, Suzuki, Subaru, and Mitsubishi) complained but not too loudly—all the Japanese carmakers knew that it was better to be restricted in volume than legislated out of business entirely.

The VRA produced some strange, somewhat unintentional, but always entertaining side effects. The domestics largely used the VRA as a means to recoup their losses from the dark, dead days of 1979 and 1980—they raised prices instead of going for lost market share. The Japanese, who have subsequently been accused of price gouging during that period, really did nothing more than what they had been doing, which is to say that they built marvelously designed, quality cars and shipped them to the United States in line with the VRA parameters at a very fair price. They could afford to do this with the yen at 240 to the dollar, so they were taking fifty- and hundred-dollar bills to the bank by the truckload. Until now we have talked largely about the government, the VRA, and the domestic manufacturers' reaction to both. What comes next epitomizes the greed that ensues when the government gets into the economy.

Car dealers are only human; their mindset became, in the words of the old Buck Owens song, "All I gotta do is act naturally," and so they did. With their supply of Japanese cars severely curtailed and with the popularity of Japanese cars ever increasing as the recession deepened, import car dealers raised their prices. Common practice became a customer walking into a Toyota, Datsun, or Honda dealership and seeing an additional label on the window. Customers complained loud and long, but in the end, when a salesperson, general manager, or dealer told them, "Fine, see if you can find this car somewhere else," they usually ponied up the price on the addendum sticker. The dealers could get away with such. The cars were so good, so popular, and so scarce that a customer would gladly pay the price after a perfunctory "Aw, come on . . . ," knowing that the price was still lower than the smallest GM, Ford, or Chrysler.

The entire sales environment became topsy-turvy because of the artificial market barriers to Japanese cars. Seriously, who would buy a GM X platform car when they could have a Datsun Sentra for $1,500 less? Who would buy a Ford Escort when the Honda Civic beckoned from the showroom? Chrysler's K-car was a stodgy box compared with a Toyota Corolla, which also cost $1,500 less. To customers desperate for transportation but who did not want to pay domestic prices, the alternatives became overwhelmingly humiliating and outright indecent. The car people were doing what came "naturally"—they had a captive market, and they knew that if they blew one customer out, another would come along. The foregoing only points out one end of the spectrum, that of a dealer taking full advantage of an artificial market situation.

Another aspect of this business was the relationship between the dealership and its facing manufacturer's representative. Until about 1986, when the yen began to strengthen against the dollar, dealers were so desperate for hot-selling Japanese models that their entreaties to facing import representatives proved surprisingly tempting. At most levels such propositions took the form of an expensive seafood lunch, paid for by the dealer, with the expectation that the memory of such a repast might incur favor with the sales rep at allocation time. In other cases such activities took the form of a round of golf at the dealer's country club. Some of the more involved encounters might entail a hundred-dollar gift card to a popular department store at Christmastime, or the dealer might ask for the rep's car keys while he and the rep went to lunch in the dealer's car. After a delightful lunch (usually four or five drinks, steamed lobster, pheasant under glass, or a twenty-ounce rib eye), the rep would fall into his company car, which had just been fully detailed; drive home; and discover in his trunk a bottle of Jack Daniel's or Glenlivet—not only as appreciation for favors already done but also in consideration of further automotive expectations.

My own experience with this type of "appreciation" involved a Honda dealer whom I had signed as a Mazda dealer in the same location. Just before Christmas 1991, I received, by courier, a $1,000 American Express gift card. Although no written Mazda policy concerning the acceptance of such largesse had ever been communicated to me, accepting the gift somehow just didn't feel right. As a good, principled, little district sales manager, I called my boss to inform him of what the dealer had sent me and to ask him if it was appropriate to send the gift card back to the dealer with a note of polite refusal. After a long silence, my supervisor said, "You can't do that." "Why not?" I said. "Because the guy sent me one, and I've already spent the son of a bitch."

Just as notable were the much more felonious goings-on at Honda during the same period. At Honda, graft, corruption, payola, and illicit entertainment activities thoroughly dwarfed anything seen at the other brands, in Las Vegas, or even in an Italian postwar government. Much of this corruption has been magnificently documented in a 1995 book, *Arrogance and Accords*, by former Honda employee Steve Lynch. Throughout the early 1980s, most of us in the industry were aware that Honda dealers, given the popularity, quality, and desirability of Honda's cars, were offering their facing sales reps pretty significant consideration for an occasional extra car. At first, the favors appeared to include a steak dinner, or a lunch at a popular strip club, or a new set of golf clubs. Sometimes the rep would shake hands with the dealer at the end of a convivial visit to find that the dealer had palmed him a crisp one-hundred-dollar bill. Other times a fulsome "young thing" would accidentally appear in the rep's hotel room with no stated purpose but with the implicit intent of an illicit evening of erectile ecstasy.

However, some dealers were not content with one extra car, or even two. To get at what they really wanted, these dealers targeted even bigger fish than their district sales managers. Honda zone managers and assistant zone managers in those days wielded significant power because of their ability to control scarce, desirable models rendered priceless because of the VRA. In some cases Honda dealers visited their zone offices, dispensing gifts of funds and flesh to Honda senior managers who would "play ball." In those days a Honda dealer, with a zone manager or assistant zone manager in tow, spent the afternoon, after a sumptuous lunch, at even more drinking and debauchery. Other dealers were not satisfied with these transactions, even though they yielded sometimes dozens of extra cars or tens of thousands of dollars of merchandising money.

The really big players targeted Honda's US headquarters in Torrance, California, where a gold Rolex President or a small briefcase full of Benjamin Franklins might "earn" them another Honda dealership. For most of us at the other import companies, hearing these stories was standard fare—the joke making the rounds at Mazda, Subaru, Isuzu, and a bit later, Mitsubishi, was that the Honda district service managers wore silver Rolexes, the

Honda sales reps wore stainless and gold, while the Honda zone managers and assistants sported gold-crusted Presidents with diamond bezels. Everybody knew what was going on, so it was with tart grins and not some small satisfaction when the news of this automotive malfeasance broke in 1991. In the end several Honda dealers were indicted, and several more Honda employees received prison sentences. Given how widespread the practice had become and how many Honda dealers and employees were involved, we were amazed that so few indictments were handed down, and so few prison terms were issued. In any case for all of us who gritted our teeth and remained true to our principles and our company's reputations, we could lean back on our decks in the evening, take a puff and swig a cocktail (from a bottle of booze we bought ourselves), and say, "There, but for the grace of God, go I."

That is not to say, however, that those of us outside of Honda had it all that bad. Because of the VRA and the quality and popularity of the cars, our jobs as district sales managers were actually quite fun. As a district sales manager in Mazda's New Orleans market, I received an allocation of approximately five hundred cars and trucks at the beginning of each month. All the dealers were begging for these vehicles. Similarly, our Japanese owners demanded quick sale to the dealers to pay off the drafts on the ships. The Japanese executives needn't have worried. Throughout most of the 1980s, I never took more than two days to finish an allocation. In many of those instances, I would have finished in a day had I not had to listen to dealers whining for more.

Some of these exchanges, which were all by telephone, usually from my home office, became, in retrospect, absolutely hilarious. At the beginning of the conversation, the dealer, hearing of his allotted share of vehicles, would complain loudly for five or ten minutes about (1) the inadequacy of the total number, (2) his belief that I was being unfair with the allocation system, and (3) his opinion of my ancestry and my dear mother's bona fides. Since I announced the allocation by model, trim level, and transmission, the dealer had a pretty good idea of what to expect during the month even if I didn't give him the color. Sometimes my recounting of the allocation led to even more vituperative vitriol. During the ensuing oral eruption, I would simply take off my twenty-six-dollar Bulova watch, lay it on the table before me, and listen to the dealer's desultory diatribe. After ten minutes or so, the dealer would suddenly realize that he was speaking ill of the man who helped him make his livelihood and would pipe down. If he didn't, I would grace the dealer with an appropriate number of cars, all in the same color, all in the same unsellable trim level with the same unsellable manual transmission. That usually silenced future outbursts. What's more, weeks later, knowing that his oratory had induced such unwanted automotive arrivals, the dealer was usually overeffusive in his praise of our brand and me personally. Many free fried catfish dinners followed such episodes. (Most of the markets I visited in those days did not even have midrange chain restaurants, much less five-star Michelin venues, so the local fish house or an ice house with a good juke box had to suffice.) For the majority of us who worked with Mazda then, these encounters were enjoyable, productive, and memorable.

Some of my dealers during this period were quite notable, and high among the denizens of that list was Herb Mead, a Buick-Pontiac dealer in Natchez, Mississippi, who also had Mazda. Natchez always made for an interesting stop on my monthly itinerary because it retained its old Southern charm through nice hundred-year-old houses, exceedingly courteous hospitality, and an entertaining afternoon with Herb Mead. Mead's father had owned the Ford dealership in Natchez, and Mead himself had grown up in the car business. Accordingly, one would think that some of the practical wisdom of the business would have filtered through to Mead—it didn't. Mead had gone to work after college in a Ford district office and ended up so bored by the monthly chores of recording sales, reading financial statements, and analyzing market penetration that by the time he entered the dealership world himself, he preferred writing plays and poems. Mead was arguably the most intelligent individual I met in the car business up to that point, but his performance as a car dealer was so poor that it confirmed my suspicions that Mead's heart and head just weren't in the game. His speech, mannerisms, dress, and grooming were more that of a medieval academic than anything else. In a location and vocation that spewed good ol' boy humor and hail-fellow-well-met personalities, Herb Mead was decidedly an automotive oddball.

Because of the voluntary restraint on imports, Mead had the best of both worlds: a midrange, quality, reputable import car franchise and Buick and Pontiac, two of GM's best car lines. Natchez, while being in Mississippi, had one of the highest concentrated, if small, clusters of Old South wealth anywhere in my district, yet Herb couldn't sell his way out of a piss-soaked paper bag. With his tendency, like General MacArthur, to refer to himself in the third person, Mead would intone, "Randy, Herbert simply cannot countenance such meager rations of your superb product." Meaning that Mead, like almost all my dealers, wanted vastly more hot-selling cars and trucks than I could provide. However, Mead complained less and philosophized more than any other dealer I had back then. After an hour or so of Mead's rejoinders, he would close his unsolicited soliloquy with "Come, let us adjourn to a delightful repast." Off we would go to a nice lunch at the Eola Hotel or one of the great catfish shacks that Natchez, on the banks of the Mississippi River, could boast in plenty.

Yet like most dealers of delightful mediocrity, Herb Mead did rather okay in the mid-1980s. The market was so good, the products of such quality, and his local clientele so well heeled that he was able to muddle through selling about ten or twelve Mazdas and twenty-five or so GM products every month, in addition to a couple of dozen used cars, mostly late-model GM trade-ins. However, in early 1986, when the yen strengthened sharply against the dollar and the domestic business took a slight dip, Mead's lack of grasp of the retail fundamentals finally got to him. Never an astute businessman, his meager monthly earnings turned to losses. With no stomach for the business as it declined, Mead sought a buyer.

Kent Richards, a very successful Honda dealer in Baton Rouge who had grown up in his father's Ford store and had a wonderful business mind, expressed interest in the Mazda portion of Mead's business. Mead, who had never bought or sold a dealership, was totally unprepared to negotiate with Richards and his fellow buyers, which included his two brothers, Gary and Doug, and a talented general manager who had come up through Ford, Danny Hammett. Richards and his team, all younger, more sophisticated, and with a nose for a deal, became so frustrated one day during the negotiations that Richards stood up, looked Mead straight in the eye, and said, "Up yours!" Herb Mead, in characteristic flamboyant fashion, followed Kent Richards to the door and yelled, "Up yours, too, my good fellow!"

To Danny Hammett, who witnessed the event, the net effect was like that of a schoolmarm yelling at a rebellious student. (Hammett actually said, "Herb got his nuts all swole up.") Eventually, the sale went through with Richards and his brothers basically ceding the business to Hammett, who went on to become a great little Mazda-Honda dealer in Natchez. For years thereafter, whenever I ran into Hammett at dealer meetings or car shows, he always had an appropriate Herb Mead story. It seems that as Mead exited the business in Natchez, all sorts of interesting phenomena emerged: cars with unpaid liens, unpaid back wages, and goofy stories of some of Mead's local shenanigans, like the annual New Year's bacchanalia hosted by Mead and a host of his nerdy friends. "Yeah," Hammett would remark, "there were a lot of turds in that punch bowl." These stories included some of Mead's associates getting truly toasted and hitting on the old dowagers whom Mead always made it a point to invite. These gentile ladies were the widows of some of the old-money merchants in Natchez who had succumbed to Herb's old-world courtliness over many years in Natchez. Hell hath no fury like an eighty-year-old heiress drunk on spiked Southern eggnog. Still, for all his shortcomings as a dealer and businessman, Herb Mead was a fun guy to be around. In many ways I had more in common with Mead than I had with most of my other dealers; we even snorkeled together in Hawaii during Mazda's 1985 new-car announcement meeting in Honolulu. He was a true gentleman, but the problem is, most true gentlemen in the car business get blasted.

An exception to this dictum was the family of George M. Roy in Lafayette, Louisiana. When I first met him, Roy owned the oldest car dealership in Louisiana. Lafayette Motors, established in 1911, represented Chrysler, Plymouth, Peugeot, and Mazda. When I was a young district sales manager for Chrysler, I had the good fortune to have Lafayette Motors as one of my dealers. At a time when Chrysler was floundering along with the rest of the industry, Lafayette Motors always made money, and they did it the tried-and-true traditional way—they merchandized consistently and effectively. They treated customers like family, which is not surprising since Roy treated every one of his employees like his own children. Roy had brought into the business his son-in-law Robert Trahan and his son Rocke. Trahan was one of the first dealership guys in the zone to take automobile leasing to a high level. Rocke Roy, for his part, was the finest merchandiser I had ever met.

George M. Roy's other employees were no less remarkable, talented, and generous with a young district sales manager unschooled in the retail end of the business (that is to say, me). Jalayne Dupree, the dealership controller, besides being loyal (to the brand she represented, as well as to her employer), effectively ran the dealership for Roy, and she ran it with an iron hand. Patient while teaching me the nuances of a dealership back office, she was tough as nails in defending the name and integrity of Lafayette Motors. The dealership salespeople all spoke of Dupree in admirable, if not outright, reverent terms. I remember one of them telling me, "Don't tell dat gal to piss up a rope—she jest maht do it."

Similarly, Rocke Roy, with his merchandising mind, his feel for cars, and most importantly, his keen sense of his local market, certainly proved my best friend throughout the time I learned the dealership business. He could take the worst car, color, interior, drive train combination, and price point and make it sell like hotcakes. In 1982, he was the first Chrysler dealer to recognize the merits of Chrysler's newest New Yorker, which was a knockoff of a high-line Chrysler LeBaron introduced in late 1981 upon the demise of Chrysler's big R-body New Yorker. He would order thirty or forty gunmetal gray New Yorkers with a gray landau roof, upgraded tires, and wire wheel covers, then price them all, along with the odd-lot blue, gold, and black New Yorkers, at $10,990, only to watch them all fly off the lots, affording himself and his father the opportunity to laugh all the way to the bank.

In short, even at Chrysler's lowest point, Lafayette Motors shone like a glittering jewel. In Chrysler's darkest days, George M. Roy proved himself a man of impeccable character. At Lee Iacocca's urging in December 1979, dozens of Chrysler dealers went to Washington to lobby their congressional representatives on the loan guarantee act. For his part, Roy traveled to bend the ear of Louisiana senator Russel Long, for whom he had never voted, as previously mentioned. The entire Lafayette Motors staff, like hundreds of Chrysler dealers all over the nation, followed suit. Roy, infinitely respected among all Louisiana dealers and all Chrysler-Plymouth dealers, was instrumental in tipping the balance of the vote.

Business was not alone among Lafayette Motors' concerns. Deeply embedded in the Cajun community, George M. Roy and Lafayette Motors always gave back to the people. Acadiana is arguably the most diverse and generous region of the United States. I realized quickly that, more than any others with whom I have dealt, the Cajuns were people of honor, integrity, and determination to the point of pugnacity. I heard stories of "swamp people" in overalls with ten thousand dollars in cash in their fist, rolling into Lafayette Motors to buy a car because it was the patriotic thing to do. The causes and concerns to which Lafayette Motors donated filled the local media. The University of Louisiana at Lafayette was built and sustained on the largesse of benefactors such as George M. Roy, Robert Trahan, and Rocke Roy. Some years later, when I was servicing the dealership as a Mazda representative, Rocke invited me on a six-mile charity run. It was the middle of July, the temperature over one hundred degrees, and the humidity about 100 percent. I finished second in the run, so I didn't see the rest of the throng of runners who braved the heat, the sweat, and the asphalt, but at a gumbo supper after the event, I met and spoke with hundreds of people who had participated solely at the behest of Lafayette Motors. The participation represented a fitting testament not only to the beneficiary but also to the wonderful organization that had staged the event.

Rocke Roy always told it how it was. The time-honored event called the Cochon de Lait staged by Louisiana dealer O. J. Scallan and his son Brent each April at O. J.'s camp near Marksville became the social event of the year for every Chrysler, Plymouth, and Dodge dealer in the state. For those not fortunate enough to have attended a Cochon de Lait, I'll describe it thusly: Seventy-five or so Chrysler, Plymouth, and Dodge dealers, along with the Memphis Zone Chrysler representatives, would descend upon O. J.'s place for a feast of boiled crawfish, Cajun cracklins, and the pièce de résistance, a whole, young pig roasted slowly over an open pit and devoured amid copious quantities of Louisiana ten-ounce beers, Jim Beam, Jack Daniel's, Old Crow, and local white lightning. To add to the esprit de corps, a hastily installed craps table enticed the assemblage of tipsy men. (Women weren't allowed, despite their contributions to the industry.) The event became a welcome break in the otherwise routine dealer business visits. All in all I had never seen more fifty- and one-hundred-dollar bills bandied about as I did the first time I attended.

Nevertheless, in 1982, as business dipped in Louisiana amid rapidly falling oil prices, a few dealers actually opted out of the generous Cochon de Lait invitation because of overriding business concerns. I called up Rocke to see if he and George M. or Robert would be attending. "Shit!" he said. "You think me and George M. gonna leave this dealership at a time like this to go to some goddamn pig roast?" He also offered that Iacocca himself had declined his invitation to the annual backwoods bacchanalia. "Shit!" Rocke repeated. "If somebody pulls the pin on a grenade at dat place, Chrysler would still be okay. It might wipe out every high roller there, but the smartest guys at Chrysler, Iacocca and George M., will still be alive to see the company through." I always trusted Rocke to tell me exactly how he saw the current state of affairs.

Other dealers were notable, not for their colorful vocabulary but for the seriousness with which they took themselves. One such dealer was a VW guy in the New Orleans area who was very successful, almost in spite of himself. He seemed to be able to make money by breaking all the rules. He would keep used cars on his lot for a year. He seemed to think used cars, against all industry wisdom, were like fine wine that got better with age. (Normal industry practice is to send a car to auction or wholesale it if it hasn't been retailed in forty-five to sixty days.) One particular DeLorean enjoyed two birthdays on this dealer's lot. This dealer also had Mazda at a time when Mazdas were in short supply. I called the dealer out on his sales and inventory practices one afternoon, citing that he had retailed only two new Mazdas the previous month, a B2000 pickup truck and a 1984 model RX-7, on which he had grossed about nine thousand dollars. The dealer erupted in Acadian convulsions: "Damn you!" he said. "I'm gonna protect the integrity of my grosses! *Both* of them." This dealer, though diminutive in stature, towered a giant in his own mind. He used to boast that he was the biggest import dealer on the West Bank. This was true, but only because he was the *only* import dealer on the West Bank.

But the guy was always good for wonderful lunches and fun, if not lavish, holiday parties. One of my best introductions to Mazda, on my initial trip through the New Orleans district, was a fantastic lunch the dealer hosted for me and my predecessor, who was just then leaving for Dallas, at Del Frisco's on the West Bank. The dealer must have spent a couple of hundred dollars doing what I thought was welcoming me to the district. "No!" he exclaimed. "I'm celebrating 'cause I'm getting rid of Dave!" (He was my colleague who had been promoted to Dallas.) "Dave never gave us enough cars. I figured if I buttered you up on the front end, I'd have better luck with you." As it happened, he was to be sorely disappointed. Nevertheless, the first Christmas party this dealer had while I was in the district was a catered affair in the service department. The dealer spared no expense on booze, étouffée, crab, crawfish, shrimp, oysters, and other assorted culinary accompaniments, but he was still too cheap to hold the affair in an event space or any place other than the service department. It's too bad, too, because at some point in the afternoon's activities, the sprinkler system activated and turned the whole to-do into a seafood stew. While I generally got along with the fellow just fine, others came away from this dealership with decidedly different opinions. "Typical short-man syndrome," said one of my supervisors after a memorable afternoon of verbal jousting with the dealer.

Another New Orleans dealer was an old Dutch lady, Maria Benton, who was the subject of contemporaneous derision and delight within our regional office. She had a small, slipshod, dirty, ill-maintained dealership on Airline Highway in New Orleans (one could not get from the showroom to the service department without walking through the bathroom), from which she sold not only Mazda but also Lotus, Maserati, and several other obscure European brands that failed to lift the store out of its automotive obscurity. She called the place "Classic Imports," and on one of my contact reports, I concurred: "This dealership is indeed a *classic*, in every sense of the word." During a 1984 visit, the toxicity of the premises proved so pervasive that I was induced to write "The service drive was festooned with Folgers coffee cans full of waste oil. The service bays were so imbued with tools, parts, rubbish, shop rags, and other assorted automotive impedimenta that one could hardly perambulate the premises."

"You can't write this," my boss said. "We send this report to California, and all hell will break loose. Take it back and write it over." I took my calligraphy fountain pen and marked a huge, thick *X* across the offending passage. In the left margin, I wrote, "Service department looks like shit." I sent it back in and never heard another word. However, at my pleas to remodel the premises, Benton did install a wet bar in the showroom. At this development the dealership became a regular Friday stop for other dealers trekking to New Orleans on trades, as well as vendors and factory people eager to start an early happy hour. One of the biggest imbibers was Benton herself, who not only took seriously her prowess as a bartender but also graciously partook of her copious concoctions. This tendency came to light in a legal proceeding about four years later. Benton was heading home one night when she was T-boned in a new RX-7 by a guy running a red light in Metairie. During the resulting lawsuit between Benton and the driver, I was tasked to give a deposition. In the offices of Fulbright and Jaworski in Houston, counsel for the driver's insurance company questioned me at length about Benton.

"Have you ever been with Mrs. Benton in a social context?" she asked.

I replied that indeed I had.

"What are Mrs. Benton's drinking habits?" she further asked.

"Well," I said, "she seldom buys."

The look of disgust on the face of the counsel for the insurance company was overshadowed by the ineffective attempts of the courtroom stenographer and Mazda's own Fulbright and Jaworski attorney, Tippy Newton, to stifle gargantuan belly laughs.

At a performance level, despite my best efforts, Benton's dealership remained a bitter, if entertaining, embarrassment for the Mazda Gulf Region. By the spring of 1987, the store was such a laughingstock that hardly anybody could take it seriously. Her tendency to jumble her words hurt her reputation as well. To illustrate, occasionally at Mazda, particularly after the yen strengthened significantly against the dollar, we used incentives to jump-start sales. In the summer of 1986, these incentives took the form of a program called "Fahrenheit 456." The program included three levels of attainment: (1) If the dealer hit a level-one objective, each vehicle paid four hundred dollars. (2) If the dealer hit a second-level objective, each vehicle earned five hundred dollars, retroactive to the first vehicle sold. (3) If the dealer hit a third-level objective, each vehicle was worth six hundred dollars, also retroactively. Astonishingly, Maria Benton hit level three, and the following day she was on the phone to me, complaining that she should immediately receive her payout for what she called her "radioactive incentives."

Because I had been her district sales manager for forty-two months, by that time nobody was taking me very seriously either. Throughout the 1980s Mazda's shortage of cars, coupled with Benton's long and persistent threats of legal action against the company, meant nobody had earnestly moved to take her on. Mazda didn't want to be perceived as beating up on a lady dealer no matter how bad her performance or hygienically disgusting her premises (except for the bar, with its natural antiseptic qualities). Then came the answer to everybody's wildest wish: I was promoted out of the New Orleans district, and the very same day, Maria Benton sold her dealership. For me, my promotion was deliverance from automotive hell. For the Mazda Gulf Region staff, the sale of her store was everybody's wedding day, Christmas, Easter, and New Year's rolled into one. Yet Benton's demise had a bitter postscript for me. The day she sold and I was promoted, my boss made a poignant note: "Gee," he said, "in three and a half years, you couldn't get rid of her. Your successor has been on the job less than a day, and now she's gone." My successor, on the other hand, was a little disappointed: "Crap," he said, "I was hoping to get a drink at that bar."

Much to my own disappointment, my promotion to Houston did not spell the end of my automotive problems. By the time I got to Houston in 1987, the nation's fourth-largest city was mired in its worst local recession ever, brought about by a skid in oil prices from sixty dollars a barrel to about nine dollars. The refineries, manufacturing plants, entire strip malls, and other businesses in Houston were shut down; subdivisions were packed with abandoned, unsold houses; and car sales had hit rock bottom. Yet desperate times beget desperate actions. And desperate actions beget entertaining acts. My Mazda dealer, Jay Marks, had taken on the comical European franchise Yugo, and while he wasn't making much of a "go" of it, he was as protective of the franchise and of his dealer rights as a kid on a playground with a popsicle. The other Yugo dealer in town, Plaza Lincoln Mercury, had long since given up on Yugo and was attempting to sell the franchise to Lone Star Ford, who proposed to relocate Yugo after the purchase to a lot adjacent to the Lone Star Ford store in Northwest Houston.

For whatever reason, Marks took issue with the Plaza action, even though Plaza's Yugo franchise was moving twenty miles farther away from his location. Even under the goofiest of Texas statutes, Marks's actions made no sense, particularly since he had to pay money to file a complaint with the Texas Motor Vehicle Commission. Marks's antics reminded me of the other kid on the playground who complained that somebody he didn't like was running away from him. I didn't get it, and neither did anybody else. Marks's general manager at the time, a twenty-eight-year industry veteran named Jim Harrell, also the father of one of my Mazda colleagues, explained to me one night at dinner that he had talked himself blue in the face to convince Marks to drop the protest. Marks refused. All Plaza Lincoln Mercury wanted was to get rid of Yugo and get fifty thousand dollars from Lone Star Ford. All Lone Star Ford wanted was to get the Yugo franchise—but for whatever conceivable reason, nobody knew.

The whole mess led to a hearing in the motor vehicle commission in Austin, where Jim Harrell, on the stand, declared (in)famously, "Guys, I don't know why the hell we're here. This is like two guys fighting over the ugliest girl at the prom." His statement, though terribly crass, was borne out in truth when Yugo cratered completely a few months later. I never knew what Lone Star Ford, or even Jay Marks for that matter, did with their unsold Yugo inventory. What I do know is that, for months thereafter, I would drive across the bridge spanning the Houston Ship Channel and see hundreds of unsold Yugos on the docks. I also know that for ten years thereafter, Yugos regularly appeared in the Westheimer Art Car Festival. Somehow they served better as objets d'art than as efficient transportation.

While sales might have sucked during that time, I was nevertheless privy to some of the most fantastic anecdotes a middling car guy can hear. Over beers at the infamous watering hole, the Forum in Victoria, Texas, I was told a story about the insatiable Buick GMC general manager who was cruising the local bars one night and picked up a beautiful young woman who intimated that she was a "player." The general manager, being a "player" himself, sprang into immediate action. As they entered his car, the lady indicated that she was married and that her husband was due in late that night from one of the oil rigs offshore, and therefore, it was too risky to go to her house to "play." The general manager, as a married man himself, couldn't very well take the lady to his house either.

Since the general manager, a notorious cheapskate, wasn't about to spring for a hotel room on some gal he'd just met, he hit upon a novel solution—the fourth fairway of the local golf course seemed an ideally secluded venue on a South Texas June evening. Things were going pretty well, according to the general manager, until the golf course sprinkler system activated. "I was just about to reach critical mass," the general manager shrieked, "when the first swath of water hit us, and the gal went screaming naked across the fairway to God knows where!" He never saw her again, but he did have one hell of a time explaining to the dealer the next day what a soaking-wet blanket and a pile of soiled women's clothes were doing in the trunk of a brand-new Buick LeSabre.

As if this account weren't enough, many years later I was told of another idiotic incident by a work colleague, a former GMAC business development manager in the Northeast. A couple of highly placed GMAC regional reps were driving separately from a Christmas party one night back over to the senior regional manager's house. Already tight from the Christmas party they had attended, the junior executive imbibed quite a bit more at his chief's house. Well into the wee hours, the junior executive, who had no business driving, announced that he was leaving for home. The senior manager recognized that the guy was in no shape to drive and said, "Look, leave your car here. I will take you home in my car and then come pick you up tomorrow morning." The junior executive's car was not outfitted for cold weather, so the senior executive hit upon (yet another) novel plan for keeping his subordinate's car from totally freezing to the ground during the night. He started the car, left the engine running, and placed a brick on the accelerator to keep the engine revving through the deep freeze. You know what comes next.

He woke up the next morning to the sound of a fire engine pulling up to his house because his junior executive's car had begun blazing. While the firemen were able to extinguish the conflagration before it spread to the senior executive's house, the junior executive's car, alas, was totaled. The senior executive was in the awkward situation of calling his subordinate with the sad news. They couldn't very well tell GM what had actually happened, so they tried to convince everyone that it must've been some kind of warranty problem. Not only did Motors Insurance Corporation not think the episode was very funny, but the warranty department also rejected the claim out of hand. In fact, the subsequent investigation revealed what had actually happened, and the colleague who related the entire episode to me not only swore up and down that it was all true but also insisted that both executives were somehow, miraculously, able to keep their jobs with GMAC.

Factory executives sometimes perform stupid stunts, but some dealer people prove equally adept at inappropriate actions. During my time at Mazda, a particular Iowa dealer became famous for peculiar and totally tasteless behavior. Breaking wind on the showroom floor in front of his staff and customers was typical for this fellow. Also, he tended to grasp at his crotch and adjust himself in full open view or pull the seat of his pants out of the crack of his ass while negotiating a deal with a difficult customer. One afternoon, when he was being visited by his Mazda road rep, he decided to invite the Mazda guy to lunch. The venue became the local supermarket, where the dealer conducted his business with the rep while grabbing food off the shelves. Packages of cookies, bunches of grapes, bundles of cherries, and even a carton of Hostess Ding Dongs, half a dozen of which the dealer hastily unwrapped and either ate himself or offered to the astonished rep, comprised lunch. After fifteen minutes of this performance, the dealer exited the store, bypassing the checkout and dumping the remains of his repast in an empty shopping cart before driving back to the dealership. To add insult to injury, this dealer, twice, made emergency landings in a light plane in the same shopping center's parking lot.

In summary, car stories can become exaggerated in the retelling. Such recounted incidents, and they're all true as far as I know, probably reflect negatively on car guys generally and dealer people more specifically. Still, from the remove of some forty years, I realize now that these episodes brought some much-needed comic relief to my first brutal year in Houston.

CHAPTER 19

STORIES FROM THE ROAD (PART II)

While dealers provide rich memories, headquarters staff have their own place in this recounting. Most of these people had never been in a dealership and wouldn't have known a spark plug from a hub cap. However, their professions of superior intellect and their absolute certainty that they knew what the hell they were talking about contrasted markedly with reality. Some of them actually needed geography lessons. Take for example the Mazda fleet manager from the late 1980s, a well-intentioned but nervous man whom we'll call "Dick" Durnin.

Like many anxious people, Durnin was always running one hundred miles per hour, and not being overly familiar with Mazda and its personnel, he would sometimes make really goofy mistakes. Several times he would answer the phone, saying, "Ford, New Holland," the name of his previous employer. Other times, when advised he needed to call a Japanese staffer or one of the vice presidents immediately, Durnin would pick up the receiver of his desk telephone but start keying the number in on his adding machine. Several months after joining Mazda's headquarters in Irvine, California, Durnin wanted to come out to the Gulf Region in Houston for a visit. Since nobody else in the Gulf Region office wanted to deal with Durnin, the job fell to a fellow named Jim Quimby, who supervised the district sales managers.

Phoning Quimby to let him know his itinerary, Durnin said, in his fast East Coast accent, "Okay, Quimby, I got it right here. I leave Orange County at ten o'clock and get there at three o'clock." On the appointed day, having heard nothing further from Durnin, Quimby was dozing in his office when he was awakened by the obnoxious staccato of his telephone. On the other line was an obviously rattled Dick Durnin. "Quimby!" Durnin said. "I'm here." Quimby responded with, "Okay, Dick, great. Where is *here*?" "The airport," Durnin responded. "Well, which one?" said Quimby. To which Durnin replied quizzically, "What do you mean?" "Well, we have two airports in Houston: George Bush Intercontinental and Hobby." Several seconds of dead silence ensued on Durnin's end of the phone. Finally, Quimby said, "Dick, which airport have you landed at?" Durnin replied, over the lump in his throat, "DFW. I thought the office was in Dallas."

Despite his obvious challenges, Durnin remained hardworking, earnest, and totally devoted to his craft as a fleet manager. Except . . . the fleet business—manufacturer sales of vehicles to commercial interests and rental car companies—had become an object of derision by the late 1980s. Successful fleet business required enormous subsidies by the manufacturers to the fleet companies because of the desperate competition. For example, if Mazda wanted to sell hundreds of cars to Hertz, Avis, Budget, or National, the company had to match or surpass the already strong fleet incentives offered by Chevrolet, Ford, and Chrysler. In Durnin's mind, if Chrysler was offering National Car Rental one thousand dollars off every Mazda that National would buy and put into rental service, Durnin had to convince the tightfisted Japanese that he needed a one-thousand-dollar-per-car subsidy to make a monster fleet deal. Since the Japanese were desperate to increase sales, they agreed to the subsidies for the rental car company.

However, this wheeling and dealing deprived other areas of the company of precious cash with which to operate. When fleet sales subsidies surpassed retail incentives in late 1992, all hell broke loose. The company curtailed bonuses, laid off several dozen employees, and cut operating expenses for items such as training and travel. When Mazda canceled merit increases for employee compensation, the fleet department became a ready target for employee disdain. For my part I decided to memorialize the prevailing attitude by capturing the vitriol and bitterness in a little poem:

Larry, Moe, and Curly Joe
Masters of Mazda's fleet you know
Selling all those rental cars
Hanging out in swanky bars
Smoking cheap five-cent cigars
Masters of Mazda's fleet

Masters of Mazda's fleet they are
They've yet to sell a retail car
Rental is their only game
Volume is their claim to fame
The discounts are a crying shame
Masters of Mazda's fleet

Masters of Mazda's fleet they be
MC staffers shout with glee
These are the only Mazda men
Who sell thousands with a stroke of the pen
Wakiya hopes they do it again
Masters of Mazda's fleet

Masters of Mazda's fleet they iz
Chieftains of the discount biz
Gotta car you wanna rent?

Gotta beef you wanna vent?
Wonder where your bonus went?
To the Masters of Mazda's fleet

Further aggravating the situation and the fleet department's status in the organization, Mazda's proposed new dealer agreement was rejected by the California Motor Vehicle Board. That autumn of 1992, Mazda Motors of America posted its largest-ever operating loss, with bonuses consequently even more severely reduced. Accordingly, the silly little poem gained a lot of traction within the company.

Sadly, the autumn of 1992 also saw the beginning of a marked decline in Mazda's overall fortunes. After thirteen years in the automobile business, I began to more consciously reflect on what I had done and what I had seen. As I replayed my career, I realized that while the cars had much improved and dealerships had come and gone, the real constants proved the people I'd met along the way at Chrysler and Mazda.

Early in my Chrysler career, a parts and service representative named Bob Baird helped me tremendously in the area of fixed operations. We traveled through Southern Arkansas and Northern Louisiana, and Baird was just a delight to work with. As it happened, Baird was an even better delight to drink with, as I discovered at a meeting of the nonprofit Ducks Unlimited in Crossett, Arkansas. After work one day, the local dealer, Oliver Couey, invited us to one of the conservation organization's fundraisers. They'd arranged a barbecued hog dinner, where the beer and Jack Daniel's flowed freely. Baird, who seldom drank hard liquor, truly relaxed for the first time in weeks but had a little more whiskey than he should have.

After the delicious dinner, Ducks Unlimited hosted an auction of hunting-themed, obviously overpriced, yet attractive items. As the auctioneer presented each item, Couey poked Baird in the ribs and said, "Bid, Bob! Bid!" Fueled by numerous highballs, Baird's hand immediately and repeatedly shot up into the air. Luckily, other Ducks Unlimited members outbid

Baird every time, that is, until the grand prize: a beautiful double-barreled, twelve-gauge shotgun, appropriately overvalued at $1,500. The bidding started at $200 and quickly rose to $900. When the auctioneer said, "Who'll give me $950?" Couey predictably poked Baird again, and Baird, in the heat of his alcohol-induced haze, predictably raised his hand but also stood up with a wobble and yelled, "I've got $1,000!" A five-second silence preceded thunderous applause and the auctioneer's enthusiastic "*Sold!*" Thus, Baird was all set to go home with a real bargain—a $1,500 shotgun for which he had no ostensible use but at a successful (if unintentional) discount price. Fortunately for Baird, later in the evening, Couey actually bought the shotgun to graciously take it off Baird's hands. (By this stage of the evening, my esteemed colleague had no idea what he'd bought or even where he was and why everybody thought he was such a great guy.) Still, for one glorious night, Bob Baird was the most popular guy in Crossett, Arkansas.

Some of the most unusual events involved more (intentional or unintentional) stunts on the part of dealers, staff, vendors, or field colleagues; well, rather they seem, in retrospect, those inevitable but unplanned events, the type of which can add color and texture to a career. Such as, in the early 1980s, while I was a young Chrysler district sales manager in New Orleans, zone management ordered three of us to retrieve a damaged Dodge Mirada from Morgan City and drive it back to New Orleans. This particular car needed repairs that a Morgan City dealer could not perform, and while the car was still drivable, the company wanted a proper diagnosis of the problem. Accordingly, I drove J. T. Meals, the New Orleans district service manager and a Chrysler certified technician, down to Morgan City to retrieve the car.

To complete the vision, for the return trip, I took the lead in my own company car, Meals drove the damaged car, and John Kelleher, the Baton Rouge district sales manager who had informed the zone of the damaged car in the first place, brought up the rear in a practically brand-new Dodge Mirada. With safety in numbers, our convoy sped eastward from the dealership in Morgan City on Highway 90, a two-lane slab of asphalt raised only about four feet above the swamps on either side of the road, where the snapping alligators lay in wait. We proceeded steadily at about sixty miles per hour until I saw an object on the right side of the highway hobble onto the pavement about one hundred yards ahead. At our rate of speed, I was already fifty yards closer before I recognized the object as a hefty armadillo. A large pickup truck was coming west, and I sure as hell wasn't going to drive off into the swamp to miss the armadillo. I believe I passed over the armadillo around the same moment the pickup truck intersected that point, but I definitely closed my eyes for a second or two in anticipation of an armored body smashing into my shiny new 1980 Plymouth Grand Fury.

When I opened my eyes, I instinctively checked the rearview mirror just in time to see the armadillo clear the roofline of the second car in our convoy. Somehow the unfortunate animal had been scooped under my car, then propelled over the damaged car and slammed with an ignominious thud into the grill of the 1980 Dodge Mirada driven by Kelleher. When I saw the emergency lights on the third car in my passenger-side mirror, I pulled over to where the passenger door was only a couple of feet from the swamp but with the rest of the car still very much in the roadway. All three of us got out of our cars in the hundred-degree heat and went to inspect the remains plastered to the grill of what, otherwise, was a beautiful car. I asked, "Is everybody all right?" Kelleher could only stare dejectedly at the mangled mass on the grill of his Mirada, which had barely twenty miles on the odometer. He swallowed and glanced at me and said nothing. Meals, over whose rooftop the creature had flown to its untimely demise, seemed clearly shaken. When I asked him again if he was okay, he lit a cigarette and said, "Just give me a minute. I still have this vision of a terrified armadillo headed right toward my windshield. I don't know who was more scared, me or the armadillo."

Fortunately, all three cars remained operable, so we continued on to New Orleans. When we arrived at Gentilly Dodge, the service writer looked incredulously at the grill on the new Mirada and choked at the sight and the smell. I had to get to another dealership, so I drove off, but I heard later that it cost six hundred dollars to fix the grill. I wouldn't be surprised if three hundred dollars of that was just to bribe some mechanic to take the old grill off.

Unfortunately, more significant problems than poor drunk colleagues and poor dead armadillos vexed the early days of my career. Since the title of this book is *This Car Sux!*, I'll confess that sometimes our cars did have problems. Consider this example: "Build-out" was the period at the end of the model year when the factory produced cars not ordered to any specific customer preference but with inconsistent results. One day a transport driver dropped off a K-car in Winnsboro, Louisiana, that sported a Plymouth Reliant front grill and hood ornament but a Dodge badge on the trunk. The Jefferson Avenue assembly plant delivered numerous cars with only AM radios, or no radios at all, when they'd been clearly dealer-ordered with AM/FM. At a dealer's specific request, I once ordered a standard half-ton Dodge truck that, alas, arrived with the wrong tires.

The plants built these automotive oddballs at the end of the model year because some plant scheduler or line foreman needed to use up excess components. Though irritated, dealers usually accepted the wonky vehicles and eventually sold them. The real problems began when the factory substituted—or eliminated altogether—bigger, more important items. For instance, the substitution of an eight-cylinder engine into a truck that a dealer ordered for six-cylinder use not only increased the price of the vehicle by as much as one thousand dollars but also entailed changes throughout the entire vehicle to accommodate the larger engine. Similarly, the accompanying transmission substitution became an even trickier issue, as in those days automatic transmissions required support components that drove up the truck's price even further.

Some of the even goofier mistakes revolved around colors. Occasionally, a car with, say, a red exterior ordered with red bucket seats showed up with blue carpet and seats. Since this era also included padded vinyl roofs, a car ordered with one color vinyl roof could show up with another clashing color. Generally, a white vinyl roof worked with anything, but a red vinyl roof on a blue car obviously did not work. Thankfully, vinyl roofs disappeared in the 1990s.

The most common build-out problem involved a car ordered with no or little optional equipment as a price leader. Such an order became a juicy target for any plant person looking to get rid of some spare parts. I saw more than one Plymouth Volaré base model show up at a dealership with a vinyl roof, power door locks, power windows, an eight-cylinder engine, cornering lights, and bumper rub strips. Thus, the most unlikely car became the most unsightly, as well as the most expensive.

Overall, these build-out cars tested the limits of factory-dealer relations. In good times the reasonable-minded dealer would groan and mumble but, in the end, accept the car; if they didn't sell it, they could probably make it a demonstrator. In bad times, when it was tough to sell even normal cars, a dealer would usually bow up their back like a hissing cat and flat-out refuse to accept the car. In this case the district manager found themself in a real spot. They had to get rid of the car, so they had to go begging other dealers in their district to take the car. I experienced this desperation on more than one occasion, and I can tell you that it is one of the most unpleasant tasks in the business. Maybe even worse than roadkill repairs.

Such spats over vehicle discrepancies tried the patience of all involved. Given the conditions that existed at the time of the 1979 Chrysler loan guarantee crisis, bad news compounded the interest and inflation problems. Chrysler was losing $3 million per day, the dealers were losing everything they had, and everybody was losing their minds. The anecdote I related in an earlier chapter about the Midwestern Dodge dealer who prayed to wake up as an import car dealer became typical of the way we as district managers handled the worst business environment in American history—yes, even worse than the Depression. The very fabric of our industry, indeed all commerce, and subsequently, even the American way of life, was changing forever. All my dealers became scared, cross, and difficult to deal with, but one in particular led the league in tastelessness.

Arthur Tait, the Dodge dealer in Shreveport, made my life miserable. A former professional football player and a bloke of bloated bombast, Tait had already gone bust in new-car stores in Memphis and Huntsville when I became the district sales manager in Shreveport in August 1980. By that time Tait's high-volume Dodge store lost thousands of dollars every month and teetered dangerously close to insolvency. For a blowhard businessman who prided himself on his past successes, his cozy relationship with Chrysler management, and his status on the Dodge National Dealer Council, his failing store became a source of supreme irritation and embarrassment. Accordingly, the arrival of a twenty-four-year-old punk, rookie district manager, specifically conditioned to constantly harass him to order cars and trucks that he did not need or want, sent him over the edge. Within a couple of months of my arrival, Tait and I locked horns; Tait's refusal to order cars infuriated me. Worse, he telephoned complaints to my superiors in the Memphis zone office about me. I became that much more frustrated since Tait's status as a dealer bigwig and chairman of the dealer council frightened the zone staff into inaction. Tait despised me so much that he enlisted his archrival Marshall Hebert, the general manager of Bob Post Chrysler-Plymouth just two hundred yards down the road, to try to get rid of me forever, such as transferred to another sales area. At this point, I realized that the two biggest dealers in my district, one the chairman of the Dodge dealer council, the other the chairman of the Chrysler-Plymouth dealer council, wanted my balls on a fork.

Eventually the zone manager, Phil Kenningham, felt the need to join the fray. Kenningham found himself in a tough spot, though: He couldn't continue to have his two biggest dealers in Shreveport, however boorish and buffoonish, stuck in such a murderous mindset. On the other hand, he couldn't very well discipline a district manager, however inexperienced, who was simply following the company directives to cajole and persuade dealers to order cars. Kenningham, in desperation, arranged a dinner at one of Shreveport's nicest restaurants, Ruth's Chris Steak House, with himself, Hebert, Tait, and me. After a couple of rounds of cocktails, Kenningham said, "It's my meeting. May I make a statement?" Hebert and Tait both nodded pontifically. Kenningham continued, "We have come too far, overcome too much, and have too much yet to do for us to have this kind of situation."

The net effect was like throwing lighter fluid on a grass fire. Tait and Hebert predictably fingered me as the source of their current plights, Chrysler's current state, the industry's and country's pathetic situation, and the potential demise of the automotive world order. I sat there stone-faced, but Kenningham propped his elbows on the table and leisurely smoked a Salem while Tait and Hebert yelled themselves out. As their complaints rose to a crescendo, and the servers brought fresh glasses of Johnnie Walker Red and Glenlivet, other diners glanced over their shoulders to see what the hell was going on. Had it not been for my own disproportionate consumption of Scotch whisky, I would have either punched both of them out or left the meeting long before they ceased their bellowing.

But then the steaks arrived, along with mounds of potatoes, creamed spinach, and by this time, a bottle of Glenfiddich. The loose-lipped dealers began to moderate their modulations; red meat tends to satiate all carnivores. Kenningham, finally able to get a word in for the first time in about an hour, explained that Chrysler's only hope for survival in the current rotten environment was a steady flow of orders to keep the plants running. The company, he explained, required a modicum of cooperation between his district staff and the best dealers he had. It sounded to me like pure, corporate bullshit, but I realize now that he was soothing the ruffled manes of his two biggest horses while throwing a reminder at me that went something like, "You better get along with these two guys because without them eating out of the palm of your hand, you're going nowhere."

The evening ended on a strained note and agreement to meet for breakfast the next morning at eight thirty for more intelligible conversation without the influence of alcohol, which had ultimately entailed another bottle of Scotch. I awoke the following morning, Wednesday, with an imperial headache that six Tylenol could barely contain. After a shower during which I thought I would drown, I dressed and stumbled downstairs to the dining room of the Regency Hotel in Downtown Shreveport. By eight thirty Kenningham had not yet arrived, so I decided to wait about fifteen minutes, supposing he would surface shortly. Fifteen minutes turned into thirty, so I called up to his room. In a gut-sore groan of agony, he answered, "Ugh, I'll be right down."

Just then Hebert arrived looking and acting as if nothing had happened the night before. He ordered coffee, three eggs over easy, bacon, six biscuits, and a bowl of red-eye gravy and had easily finished off this repast when Kenningham arrived, clear-eyed, hair in place, tie done in a natty knot. He surveyed the various glasses of milk, orange, tomato, and grapefruit juice in front of me and said, "It looks like you're having breakfast in Technicolor." Kenningham shook his head at me and ordered a Bloody Mary, which made me kick myself because I should have thought of doing the same. He then said to Hebert, "I don't like to drink alone. Why don't you have one with me?" and Hebert readily agreed.

Badly hungover and fighting the onset of a nasty cold, I honestly cannot remember another detail of that morning, except that Tait never showed up. I remember shaking hands with Hebert while precariously standing up to take Kenningham to the airport. Hebert looked me right in the eye and said, "When you come out of the ether, give me a call, and we'll get those orders taken care of." He even winked and gave me his big, yellow-toothed grin. The only thing Kenningham said to me on the way to the airport was "You're okay with Marshall, but I don't think we'll ever get Arthur to a point where he can work with you." And he was right. Two months later I was promoted to district sales manager in Lafayette, Louisiana. I got a pen and a bottle of whiskey from Marshall Hebert when I left for Lafayette. I didn't get so much as a "good riddance" from Arthur Tait, though I'd graciously toned down my discussions with him.

But life has its odd twists and turns. I did well enough in Lafayette to be promoted again in a year and a half to be the district sales manager in New Orleans. I would see Hebert several more times during that year and a half, and he always greeted me amiably, so we got along fine. Tait would continue to refer to me as the worst factory rep he had as his store continued to derail even when business improved and Chrysler paid off its loan guarantees. Many years later, when I worked as the dealer development manager for Mazda in Houston, the Mazda regional manager, Pete Lassen, came into my office and put a letter in my hands. At first, the letter appeared to be like a lot of letters I got during that time, mostly from domestic car dealers stumbling through the economic downturn after the first Gulf War and looking for a Japanese import franchise to try to save their businesses. The letterhead read, "Tait's Shreveport Dodge" and was addressed to "Dealer Development Manager, Mazda Gulf Region." The letter extolled the virtues, profitability, and desirability of Tait's Shreveport Dodge representing Mazda in Shreveport. It was signed, "Very truly yours, Arthur Tait." On a small pad, I wrote to Lassen, "This dealer is the biggest uncouth bastard I ever met, and I intend to call him and tell him that Mazda will not offer a franchise to such a deplorable dunce." I stapled the memo to the letter. He sent it back with a memo of his own. "Tell him," Lassen's memo said, "thanks for the letter, but no."

No book recounting the good, the bad, the ugly, and the just plain dumb would be complete without recounting my role as one who was just plain dumb. In this case, though, it was dumb luck. In December 1980, Chrysler still felt the ill effects of the recession, the backlash of the loan guarantees, and the consequences of the deplorable "sales bank"—the end-of-year rush to sell off remaining stock. Sales bank consisted of the unsold new vehicles assigned to the zone. All the manufacturers shut their plants down in the week between Christmas and New Year's. At Chrysler, however, while the plants closed down, the district sales managers remained ensconced in the zone office at 5:00 p.m. on Christmas Eve. We had been "dialing for dollars"—that is, calling up all our dealers and begging them to take the last of the unsold 1980 model cars. These cars constituted the last of the last and the worst of the worst. Most had no air-conditioning, and many had no radio. Others sported such god-awful paint and trim combinations that no sane dealer wanted to take these cars, especially since interest remained well above 10 percent, business still sucked, and everybody's head was already out of the office and into the holiday season.

By late afternoon we had whittled the sales bank list down to the most unsellable cars you can imagine. Detroit, through our zone management, ordered us to stay there until all the cars were sold, so we divvied up the last of the ugly butts. I drew two 1980 mid-level Aspen wagons with four-speed transmissions and fake wood applique on the exterior. Both were white, both had an AM radio, one had red interior, and the other had tan. All we wanted to do was to get rid of these dregs and get home to our families. The tension in the room grew as thick as the cigarette smoke as twelve men trapped in a room for ten hours reached unbearable levels of near-screaming nervous fatigue. As it happened, my two sleds looked like the worst of the bunch. Finally, at about five o'clock, all of us committed the most unpardonable yet most common sin that a district sales manager can commit: to "airmail" some really unwanted Christmas presents to our dealers.

Now shipping a car to no particular dealer order technically could get a guy fired. By this time, however, we frankly didn't care. As I anxiously puffed a cigarette and became increasingly conscious of the tightening muscles in my neck, I looked down my dealer list thinking I might find a giftee for my two matching Christmas presents. The only one I could find, as in the only dealer who had not ordered a car from me in a month or more, was a small Chrysler-Plymouth-Dodge dealer in Fordyce, Arkansas. I did some quick calculating: It was 5:15 p.m. on Christmas Eve, and if I entered these cars right then, nothing would happen in our system until possibly December 26. (Even Chrysler observed the sanctity of Christmas Day.) I figured that the order would take all day on the twenty-sixth to batch and probably not be transmitted to the trucking company until sometime on the twenty-seventh. The cars were in Newark, Delaware, and would probably be railed to Memphis, put on a truck, and maybe, just maybe, take as long as the twenty-ninth or thirtieth to get to the dealership in Fordyce. But I miscalculated.

At eight o'clock on the morning of the twenty-eighth, my phone rang; it was the Fordyce dealer. I was shocked but not really: I suspected the dealer had gotten an advance shipping notice and was ready to give me a well-deserved tongue-lashing. But as soon as I picked up the receiver, the dealer said, "Randy, I just wanted to say I hope that you've had as great a holiday season as I have. I just got the greatest Christmas presents I could get." *Wow*, I thought, *this guy really knows how to lay on the sarcasm*. "Jim—" I said, but he cut me off again.

"No, now listen," he said. "First thing this morning, this transport with two white Aspen wagons showed up, and I was sitting there scratching my head just knowing that neither me nor my wife had ordered anything from you. We brought them off the transport, and I was just about to call the bank and bounce the drafts when these two gals came in and said they drove down from Little Rock to buy a car. Well, it was a mother and daughter, and they had done seen both them cars when they drove up, and they thought they were pretty. Well, the mama had not had a new car since her '49 Hudson gave up the ghost. But *her* mama had left her ten thousand dollars, and that ten thousand dollars was burning a hole in her purse. So I'll be damned if this gal didn't buy both them cars. When I came back in my private office here to call you, they were both tickled pink, but they was arguing like a couple of old hens over which one of them was gonna get the red seats or the tan seats. I tell you, Randy, I ain't never sold two cars so quick in my life. And I was just callin' up to see if you got any more of them sons of bitches."

I said, "Well, Jim, that's just great, and I'm sorry we don't have any more for you, but it sounds like you did pretty well."

"Yeah," said the dealer, "I full popped them both, and I'll be danged if they didn't sign both five-hundred-dollar rebates over to me. Now I ain't a saint, but I ain't no thief either, so I told these gals to send the rebate forms to Detroit and get their five hundred dollars apiece. So you have a good New Year's, and if by chance you get a couple more cars like that, you just remember your ol' buddy Jim down here in Fordyce."

I felt so shocked (genuinely, this time) when I hung up that I didn't even realize that I had smoked my cigarette halfway down through the filter. All I could do was snuff it out, fold my hands, bow my head, and offer a prayer of thanks. I had just dodged disaster, or more to the point of this particular tale, I had just experienced life's greatest stroke of dumb luck.

While dealers and customers livened up my days during my years at Mazda, my district sales manager colleagues provided, by far, the best and most entertaining memories. When I was a junior staff member in Mazda's Gulf Region, we hired a guy who had most recently been with Toyota in Iowa. He was a big guy whom we'll call Mike Trejo. Everything about Trejo was big: his height, his girth, his ego, his talk. He made comparisons of Mazda to his erstwhile Toyota experience, to the point where we all began to wonder why the hell he had left Toyota to come to a second-tier import in the first place. While his general big talk remained wonderment enough, some of his specific claims of attainment defied credulity, such as his boast of being the biggest wholesaler in his Toyota region. We wondered how true this particular boast could be, as we knew Trejo had served in the fixed operations department and had probably not ever had the opportunity to wholesale a car. Tall tales aside, most of us made a good-faith effort to welcome him to the region and to wish him luck in his new position. Nonetheless, his tendency to call everyone "brother," even the women on staff, annoyed even the best of us. One of the distribution clerks quipped, "Even if I were his brother, I wouldn't admit to it."

What really made Trejo famous in Mazda lore, however, were his gastronomic exploits. During one staff meeting, all the guys adjourned to a nearby Olive Garden for lunch. Trejo ordered the "endless" soup, but when the order arrived, instead of laying his napkin in his lap and taking a spoon in hand, he tucked the napkin into his collar like an epicure in a 1930s movie, chucked his silverware aside, picked up the bowl, and proceeded to chug the soup as if downing a twelve-ounce can of Pabst Blue Ribbon. While this singular act constituted remarkable behavior for a grown man in a midrange Houston chain restaurant, the fact that he repeated the performance twice more made it truly outstanding. Even before the third refueling, most of us had lost our appetites by the time our entrées arrived.

Trejo's crowning nutritional achievement came several months later during another group lunch at a popular seafood restaurant not far from the Mazda Gulf Region office. While decorum, to say nothing of the fact that we still had a full afternoon of work ahead of us, dictated that we all exercise some restraint, Trejo took a full plate of boiled shrimp from the buffet table back to his place and proceeded to scarf every crustacean well before the rest of us chose our items from the buffet and sat down at the table. As in the soup episode at Olive Garden, Trejo repeated this feat twice, each time ladling more shrimp, lemon wedges, and cocktail sauce. By the end of this delightful repast, Trejo's white shirt was festooned with specks of cocktail sauce and shrimp remnants, and he had been officially dubbed "The Face That Lunched a Thousand Shrimps." The name stuck; in the past twenty-seven years, anyone with Mazda at that time remembers fondly the story of the shrimp buffet. Many remember that the majority of the crustaceans consumed were not even peeled.

The biggest guy I ever knew in the car business, however, was of sterner stuff and far higher character than Mike Trejo. When I met Andy Barter in the fall of 2016, he worked as Kia's district sales manager for Northern New Jersey. We called him "Big Dog," and for good reasons. He stood at least six foot three and weighed well over three hundred pounds. He was also known as Big Dog because his performance as a district sales manager led all others during his tenure at Kia's East Region. Everything about Andy Barter was big but in a very positive way. A former army officer, Andy spoke with a booming voice that commanded attention; at the same time, he projected an authentic bonhomie. His smile was bigger than his heart, and nobody ever heard him say an unkind word about anybody. After his army service, he spent a number of years as a trainer and a recruiter for Dunkin' Donuts, the now-famous doughnut chain that began in the Northeast. He also spent a number of years as a sales manager and then general manager of a Chrysler dealership in Pennsylvania, so he certainly knew his way around a dealership. An all-around likable guy, he commanded the respect of his peers, dealer people, and headquarters people. Because of a promotion in my department, Andy joined my dealer development team in Kia's East Region in the fall of 2018. He assumed the role of a facility and signage manager and fell into the work with an enthusiasm and energy that made me very glad to have him on board. The work required constant collaboration between dealers, vendors, municipalities, and our headquarters people, and in this role, he proved effective from the start.

Shortly after Andy joined my team, the regional sales manager for the northern part of our region, Werner Mersch, decided to retire after more than thirty years with VW and Kia. Andy would have been a great successor for Mersch, even though I knew I would have a tough time replacing him as facilities and signage manager. As the weeks wore on, though, we couldn't discern any significant progress toward replacing Mersch. Also in early May 2019, we began to hear rumors of a pending workforce reduction in the company. Soon we were informed that my entire department, except for me, was being eliminated. Though not totally unexpected, the news jolted all of us. Although Andy and the two additional members of my department were allowed to interview for other open jobs within the company, the situation stank. However, Andy took the news with characteristic strength. Now he could interview for the open regional sales manager's job. Yet at about this time, Andy received more terrible news. A bad left knee exacerbated by his weight forced him to start using a cane, and he was diagnosed with prostate cancer. Andy continued to do his job effectively in between driving from his home in Pennsylvania to his cancer treatments in Bergen County, New Jersey, while also exploring other opportunities both within and outside the company.

Meanwhile, those affected by the workforce reduction were impacted in different ways. Fortunately, my open point man, Keith Tooley, who had not taken the news of the job loss well, was able to slide into a district sales manager's slot, thanks to some deft maneuvering by our regional manager. My dealer development administrator, Lease Johnson, was able to interview for what amounted to her old job and therefore stay in my department, which remained effectively at half-strength.

Andy, unfortunately, found himself in a curious and untenable position. He had interviewed for a district sales manager slot in Kia's Central Region, but he really wanted a shot at Werner Mersch's old regional sales manager job. The company, which had behaved very badly throughout this whole charade, at this moment did its damned level best to make things more difficult for Andy. Although our Central Region wanted Andy badly, our HR jokers offered no assurance that Andy could have the district sales manager job in the Central Region if he interviewed for the regional sales manager job. In pain and worried about his knees and his prostate and wondering how he would take care of his family if nothing worked out, Andy refused to get worn down. He had a telephone interview for the regional sales manager's job with the vice president of sales, who, it appeared, had concocted the workforce reduction in the first place. In the presence of our regional director and with all of us cheering him on, Andy gave a good accounting of himself in the interview. In the end he did not get the regional sales manager's job, but he was able to transfer to a spot in our Central Region, eventually becoming Kia's district sales manager in Cleveland. The arrangement meant several months away from his family in rented housing while getting used to new dealers, a new job, and still traveling a couple of times a month for his prostate treatments. Between the work schedule, the relocation, the treatments, and the company's crappy behavior, Andy stood tall, never complaining, never uttering a foul word about any of it.

Luckily, some things work out. I talk with Andy about once a quarter, and as of this writing, Andy remains the number one district sales manager for Kia in the nation. He is practically free of prostate cancer, has lost a ton of weight for his health, and doesn't have the nagging pain in his knee. Andy stands as the best example of grace and guts I've ever seen, and when I call him, he still answers the phone in that big voice of his, exclaiming, "Hello, good sir!"

CHAPTER 20

CHARM SCHOOL (PART I)

When I joined Chrysler in October 1979, I knew practically nothing of my job responsibilities, the company, or even the automotive business. But I knew that the country was heading into a big recession, I knew that as a result the automotive industry was suffering from a disastrous downturn, and I knew that Chrysler had become the worst car company on the face of the earth. I also knew that I had five dollars in my checking account, no vehicle that I owned, and no other job prospects. Finally, I knew that at twenty-three years old, I did have the opportunity, desire, ambition, and determination to make it work.

I started at Chrysler with the title of administrative trainee. Steele Molloy and I were two of three trainees in Chrysler's Memphis zone. A fellow named Jack Wood, who had been a trainee for about a year, worked in the zone's business management department, logging in dealer financial statements, keeping track of dealer rental cars, and assisting Nell Pewitt with market representation assignments. Since neither the company nor the zone had a formal training program, Steele and I were stuck in the distribution department correcting faulty dealer car orders for production scheduling. For a couple of inexperienced nobodies, "correcting edit errors," as the car guys had christened this exercise, actually became quite important work:

The paper car orders had to be reconfigured to go through Chrysler's computer system for transmission to the various plants as cars were scheduled to be produced. We easily got the gist of the most common dealer mistakes in ordering vehicles and learned how to correct them. We were supervised by a car coordinator, a great old guy named John Barnes. Barnes, who had entered the business with Ford in 1934, was nearing retirement and loved showing us the ropes because he was bored as hell. The truck coordinator, Roy Dickson, helped us with truck orders since ordering trucks was a vastly more complicated exercise than dealing with cars. Barnes and Dickson watched us closely because, with orders already scarce, the plants had a voracious appetite for clean orders to build. It was good experience, but it was not solid training.

After the first week in the distribution department, Molloy, Wood, and I went to lunch. As none of us had any money, we relied on fast food or the vending machine. Over fish and chips, Wood told us about his year as a trainee. After about six months in distribution, doing car edit errors like us, he moved over to business management and had been there ever since. Molloy and I asked Wood if there was anything more to working at Chrysler besides doing car edit errors and correcting financial statements until it was time to become a district sales manager, which allegedly was the end goal of the informal training program. At that, Wood chuckled lightly and said, "Yeah, there's always taking a zone manager's car to get it washed or filled up with gas." But the job included other nice little perks; for example, occasionally, we were given the chance to drive a shiny new Chrysler for the weekend. Since I didn't have a car of my own and relied on Molloy or Nell Pewitt to get around, this particular perk was a real treat. One Friday I was handed the keys to a 1979 Dodge Diplomat Station Wagon with crimson paint, exterior fake wood applique, a luggage rack, power steering, power brakes, power door locks, power windows, and a 318 cubic-inch four-barrel V8 engine. I was so overjoyed that the next day I drove up to Jackson, Tennessee, to show all my buddies the trappings of my new trade and take my girlfriend to dinner (which turned out to be Shoney's because that was all I could afford).

Other notable small boons came our way eventually, like when we were assigned the task of ordering cars for the "sales bank," the aforementioned notorious Chrysler term for leftover cars built to no specific dealer order. This chore proved great fun because we could configure the cars of our dreams. One of my first valiant efforts was a 1980 Plymouth Volaré Special, which, by the time I got finished with it, seemed "special" indeed. The car had steel blue metallic paint with gray carpet and vinyl seats, power door locks, cornering lights, and an AM/FM radio with an eight-track tape player. Since the Volaré Special was conceived as a no-frills, midsize sedan with power steering, power brakes, and maybe an AM radio, the masterpiece order I'd built was quickly snatched away by Barnes, who shredded it into tiny strips and tossed it into the wastebasket. In my joy to create an automotive artwork, I had taken what was supposed to be a $5,500 car and turned it into a $9,100 unsellable warthog. Molloy's effort wasn't much better. He had taken a 1980 Dodge long bed 131-inch wheelbase pickup truck and added off-road tires, a 318 four-barrel engine, sliding rear glass, rear cargo light, and four-wheel drive. In a market in which trucks were not selling anyway, this creation was truly an automotive monster. Dickson took Molloy's order and put his Zippo lighter to it. After that we confined our efforts, with continued careful supervision, to more practical products. We quickly learned that cheaper was better as long as you included power steering, power brakes, and since we were in the South, air conditioning.

After about sixty days, Wood and I switched places. I became the business management trainee, and Jack went back into distribution. Given that one of our district sales managers had recently retired, we knew one of the three of us would be going out into the field as a district sales manager very soon. None of the three of us was properly trained or ready. Nevertheless, on the last day of February 1980, I was called into the zone manager's office and told that I was going to be the district sales manager for Northern Mississippi and Eastern Arkansas. The zone manager said he knew I wasn't ready but that I would get whatever support the zone could offer, which turned out to be a new 1980 Dodge Mirada, a road map, and reservations at the Holiday Inn in Greenville, Mississippi. The following Monday night, I checked into the aforesaid Holiday Inn at 11:59 p.m. I was on top of the world: I had a flashy car, an expense account, and an eleven-dollar hotel room with a color television and an ashtray. This was the life indeed!

The life indeed turned to pure crap Tuesday morning when I met Dodge dealer Bud Billings. Billings had no more time for me than I had the wherewithal to do anything at all for him. After seating me in his office across from his nice chair behind a large desk, Billings proceeded to chew my ass like I had never experienced before. He complained about Chrysler's nonpayment of warranty, nonpayment of incentives, Chrysler Credit's inability to fund any of the proposed contracts he sent to them, the prices of the new 1980 cars, and the 21 percent interest rates that were killing everyone. I learned more in two hours with Bud Billings than I learned in any subsequent dealer meeting. I also learned how woefully unprepared I was for my chosen career. But curiously, the ass-chewing became the best practical training I'd had in about four months of being a Chrysler "trainee."

Much of the next year and a half entailed the same: drive to the dealership, meet with the dealer or general manager, receive all kinds of complaints, get cursed out royally when I asked the dealer to order cars (at the time nobody needed new cars), and generally get an earful from the dealer on how lousy Chrysler was and how unlucky it was to be a Chrysler dealer. The worst of the job revolved around inventory, floor plan costs (because of the prevailing high interest rates), or the dealer's distaste for the practice of Chrysler's representatives shoving unwanted sales bank cars down their throat.

However, I got something of a break in June 1980, or at least a welcome change of scenery, when I was transferred from North Mississippi to Baton Rouge. Because the Baton Rouge district was more than three hundred miles from Memphis, I was able to fly down to do my job every week instead of drive rural back roads behind tractors or cotton pickers to get to the dealerships. And because Louisiana's oil-based economy was significantly better than that of the rest of the country, I had some moderate success with my dealers. The dealer concerns remained the same, but since the dealers in Louisiana were still selling cars and generally making money, their bite and bark were not as bad as that of the dealers I had been calling on before.

Baton Rouge seemed a picnic compared with my first district. But such was Chrysler's condition that on August 1, 1980, the company was forced to lay off a significant portion of its workforce. In our Memphis zone, we lost four or five district sales managers and several secretaries. The zone experienced a total realignment, and by Monday, August 4, I was the district sales manager in Shreveport, now covering an area including about fifteen dealerships in South Arkansas and North Louisiana. My new territory included dealers in an agricultural belt that had been hit hard by the recession. Unlike the Baton Rouge dealers, these guys and gals had no oil business to support them. Accordingly, their attitude toward me and Chrysler was generally about like that of Bud Billings. Such conditions made for a tough assignment.

Through all this, I was learning the business the really hard way. A typical week involved flying to Shreveport, picking up my field car, and spending the week driving from dealership to dealership practically begging dealers to order cars or, alternatively, begging them to purchase one of the sales bank cars stowed behind a fence in the mud and snow up north. Neither was an agreeable task, and my success at both was decidedly mixed. After over a year of this daily struggle, even at twenty-four years old, I was pretty worn down and began to seriously think about doing something else for a career.

And then, as often happens at critical times, I got another couple of breaks. Knowing that my relationship with the Shreveport dealers had turned so sour, the zone transferred me back to South Louisiana, this time to Lafayette. At the time, the Lafayette district in the heart of Cajun country was also the center of the US oil industry. The oil field was rocking; people still had money, so the dealers were still selling cars—a dramatic change for me. What came next solidified my intention to remain with Chrysler. The zone informed me that I was selected to attend district manager training in Detroit, also known within the company as "Charm School." This proffered opportunity was significant for two reasons: First, it proved to me that the zone and the company had enough confidence in me to invest several thousand dollars to put me through some decent training in the capital of the automotive world. Second, from my own point of view and narrow self-interest, the training was a chance to escape, however temporarily, the grind of flights and three-hour drives, not to mention regular battles with dealers and general managers over inventory and Chrysler's problems. The training was scheduled to take place at the new Renaissance Center in Downtown Detroit, where all the attendees would also be housed. I would be gone for two weeks, all on the company's dime. Around the country, two dozen other district sales managers and two dozen district service managers got the same opportunity. We all flew into Detroit on a Monday in mid-April of 1981.

To really appreciate the effect of this opportunity, you must remember that all of us had, for over a year and a half, been pounded by respective zone managers to get dealer orders placed, get dealer financial statements submitted, and get dealer facilities upgraded while at the same time getting vilified by the dealers themselves for simply doing our jobs. The idea of flying someplace for two weeks away from the nagging phone calls, the dealer bitching, and the grind of travel to spend a couple of weeks in a luxury hotel with decent meals and liquor paid for by the company made this experience a tremendous treat. Indeed, for some of them, the training in Detroit marked the first time they had ever been out of their zones.

I checked into the hotel in the Renaissance Center after a lovely flight from Memphis to Detroit. My room on the thirtieth floor faced the Detroit River overlooking Windsor, Ontario, and offered a fine view of the iron ore ships moving up and down the waterway. The king-size bed was comfortable and remarkably free of the bed bugs that infested most of the hotels to which I was accustomed. Unlike your garden-variety Ramada Inn, the showerhead worked perfectly, and since breakfast in our meeting room didn't start until 8:00 a.m., you could actually relax a little bit after waking up instead of shaving at the speed of light, packing and dumping your stuff in your trunk, then driving off to the next dealer contact.

On the first day of our training, we were greeted by Dirk Newell, Chrysler's head of training, whom I didn't even know existed. A buffet breakfast on one side of the large meeting room included waffles and pancakes, toast, pastries, bacon, sausage, ham, eggs and omelets cooked to order, all kinds of juices (some of which I didn't think had been invented yet), and gallons of coffee so black and strong as to disintegrate a spoon. For all of us, this splendid vision was a far cry from the dingy motel dining rooms that offered vastly inferior fare. On top of that, we were given an hour to eat. At 9:00 a.m., Newell revealed the two-week agenda and said how happy he and the Chrysler staff from Highland Park were to have us all there. He grinned broadly and said in a loud voice, "Welcome to Chrysler Charm School." The overall effect was fantastic—we all felt like normal human beings for the first time in months. We were to be put through a rigid schedule of training in financial statements, product development, manufacturing, market representation, and advertising, and to top it all off, we were divided into groups and given a specific, hypothetical dealer problem to work through. The rest of that Tuesday consisted of introductions to the heads of the departments who would put us through our paces for the next two weeks.

On Wednesday, the organizers assigned us to groups to tackle our dealer problems. My group received the task of helping a fictitious dealer get a capital loan to help grow the business. We only had a few minutes to discuss the problem before an in-depth study of the Chrysler financial statement consumed the rest of the day. At the end of the day, we all adjourned to an even larger hotel meeting room set up for cocktails and heavy hors d'oeuvres and attended by some of Chrysler's leading managers. Most of these luminaries—Tom Pappert, vice president of sales; Bud Liebler, the head of marketing; and Steve Sharf, the head of manufacturing—I knew only through the company videos that came out of Detroit from time to time. As you might guess, we had a blast. We were able to talk with these guys on a one-on-one level and really get to know them. Pappert, in particular, we found most interesting. Because he'd been with Chrysler since 1960, he not only knew where all the skeletons were buried, but he had a vast reservoir of anecdotes as well, even some about the antics of our zone personnel long before I knew them. After forty minutes with Pappert, I really began to appreciate the industry, the job, the company, and my role in it.

Additionally, all the district manager attendees had the chance outside the confines of the meeting room to get to know one another and share common problems. Gratefully, I learned that the other attendees felt the same way about some of our policies, procedures, and programs, and that they had the same issues, experiences, and opportunities I did. Best of all, I met some guys who would become trusted friends and resources throughout my career. A fellow named Frank Stanchik from the Pittsburgh zone told the funniest stories about goofy dealers I had ever heard or have heard since. The Los Angeles district manager, Steve Rojas, let it be known that his real ambition was to become a successful car dealer. Charm School also introduced me to Keith Heatherly, who remains a great friend to this day and with whom I was eventually reunited in 1995 when we were both at Gulf States Toyota. These relationships and the ability to ask for advice, counsel, and solace bolstered my determination to stay in the business over the next tough two years.

By Thursday morning, loosened up by several dozen gallons of free booze and premium crustaceans, and after three full days of intense in-classroom training, we were all looking forward to enjoying ourselves a bit on Thursday night. For the life of me, I cannot remember the subject matter of Thursday's session beyond a group meeting on our assigned fictional dealer's working capital problem. We had made some good progress and thought we were headed toward a good resolution when the day ended. At that point two of the Detroit managers suggested that we escape the hotel for some of the area's finest night life.

Off we went to points north. A bunch of us crammed into a nondescript 1979 Aspen Coupe. In those days, when cigarettes burned freely and the booze flowed like water, I was stuck in the back seat with Molly Hoover on one side of me and Stanchik on the other side, riding the hump of the Aspen's drive train up Gratiot Avenue to God knows where. I didn't know if I was going to die of asphyxiation or drown before we got to God knows where. God knows where turned out to be a dive bar on 8 Mile Road, an area that had already acquired a notorious reputation long before Eminem memorialized it in song. The dive bar itself wasn't just any bar, either, and although I can't remember its proper name, I certainly remember its unusual ambience. Upon entering we were seated around a large tank that appeared to be filled with a combination of mud and motor oil. No sooner had we ordered the first round than two healthy blondes emerged, totally nude, from an alcove just behind the tank and proceeded to wrestle in the toxic-looking substance. Their performance defied anything I had seen at the lady wrestling events in West Baton Rouge back in my home district. While the combatants indulged in all manner of provocative maneuvers, most of us sat spellbound with our swizzle sticks in the corners of our mouths. Never had any of us seen such corporeal depravity in our lives. Our Detroit-area colleagues, knowing that they had succeeded in rendering us speechless, smiled with smug self-satisfaction and ordered more booze. The next day the meeting room buzzed with stories about our trip to "the Mud Farm." I never learned the real name of that bar, but in Chrysler Charm School lore, it remains, indelibly, "the Mud Farm."

The next day, Friday, consisted of more work on our dealer working capital problem and a presentation by Jack Casement, the director of Chrysler Market Representation. Before this day I had only a vague idea of what market representation might be. Casement outlined the classic steps of putting a dealer in business. After Casement's presentation, Hank Savoy, who had just been promoted to Chrysler's vice president of dealer relations, took us through the paperwork process of appointing a new dealer. To a guy who had spent the last year and a half doing not much more than begging dealers to buy cars, I was finally learning new, different, and interesting stuff. Even though I had spent considerable time talking with dealers, I hadn't the faintest clue how they actually got into business, nor did I know how much money it took to establish a dealership, staff it, and keep it viable. At the end of the day, I felt totally energized; this Friday was the single most significant day, and the end of the first week, of Charm School. It opened up a facet of the business that I eventually resolved to make the focal point of my career.

CHAPTER 21

CHARM SCHOOL (PART II)

The weekend marked the midway point in Charm School. No classes were scheduled for Saturday or Sunday, and while we remained free to travel back to our homes as long as we returned by eight o'clock Monday morning, Newell had made clear that the company would not pay for such a trip. All but one of us stayed in Detroit over the weekend. Besides, Detroit offered lots of interesting sites, and having made new friends of our fellow attendees, we all wanted to be together anyway. So about ten of us piled into the company-provided vans and drove to Dearborn, where we toured Greenfield Village and the Henry Ford Museum. I fell in love with the museum—in addition to all the great old cars, the sense of history in the place overwhelmed me, but in a good way. From the convertible limousine in which JFK was assassinated to the largest steam locomotive ever built to a 1959 tomato harvester, the place proved a history major's dream. On such a typical upper Midwestern early spring day—bright, clear, cool, and dry—touring Greenfield Village was pure pleasure. A thousand miles from home, with no obligations that day, nowhere to be at any set time, and no laundry or paperwork to do as would normally be the case on a Saturday, we all let go completely and enjoyed ourselves thoroughly.

Since most of us were still a little bit hungover (and still slightly horrified) from our Thursday-night saturnalia at the Mud Farm, we decided on a quiet dinner at a Dearborn restaurant. But the dinner didn't stay quiet for long. While everybody was jovial and convivial during the meal, what happened next is what normally happens when you get a bunch of car guys together. Over unceasing rounds of drinks, we all took turns entertaining each other and ourselves with ribald stories of goofy dealers, stupid salesmen, and warranty clerks. As the night wore on, we even began to share the occasional saga of sexual exploit not so atypical of single sales guys on the road. One of the best stories came from Frank Stanchik, of course. Between gulps of Budweiser, Stanchik related the story of a contentious meeting that he and his service rep had with a well-known Pittsburgh dealer. Although the dealer had previously agreed to meet with Stanchik and his colleague to discuss an operational issue, the dealer laid into them as soon as they were seated in his office. Pounding his desk, the dealer covered the waterfront: floor plan interest, high new-vehicle prices, inadequate incentives, inventory pressure from the factory, and warranty policies and procedures. About the time Stanchik thought the dealer might have talked himself out, the service rep said, "Okay, Rob, do you by chance have anything good to say?" but in a manner with just enough sarcasm to get the dealer spinning again. The effect was like putting a match to a puddle of kerosine.

All of a sudden, Stanchik and his service rep found themselves personally berated. This diatribe went on for several minutes, during which time Stanchik attempted several times to speak, only to have the dealer snap, "Shut the fuck up!" each time. The dealer totally humiliated Frank and his service rep, but since the dealer was one of the strongest in his district, Stanchik figured he'd sit and take it with the expectation that the dealer would lighten up and then all three would go to lunch together. After about the fourth crass rebuke, Stanchik's service rep slowly got up from his chair. Stanchik thought the guy simply had enough and was preparing to walk out of the dealer's office. Instead, the service rep took off his sport coat, rolled up his sleeves, and walked around the side of the dealer's desk until he was directly behind the dealer. Stanchik didn't know if the guy was going to strangle the dealer or slam his forehead onto the desk. What happened next defied all expectations. The dealer, who at the service rep's actions, had finally shut up, was now quiet, eyes wide as saucers, likely because the service rep was over six feet tall and had been a college wrestler. The service rep began picking through the hair on top of the dealer's head. The dealer began gesticulating and yelled, "What the hell are you doing?" The service rep stated flatly, "Rob, you're a prick, and I'm just looking for the pee hole." One might have expected nuclear war, but according to Stanchik, the stunt totally diffused the situation. During the subsequent lunch, the three finally conducted substantial business in a more civil atmosphere.

Not all the stories told at the Dearborn restaurant that night had such happy endings. The Kansas City district sales manager told of a Chevrolet district sales manager, a rough, gruff, and older guy with few manners and less class. Finally getting in to see the dealer after a wait of almost half an hour, the Chevy rep made an off-color remark about the rather portly, mature dealership secretary who had exited the dealer's office at the same time he'd entered. Although nothing notable happened in his twenty-minute discussion with the dealer, the Chevy rep was immediately called in to his zone manager's office when he arrived back into the zone later that afternoon. "Gimme your keys and your field kit," the zone manager told the rep. "The zone secretary has already called a cab for you. You're done at Chevrolet." Later that night one of the guys from the zone office called the rep to see if he was okay and to remind him to be careful of anything he ever said to a dealer again. "Why?" protested the rep. "I talked with the dealer for twenty minutes, and nothing happened. He seemed fine." "Well," said the other guy, "that dame you mentioned to the dealer may not be the prettiest secretary in the office, but she's certainly the dealer's wife." Deplorable behavior and language, both then and now, I know, but typical of the situation. At least the crotchety Chevy rep got his due in this case.

In all, the evening was great fun for all of us because we found that factory people everywhere seemed to have the same experiences, but we just dealt with them in different ways. All of us found some commonality in the problems we faced—the constant clambering for orders, the nagging of the zone office for financial statements, enrollment in goofy programs, and the other dozens of minor issues and interruptions that filled our days.

When the training class resumed on Monday morning, Newell informed us that we were to prepare a three-minute presentation that would be filmed for posterity. Since videography was novel stuff for 1981, everybody got a little pit in their stomach, a wiggly worm of unease deep in the bowels. We had about an hour to prepare our presentations before the shooting started. Our only ground rules were that we were to stand behind and speak from a podium in front of all the attendees, the talk was to be three minutes (with an allowance of twenty seconds beyond or below that point), and we could talk on any subject we chose as long as it was germane to the car business. Further, to our horror, Newell informed us that each of the videos would be played in front of the assembly later in the week. Appearing in your home movies at a family gathering is one thing; appearing on screen in front of your professional peers is quite another. Accordingly, some of the guys got wound pretty tight.

Frankly, I cannot remember what I spoke about, nor can I remember the actual speech being taped. What I do remember is being called out by Newell for mispronouncing "palatable." Since I was a Southerner by raising and had just spent a couple of years in Europe, my English at the time didn't have a lot of polish; some of my peers remarked that they thought I actually said "platypus." I wouldn't know; all I know is that when my three minutes were up, my hands were shaking, my heart was pounding, and alcohol-induced perspiration was dripping down the crack of my ass.

Predictably, I was not the only guy to exhibit these symptoms or blow some key pronunciations. On a day when our proper business English had not a chance in hell, I heard at least two accidental cuss words, and Iacocca's name was mentioned ten times but mispronounced at least a half a dozen.

Worse yet some speakers displayed unusual and unseemly physical quirks. One guy from California couldn't keep his right forefinger out of his right ear. Another guy couldn't keep his left pinky out of his right nostril. Another guy might as well had been nicknamed "Wink'n & Blink'n" because he had obviously memorized his speech and stared directly at the camera at the back of the room for his entire three minutes, blinking about a hundred times a minute. The moment of highest humor, however, occurred when the Dallas district service manager—I can't remember his name—planted his five-foot-one frame behind the podium and was instantly lost from view. This problem was quickly corrected by the use of a step stool, from which he acquitted himself more than admirably. In short, if you'll pardon the pun, he was probably the best speaker in the bunch.

At the end of the day, we all learned a great deal from the whole harrowing experience. On the one hand, the videos demonstrated how certain personal quirks could hinder effective business communication. But on the other hand, the exercise taught us that while none of us were gifted public speakers, a little preparation and practice would make us much better business presenters.

Tuesday was a big day for all. We boarded a comfortable charter bus for the twenty-five-minute trip north to the Jefferson Avenue Assembly Plant, which had been converted for the installation of ROBOGATE welders the previous year, just in time for the production of the famous 1981 Plymouth Reliant and Dodge Aries Model K-cars. In fact, the bulk of the first drawdown Chrysler made on the 1979 loan guarantees had gone to convert the line in the Jefferson Assembly Plant. For obvious reasons, like lack of available funds, Chrysler had arrived late to the automation party. Once on site and through security, we all donned hard hats and safety glasses for the trip down the assembly line. Since all of us were in business suits, we were warned to be mindful of the sparks generated from the welders. Although the ROBOGATE welders made the manufacturing process more efficient, the shower of sparks they produced could shoot out fifteen feet or more, creating an impressive show and a bit of a hazard. We also learned that the majority of the workers we saw were not putting parts on body frames or welding key joints on the car bodies. They were actually tending the ROBO-GATE machines. So automated had the manufacturing process become that tasks formerly performed by three or four workers on the assembly line could be handled by one person at a computer panel controlling a couple of robot welders.

We proceeded from the welding shop to the paint shop, then on to the point where the 2.2-liter transaxles were installed in the cars from below. Those of us who remembered when the engine and transmission assemblies were manually lowered into the engine compartments via chains from above found ourselves astounded by the sight. Even though the work at this station was performed by human beings instead of robots, the process and tooling were entirely different from even the model year before. From there we viewed the dash, interior, and glass installation. In an hour and a half, we had seen the entire process of how a car was built. For me, having worked in a plant only two years previously, the experience remains poignant—the industry, and Chrysler, had come a long way.

At the end of the tour, we received some optimistic remarks from the plant manager that exemplified how all of Chrysler was feeling at the time. In the dark, dead days of 1979 and 1980, when the plant was manufacturing midsize cars, they suffered repeated shutdowns simply because business was so bad overall. With so few plant orders, Chrysler had no choice but to shut the line down again and again. However, now the plant manager could enthuse that the line had been running nonstop since August 1980 as the K-car continued to sell well, and orders rolled in. The plant manager's attitude was mirrored by the line workers themselves—all of them were more than happy to have steady, valued work, and the pride showed through as the K-car enjoyed sustained success in the market. In summary, the Jefferson Avenue Assembly Plant tour was perhaps the highlight of Charm School because we were finally able to see, with our own eyes, the result of all those car orders we had been begging the dealers for. Further, since customers were buying K-cars in numbers that outstripped those of the earlier Aspen and Volaré sedans, there was hope, not only at Jefferson Assembly but also throughout Chrysler, for the future.

On the bus back to the Renaissance Center, we heard an amazing story told by the Detroit area district sales manager, who not only swore that the story was true but also added that it had been related to him directly by a line foreman during the plant tour that very day. This particular plant guy had worked for years in the Hamtramck plant, one of Chrysler's oldest, and in fact one of the oldest plants in the country for any brand. The plant had been shut down permanently in the winter of 1980; nobody was buying Aspens and Volarés, and in any case these old F-body cars were to be discontinued at the end of the 1980 model year. The property was sold to GM, for one dollar, I think, and Hamtramck was to be demolished. This plant guy, apparently, had been transferred to Jefferson Assembly to work on the successor K-cars, the Plymouth Reliant and the Dodge Aries. Less than a year later, he'd learned that when the bulldozer was chugging through the waist-high weeds in one of the plant's holding lots it hit something and came to an abrupt halt. The driver got off the bulldozer, walked to the front of the blade, and found a 1980 Dodge Aspen sunk to its axles in the mud. Normally any car built is accounted for. This car, probably a sales bank car built to no specific dealer order, had been driven off the line, plopped in the holding lot, and totally forgotten about while cars all around it eventually made it to the railhead, where they were loaded onto a train and later trucked to dealerships around the country. Such was the state of business at the time, and so poor were Chrysler's internal controls, that this particular car was unintentionally abandoned until some demolition guy ran into it with his bulldozer.

At a group dinner that night in the Renaissance Center, we all were still excited from the plant tour, especially those of us who had never been in an assembly plant before. The tour dispelled everything we had been told about car plants, assembly workers, the union itself, and the company's issues. Based on stories from the older managers in each of our zones, we had been led to believe that the plants were dirty, poorly run outfits staffed by insubordinate, drugged-up workers who at times didn't even show up for work. The reality, which we had seen with our own eyes, revealed the opposite. The plant floor appeared as clean as an operating room. The line workers who did talk to us seemed enthusiastic and excited. (We had been told before the tour not to converse with any of the workers; however, on several occasions the plant workers had called us over and, unbidden, told us about their specific responsibilities on the line or the capabilities of the machines they were running.) During the dinner, several of our group noted the timeliness of the training, particularly the plant tour: for over a year, most of us had been beaten up by the dealers, general managers, sales managers, and even our own zone managers so often that it was a real joy to explore outside of the dealer and zone environments to gain a broader perspective. While we all knew that Chrysler was not out of the woods yet, we were readier than ever to persevere.

Thus inspired, we entered the meeting room the next day to present our specific dealer cases. My group's hypothetical case involved a dealer who, while profitable, was beginning to outrun his working capital: a classic scenario of an effective dealer needing more resources to grow. Our group was evenly divided between two options. One possible solution, which I wholeheartedly supported, would have the dealer go to his bank or his captive (in this instance, Chrysler Credit) for a short-term loan. The other option entailed soldiering on and risking running out of money, then possibly missing payroll and suspending vendor payments. Stiffing a vendor makes for poor business, and an even worse error a dealer can commit is to fail to pay his people. My pro-loan camp argued that going to Chrysler Credit made much more sense and offered a safer choice overall. By sheer force of business logic, we prevailed upon the naysayers in our group to adopt our position so that we could show a united front when we made our presentation to Dirk

Newell and the executives. We must have made a convincing case because the judges, hearing all the presentations, not only supported our proposal but also voted ours the finest case study in the entire training class. Through teamwork, and by demonstrating our collective knowledge of dealer thought processes, we impressed the bigwigs and increased the momentum of the good feelings flowing among all the trainees.

The next day we heard a presentation from the import group. Now you may think, *What was a domestic car company doing with an import group?* As it happened, Chrysler, several years before, had formed a partnership with Mitsubishi Motors. As one of the oldest Japanese manufacturing concerns, prior to their alliance with Chrysler, Mitsubishi was known in the US primarily as a maker of the aircraft that attacked Pearl Harbor and terrorized the US Navy in the early days of the Pacific War. By the early 1980s, however, Mitsubishi was a builder of such quality small cars that their offerings in the United States through Plymouth and Dodge dealers became much more sought after than Chrysler's own domestic models. The cars were more comfortable and reliable, got great gas mileage, and because they were denominated in yen, much less expensive than the domestic cars. The Mitsubishi-Plymouth offerings were the Champ, in two-door and four-door versions; the Sapporo coupe; and the Arrow pickup truck, which at the time was probably the most reliable compact truck in the US market. The equivalent Mitsubishi-Dodge offerings were the Colt hatchback, also in two- and four-door versions; the Challenger coupe; and the D-50 compact pickup truck. As district sales managers we were familiar with all these import products; since these cars were allocated separately from the domestic cars and because there were never enough of them to please every dealer, the phone allocations always ended up being quite contentious. Because of their quality and pricing, the dealers literally begged for them. I remembered from my days in the distribution department the dozens of calls we got every week demanding to know why the imports remained in such short supply.

The poor guys whom the import department had sent to present to us obviously had not been briefed on their audience and their reason for coming in the first place. These two staffers merely thought they were there to give us product presentations. We already knew the product; we wanted answers to questions concerning the supply. Accordingly, the import guys were caught completely off guard when our questions began about five minutes into the presentation of the AM/FM stereo in the Sapporo and Challenger. Their reaction was to look anxiously at Darryl Davis, a senior manager in a different department who had previously worked in imports.

Much to their relief, Davis took over the remainder of the session, and while he couldn't answer all our questions, he filled in a lot of gaps in our knowledge of the situation. One thing we learned, and it was important, was that the Japanese were becoming very sensitive to the reaction in the US to the flood of Japanese cars coming into the country from Toyota, Datsun, Honda, Mazda, Isuzu, Subaru, and Suzuki. (Mitsubishi did not yet have its own sales channel in the United States at that time, as Mitsubishi Motors of America would not establish itself until several months later. Thus, Chrysler was the only outlet for Mitsubishi sales in North America.) As Davis spoke, the import concerns started to make some sense. Davis told us about the upcoming voluntary restraint agreement. The initiative ultimately proved a prudent move on the part of Japan, who recognized that it was smarter to limit their exports to North America than to be legislated out of business by a pissed-off Congress.

Accordingly, not long after our Charm School, the US and MITI (the Japanese Ministry of International Trade and Industry) agreed to the VRA: the necessary but complicated system of allocating Japanese exports to the United States by manufacturer. The only problem was that Toyota, Datsun, and Honda ended up with the biggest shares of the initial year's allocation of 1.7 million units. The smaller fry—Mazda, Subaru, Isuzu, and Suzuki—were held to significantly lower allocations. Nevertheless, as noted before, the VRA had the dual effect of offering the domestic manufacturers some breathing room and took the heat, at least temporarily, off the Japanese.

Curiously, though not unexpectedly, the domestic manufacturers, including Chrysler, raised prices on some of their most popular models within a year of the inception of the VRA. Breathing room, it seemed, had become an opportunity for a little profiteering! In any case all of us trainees had received an important lesson in the complexity of our business.

That evening's final gathering was punctuated by a short talk by Tom Pappert, who spoke extemporaneously from the same podium where we had delivered our presentations earlier in the week. He shared his hope that we all would take the lessons learned in the previous two weeks back to our jobs in our respective zones and home districts. He echoed the same optimism that the Jefferson Avenue plant manager had expressed during our plant tour, and he reminded us that we were the face of Chrysler to our dealers, salespeople, and the community at large. He acknowledged how hard we all had been working over the past year and a half and he reminded us that everybody in Detroit was working just as hard, if not harder. Afterward, since it was our last night together in Detroit some of the attendees wanted to hit the town for one last round of merriment. I was totally exhausted from the previous two weeks' activities, so I took the elevator up to my room, showered, and slept like I hadn't in a couple of years.

The next morning we attended one last classroom session. Gar Laux, one of the old Ford executives whom Iacocca had lured out of retirement, spoke to us for about ten minutes. He told us that while the K-cars were selling well along with the Omni and Horizon models, the orders for Cordoba, Mirada, and the other rear-wheel drive cars were not coming in at a rate that would allow the plant in Windsor, Ontario, to keep running. The loan guarantee agreement, as well as Chrysler's separate agreement with the Canadian Auto Workers union, wouldn't allow for a plant closure. Secondly, the company didn't want the negative publicity—for the last two years the press had killed us whenever we brought a plant down or had a bad ten-day sales report. Consequently, Laux told us to expect a push on rear-wheel drive cars the following week. We were all taken aback, particularly after all the upbeat vibes of the last two weeks, but Laux tried hard to accentuate the positive: sales of the K-car were more than covering the sales deficits of the rear-wheel drive cars. Laux then introduced a young executive named John Cesny, who gave us a rah-rah speech on how to push for orders for the Miradas and Cordobas for the time being. The light at the end of the tunnel: The old M-body LeBaron and Diplomat were to be replaced that year by K-car derivatives, also to be known as the Chrysler LeBaron and the Dodge 400, both with rather favorable early reviews in the automotive press. Then Dirk Newell ended the meeting by thanking us for our participation just before we all boarded a bus for the airport to catch our flights home.

I had several hours before my flight back to Memphis, so I had lunch and drinks at the airport with Bill Doucette, the district sales manager from Boston. Doucette's stories of his ordeals with the New England dealers made my experiences look tame. More than once Doucette had been shown the door by a dealer simply for asking for the orders. Because of terminations, Doucette had probably bought back more cars than anybody else in the company, yet he took it in stride: "Just watch," he said. "We're gonna get back to our zones on Monday, and within a day we'll have totally forgotten everything we experienced in Detroit."

On the flight home, I half-dozed and half-reflected on the previous two weeks. Some of the skills I learned have stayed with me ever since, like my ability to analyze a dealer's financial statement and find solutions to very practical problems. Perhaps even more importantly, I remained friends with some of my fellow attendees for years thereafter, even through long stints with Mazda and Toyota. In fact, some of them left Chrysler shortly after the training. Trey Underhill, a talented district sales manager out of the Pittsburgh zone, was hired by Gulf States Toyota, a private distributor in Houston, only a few days after Charm School ended. Underhill went on to have a great career at Honda after leaving Toyota. Keith Heatherly, a district sales manager out of the Dallas zone, eventually also went to work at Gulf States Toyota as a district sales manager in Oklahoma and was still in the same job when I joined Gulf States Toyota fourteen years later. Steve Rojas did indeed become a successful dealer in Los Angeles through Chrysler's minority dealer program. Molly Hoover, the Portland district sales manager, eventually went to work for a Salem, Oregon, dealer before striking out on her own with a consulting business that helped dealers improve customer satisfaction, long before the industry (and the individual manufacturers) began pounding the concept into the dealers' heads. Many years later, on a long drive between dealerships in Texas, I turned on NPR in time to hear Hoover in a radio interview promoting a book she had written on the subject. (Some of the other participants I met again on a follow-up training visit to Detroit in December 1982. I enjoyed seeing them all again; we relived the highlights of our previous stay while gaining yet more vital industry knowledge.) When I got back to my apartment that night in Memphis, two weeks' worth of company mail, messages from dealers, and nastygrams from the office awaited—we had no cell phones or laptops in those days, and nobody did this shit for you when you were away.

CHAPTER 22

"WHAT HR DEPARTMENT?"

The human resources department has become a necessary part of any current business enterprise. At a small-business level, the HR department, as we'll call it hereafter, may consist of one individual with portfolio ostensibly to hear and air employee complaints. In an automobile dealership, this person is more likely to be on staff to curtail, prevent, or eliminate any legal entanglements that can ensue from a dealership's reaction to an employee's out-of-line behavior. Let's face it, the last thing a dealer needs or wants is trouble arising from an employee complaint regarding pay issues, mistreatment by a dealership manager, or more often a harassment claim, sexual or otherwise. In large dealership groups, whether public or private, the HR department is often headed by a trained personnel professional with a staff of equally competent subordinates primarily to keep the dealer out of court.

Automotive lore abounds with instances of biased, sexist, and unfair practices. From customers or employees discriminated against to dealership managers getting their jollies by pimping the pay of their people, the misbehavior, high-handedness, and sheer managerial stupidity have always been there. Technology (cell phones, as you know, can record voices, take photographs, and send obscene messages, *as well as* dispatch and receive phone calls) has made HR issues much more visible, much more quickly, and in much more volume. Somewhere along the way, the crescendo of misdeeds has simply become too much for dealers, managers, and lawyers to handle.

Enter the HR professional, a highly trained individual hired by the organization to ensure uniformity of policy in the dealership as well as fair and equitable employee treatment. In reality, human resources representatives in small businesses, and none more so than in automobile dealerships, live a surprisingly moribund existence—that is, until an incident ensues. Then the HR professional proves their value. The HR professional schedules a meeting, sometimes with the dealer's attorney in tow. The HR representative then counsels the employee on whatever policy contradiction has led to the intervention. The attorney is there to be sure that the legal nuances and niceties are noted and observed and to provide some rhetorical muscle in the event the employee challenges the HR person.

This scenario plays out somewhat similarly in an automobile manufacturer's or supplier's world. Human resources, of course, exists in the corporate world to ensure adherence to company policy. Nevertheless, some long-tenured employees feel HR's primary function has changed over the years from a service arm to help balance employee and company relations to a risk aversion and policy enforcement division. Some feel the advancement of political correctness, the desire to keep anything controversial (politics, race, religious persuasion) out of the workplace, and the onset of the #MeToo movement have persuaded executive management to empower HR with policy and procedural controls far beyond HR's purview. In truth, however, instances of an HR staff jumping on a report of misbehavior like a fumble in a football game are way overblown. Today's HR professionals, overall, have better communication skills and more practical experience in their field than their counterparts of twenty or thirty years ago.

Yet for all the vast improvement in employee behavior, the darker side of human nature still seeps into the workplace. The term "weaponize" seems a bit strong, but sometimes supervisors hold such negative views of employees that they enlist HR to help carry out disciplinary vendettas against employees who violate not general company policies but personal pet peeves. A field manager who has great close-point relationships with dealers but is slack in paperwork may get a write-up from his supervisor, whereas coaching and counseling by the supervisor may help more effectively and diplomatically correct the "deficiency." Still, I have seen, on more than one occasion, a supervisor take their ire to HR with a view toward demoting or even terminating the employee. When this type of gamesmanship occurs, the supervisor already has painted a target on an employee for whatever reason. Up until only about ten years ago, such behavior has occurred for infractions as innocuous as writing or speaking or dressing in a manner inconsistent with a supervisor's expectations. Human resources all too often has bought into a mindset that if a supervisor says it, it must be so.

Over the years, I also saw HR involved in force reduction initiatives to trim personnel expenses, particularly in payroll and benefits. Often these actions target older, more highly compensated employees. Fine, but such actions have side effects. First, older employees have valuable experience in the industry and critical knowledge of the organization. Second, companies tend to eventually replace tenured cashiered employees with younger, less experienced new hires. Mazda and its vaunted management have become infamous for this type of practice: In 1990 and again in 1993, Mazda showed the door to dozens of hardworking men and women over the age of fifty with hundreds of years of combined industry experience.

Not surprisingly, the growth, both in the size and importance of the HR department, has been a boon to employment law offices. Human resource's involvement in everything from hiring decisions, promotions, compensation, and benefits establishment to standards of professional behavior has led to an explosion in lawsuits by employees against the car companies.

There was an incident that led to my promotion to an area executive position at VW in 2003. The incumbent area executive was a well-meaning but ineffective manager. Earnest but not bright, he inadvertently made decisions that HR felt put the company at significant risk. By accepting favors like football game tickets from dealers in exchange for extra allocations of cars, the manager crossed a line of propriety. Human resources, injecting itself beyond behavioral reproaches, prevailed on the man's supervisor to put the employee on a performance improvement program.

This classic example of a nonautomotive entity involving itself inappropriately in a business matter, solely for the purpose of removing the employee from the company, still occurs. A more appropriate approach may have been to reprimand the employee for his judgment lapses and then systematically counsel him on business and self-improvement opportunities.

In the end the employee was terminated, whereupon he promptly filed suit for wrongful termination. After considerable discovery, numerous depositions, and several thousand dollars in legal fees on the part of the company, a settlement was reached that cost the company even more money. Consequently, while I relished the advancement opportunity this unfortunate incident afforded me, I had always wondered if this situation, and thereby this employee, could have been salvaged through some professional counseling and customized dealer-contact training.

For the most part, the HR personnel I have encountered over the years have worked well with their peers, applied the company rules firmly but fairly, and done their best to hold themselves and all employees to the highest standards of performance and decorum. The problem is a few of these HR people forget that the primary end objective is to sell cars, make money, and keep the customers happy in the process. More importantly, happy employees help foster happy customers. At the same time, the increased professionalism on the part of both employees and companies is recognized and appreciated by customers. Companies with HR professionals who strike a balance between policy and empathy earn employee trust.

Sometimes policy decisions come from people at a higher level without vision. More often than not, in the execution of such strategies, while HR must be brutally and coldly efficient, they should be commended for inflicting wounds with as little bloodshed as possible. Two fine examples come to mind.

In the autumn of 2007, I had just rejoined VW, a company with whom I had worked earlier in the decade. The company had just moved me from Texas to Michigan as I assumed a general manager position. The day after my possessions arrived in Detroit from San Antonio, I was called into a session with a senior HR staffer. I was informed the company was relocating the entire headquarters from Detroit to the DC area, and I was invited to come along. The inducements offered in connection with the relocation were very favorable.

But I was one of the lucky ones. Many employees were not invited to relocate to Washington. In those cases, the employees received a stay bonus for remaining in their current jobs for six months while the relocation transition ensued. Their salaries would continue for the six months. These employees were also offered employment counseling and outplacement services, again fully paid for by the company. These stay bonus arrangements were consistent across all departments and all employees and were delivered by HR all on the same day with an efficiency to rival an execution squad.

Yet, in the case of many of these employees, while the loss of their job was certainly a jolt, the news was actually okay, if not a blessing. The company had been in the Detroit area for over thirty years, and this generation of employees had their relatives, homes, and support systems established. Many of them also were in mid- to late careers, and relocation of one thousand miles to a much more expensive market would have been an even greater jolt. Therefore, I would have to admit that the company got this one right. The company remains a viable concern in North America, and many of the employees who took the stay bonus were able to find employment. Because of the timing of the relocation and upheaval (it occurred during the early stages of the 2007–2008 Great Recession), other employees in the Detroit area had a difficult time for as much as six months to a year afterward.

For as efficiently as VW handled its corporate relocation, the most ham-handed corporate chicanery came from none other than American

Suzuki Motor Company. For years, at least since Suzuki's small SUV fell victim to a rollover issue in 1988, Suzuki had struggled in the US market. For two decades, Suzuki limped along as a third-tier franchise and arguably the worst of the worst. It wasn't that the cars were that bad—in fact, from a quality standpoint, the product got good ratings. However, in a market where Toyota, Nissan, Honda, Subaru, and Mazda were gathering most of the import market, Suzuki couldn't generate any traction at all. The product offerings, while good, were just too limited; for example, Suzuki had no pickup truck, nor did it have a good range of offerings in the still viable passenger car segments. Rather, Suzuki's problems emanated from a weak dealer base, a much smaller advertising budget than a top-tier import line like Honda or Toyota, and deplorable senior management.

Suzuki's status wasn't helped by the fact that its facility program for dealers was horribly inadequate. The facility scheme called for large square, bright-red arches in front of the store—they reminded me of gaudy gallows. In those instances where Suzuki managed to get a good dealer, the Suzuki brand was usually relegated to poorly located smaller facilities that they insisted the dealer renovate to the Suzuki scheme. Imagine an AT&T or T-Mobile retail storefront painted over red with four large rectangles out front, doing nothing more than chewing up valuable display space or customer parking. Further, even good dealers got into the habit of relegating their poorest-quality personnel to the Suzuki showroom. Not even a great car could overcome the deadly combination of bad management, bad facilities, poor salespeople, lousy location, and curb appeal that induced indigestion. Interestingly enough, a few unlikely dealers managed to carry the Suzuki brand well into 2012, each selling one hundred cars or more a month and spending big money to promote the brand.

However, Suzuki didn't have enough of this type of dealer to sustain any staying power. So Suzuki's Japanese management, rather than going for the old college try and upgrading its marketing and adding new models in key segments, decided to take the chickenshit approach. In the third quarter of

2012, Suzuki employees throughout the United States woke up to find their bank accounts heavier than expected and their management curiously quiet. When these employees called their field offices with questions, they were informed that the deposits were their severance pay and that they were now out of a job because Suzuki was exiting the market.

Suzuki's actions ran counter to American perception of Japanese honor and business acumen. To those of us who were students of the industry and had seen the decline in the quality of Suzuki's representation, the company's stance wasn't that much of a surprise. It was a shame, though, as the product, while limited in range and offerings, was definitely solid. The entire episode became an HR and public relations fiasco. The brand, along with its employees and dealers, deserved much better than they received.

The Suzuki story illustrates why a strong, professional human resources department is so vital to any company. Several months after Suzuki's late 2012 exit from the country, I was part of a team interviewing a former Suzuki manager, a victim of Suzuki's withdrawal from the market the previous autumn, for a position in VW's Southeast Region office. Another member of the interview team asked the candidate about the Suzuki experience, whereupon the candidate recounted the events similarly to how I related them above. "That sounds terrible," my team member said. "Where was the Suzuki HR department during all this?"

The candidate tilted his head slightly and replied laconically, "What HR department?"

CHAPTER 23

IT'S SHOWTIME!

The major auto shows, which hit their highest popularity in the late 1980s and kept going strong until about 2010, exemplified the limits of class and style in the business. Almost all the manufacturers pulled out all the stops for the major auto shows, such as Los Angeles, Detroit, Chicago, and New York. Some of the displays at these shows consisted of as much as forty thousand square feet jammed with bespoke displays, branding items, and shiny new cars. To properly frame their brands, the manufacturers hired hundreds of fashion models from agencies usually based in Detroit. During the glory years of the auto shows, these models were overwhelmingly female, under thirty, very attractive, and exceptionally well researched—the manufacturers wanted only the best to represent them at these high-profile events. In short, the major shows, which lasted two weeks, sparkled like a Hollywood premiere.

Manufacturers would kick off the show with a black-tie gala event. White-gloved attendants served premium alcohol and culinary delights to a special invitee list of VIPs and manufacturer executives. I attended several of these events, and I can tell you there is nothing like rubbing elbows with a service and parts vice president of your company. Only a few feet away, one of my biggest dealers would be enjoying a Jack Daniel's and water. Sometimes a reporter or factory representative got gregarious enough to put the moves on a hired model or a dealer's wife. Often careers were unceremoniously ended when the effects of the refreshments made themselves . . . ahem . . . felt.

But I digressed. Whether the show was for selling, as many of the smaller regional events were, or whether they were major stops on the auto show circuit, the main purpose was to get the brand and its vehicles in front of the public. As noted, manufacturers deployed teams of well-dressed, attractive presenters, and seeing a practiced, professional full walk-around on a new car took the selling (and buying) experience to a much higher level. More importantly, to maintain a cadence and provide some momentum for the new-car experience, the major auto shows were spaced chronologically for effect.

The Los Angeles Auto Show usually occurred in November—it was a chance for the executives and the automotive press to get in a little fun in the sun before heading back to Detroit for another lousy winter. Also, in the early 1980s, everybody in the industry recognized that California ranked as the trendsetter for the rest of the country. The Los Angeles show became an opportunity for the manufacturers to see how their concept cars and new models would be received in the culture and style incubator that California had become. Everybody looked forward to the Los Angeles Auto Show with a longing out of all proportion to what it actually entailed. The customers loved it because it presented a chance for some pizazz in the dull time between Halloween and the holiday season. Similarly, the auto executives looked forward to getting the hell out of Detroit just as the snow arrived.

Speaking of snow, for years the Detroit show in January was the hottest ticket on the circuit despite the aforementioned lousy weather. Detroit offered the thrill of seeing some of the experimental or concept cars that the manufacturers might not have displayed in Los Angeles. The Detroit Auto Show, formally known as the North American International Auto Show, became the perfect platform for the launch of many flagship models over the years. To illustrate the esteem the Detroit show held, it was grand enough to draw great crowds to Downtown Detroit in the middle of the winter.

The Chicago Auto Show in early March didn't have the glitter of the

Detroit show, but it occupied an important place on the industry's calendar. Chicago was eagerly monitored not only by the manufacturers but also by the automotive press as a bellwether of how mid-America reacted to the manufacturers' new offerings. Chicago also became important as an event coinciding with the beginning of the industry's traditional spring selling season. In many years the biggest manufacturers—Ford, GM, and Chrysler in particular—received a big jump in sales in March.

The New York Auto Show occurred on Easter weekend. This show was revered because of the glamour of America's biggest city, a journalistic capital. As the last major auto show of the season, it served as a proper kickoff to the summer selling months. Everybody loved traveling to New York. The executives liked hobnobbing in some of the most famous restaurants in the world with both Broadway and political types. The writers and the editors of the automotive press loved getting smashed in the city's watering holes on somebody else's dime. Additionally, the venue, the Javits Center on Eleventh Avenue just south of Hell's Kitchen, was so massive that the manufacturers almost always had their largest displays of the season in New York. This show also lasted longer and sported more press conferences than the other majors, and let's face it, some of the executives were always good for laughs and gaffs. Engine Charlie Wilson famously said, "What's good for General Motors is good for the country," at the New York show in 1953.

While the national shows became the flame that really fired the senses of the manufacturers and the press, the smaller regional events came into their own in the mid-1980s and served as vehicles by which the carmakers could show their offerings to customers who, until then, had to visit a local dealership to get a look at new cars. Many customers viewed auto shopping (quite rightly) as akin to having a root canal. These customers preferred to see vehicles of twenty or more carmakers under one roof. The price of admission to these smaller regional shows was usually a third to a half of the price of those in the major cities. These shows were shorter, a work-week bookended by a couple of weekends. The manufacturers loved having so many customers in the middle of America see their new offerings. If a regional show was a selling event, salespeople relished the opportunity to see more customers over the course of the day than they would in a week. The banks and captive finance sources loved seeing an uptick in their business since a majority of people financed their vehicle purchases. Practically everybody loved the regional auto shows, but . . . there were exceptions.

Since the manufacturers spent so much money on the major auto shows, the burden of staging a regional show fell largely on the local dealers and the dealer associations. For example, the Chevrolet dealers in a market such as Memphis had to split the cost of the square footage allotted for their brand. The manufacturer might come to the table with only a few thousand dollars to help with the cost of transporting the expensive brand displays to the arena. The manufacturers did make the display cars available for the brand's dealers to divvy up; for Toyota, Nissan, Subaru, Mazda, and particularly Honda, this practice became one of the dividends of a regional auto show. Import cars remained scarce, so dealers or sales managers had to fight over the hottest cars, and consequently, an unlucky regional or district manager usually had to referee these donnybrooks.

Along with staging, staffing became yet another issue at a regional show. Staff might relish the chance to talk to dozens of eager customers in one day, but they often bickered over schedules, shifts, break times, and who would have to work the show versus who remained at the dealership to maintain the normal course of business. The added drag of working two weekends in a row rankled many. Again, the regional managers would have their hands full with extra work on top of extra complaints.

In connection with the regional auto shows thus far, we had glimpsed the roles of the manufacturers, the dealers, the dealer associations, and varied retail sales personnel. Eventually, an important consideration surfaced: No regional auto show would succeed without the active participation of the manufacturers' local or regional office personnel. Specifically, the regional distribution manager monitored the shipment of the cars to the auto show venue—no minor task. Coordinating a couple of truck transports to arrive at a specific convention center within a set window of time with the correct personnel on hand to stage, clean, spot, and prepare the cars for the display required a considerable block of time for a guy (or gal) who was already the busiest person in a regional office. Sometimes the regional distribution manager was tasked with actually ordering the auto show cars. No matter how carefully a regional distribution manager performed this work, somebody was going to be perturbed. The model mix, the colors, the engine-transmission combinations, the interiors, and the style of wheels were second-guessed by everybody from the regional manager to the salespeople to the head of the dealer association. Too bad. Once a show car was on the floor and in place, it was there for the duration of the show.

At the regional level, local dealer personnel became the only resources available to staff the show. Truly, the last task a dealer, general manager, or sales manager wanted to take the time to do in a busy day was schedule people to work shifts at an auto show. Enter the district sales manager. Alone among manufacturer, dealer, or regional personnel, the district representative (or representatives) handled staffing at an auto show. Blessed with this opportunity a couple of dozen times over a forty-plus-year period, I could say that auto show staffing remained probably the most reviled duty, surpassed perhaps only by airmailing cars. If the district sales manager cultivated excellent working relationships with his brand's general managers and sales managers, he could sometimes get these individuals to help work out a schedule assuring that the auto show display was staffed properly.

If the district sales manager was a representative of a hot franchise (Honda, Toyota, Lexus, Mercedes, Audi, or Porsche), the whole task was much easier. Not wanting to anger the person responsible for getting him hot cars, a general manager or sales manager would usually comply with a request to assist. As I worked with brands that were not as popular, I could tell you that the task usually involved some measure of vehicular bribery. Here was how that went:

District Sales Manager (DSM): Joe, I need two of your guys to man the auto show display from noon until 4:00 p.m. on Saturday.

Sales Manager (SM): Screw you! Twelve to four on a Saturday is our busiest time. I have six deliveries scheduled, and that's when we get our heaviest traffic. Ask one of the other losers at the other dealership.

DSM: Look, we need the coverage, and the other two dealerships have offered to take 4:00 p.m. till closing.

SM: Fine, so you don't need my guys.

DSM: No, we need them. You know noon to four on Saturday is one of the best shifts in the entire show.

SM: Look, stud, if I'm gonna strip *my* floor during the busiest time of the day, I gotta get something in return.

DSM: Okay, I'll give you eternal recognition. Plus, I'll throw in the gray diesel four-speed short-bed pickup truck with no air.

SM: What a jerk. I'm giving you my heart and soul, and you're offering up a turd in the punch bowl. If I'm gonna take that piece-of-crap four-banger with black shoes and no breeze, I gotta have some candy.

DSM: Really? I'll throw in the candy-apple red SE-5 Cab Plus.

SM: Shit! What do I look like? A home for ugly cars? Two trucks? There's probably not a grand of gross in both of them put together. You're killing me, man.

DSM: Okay, scratch the gray diesel, and I'll throw in the five-speed Barney car instead.

SM: Crap! I could sell the Barney car, but if I'm gonna take these other ugly cars from you, I gotta tell my general manager I'm getting something of value.

DSM: Who the hell do you think I am? Monty Hall? Remember, I've got to be fair when I divvy up. How about the 626 sedan in silver with the automatic transmission?

SM: No dice. If I'm taking your cheap slugs, I want the Miata Package B in blue.

DSM: Okay, fine. I can book it, but your guys better show up at noon, and they better be good—washed up, suited up, and ready to roll.

SM: I've got the perfect pair: Jerry and Mrs. Labrier.

DSM: Come on, Joe! I need pros!

SM: All right, come to think of it, Jerry's got a delivery at two thirty, first car he's sold this month. I'll send Rasmus instead.

DSM: Deal. I'll send you over the invoice. But Rasmus and Mrs. Labrier gotta be here at a quarter to twelve so I can give them the orientation.

SM: Okay, but you better send me over their badges so they can get in. And another thing, Rasmus is always broke, so you'll have to pay his parking.

DSM: No friggin' way! I'm already out fifty bucks for buying lunch for the guys from the office who staged all these cars because all you *dealer* pukes were too *busy* to help our distribution manager get these cars in here and all prettied up.

SM: Fine, man, but this is gonna cost you three beers and a plate of crawfish étouffée at Pappadeaux when this shit is over.

This kind of exchange became a ridiculous standard, and the seemingly off-color language was pretty tame compared with similar conversations. But the recreated episode demonstrated the extra toll a regional auto show took on dealers, their people, and particularly regional office representatives. Besides the auto show responsibilities, cars still needed to be wholesaled, reports written, phone calls answered, fires doused, and general business conducted.

But the show had to go on, and it did, at least until the late 2000s. Reasons abounded for the decline in the popularity of auto shows, particularly at the regional level: With budgets busted and customers scarce, most manufacturers drastically curtailed their participation in the regional auto shows, and after about 2015, some of the marquee manufacturers began pulling out of even the *major* auto shows. Porsche was a good example. With only about 190 dealers in the United States and a greater interest in Europe, the luxury European manufacturers thought it better to focus on Geneva, Switzerland, and the other major European auto shows. Additionally, the plethora of new-car launches throughout the year somewhat diluted the marketing pizazz of the larger auto shows. By 2017 long gone were the days of having all the new-car launches stacked into September and October. Also, the trickle-down effect of moving the Detroit Auto Show from January to later in the year took a lot of momentum out of the overall experience. The final blow came in the late winter of 2020 with the continuing COVID-19 pandemic. The New York Auto Show was postponed as the people in New York and New Jersey, dying by thousands, had more immediate concerns.

With dealerships largely closed for more than ninety days and the buying public losing jobs and quarantined, a multimillion-dollar new-car bash in the spring of 2020 didn't make much sense.

Since the pandemic has abated considerably, auto shows in the major markets have enjoyed a modest revival, but the splash and the glitz are just not there anymore. To illustrate, in closing, the November 6, 2023, edition of *Automotive News* reported that Stellantis, the parent company of Chrysler, Dodge, Jeep, and Ram Trucks, was skipping the Los Angeles Auto Show, thereby missing a great opportunity to showcase its new electric vehicle (EV) offerings. The news that one of the Detroit Big Three has opted out of one of the major auto shows indicates just how much has changed in the auto show environment.

Great advances in technology, specifically social media, also have eaten into the allure of auto shows. If a customer can view all the new cars they want by clicking on their computer in the comfort of their own home, why pay forty dollars in tolls to cross the Verrazzano-Narrows or the George Washington Bridge and then fork out twenty-five dollars on top of that and fight New York City traffic to the Javits Center? Some of the same technology that enables a customer to shop for cars online will, I predict, morph the auto shows into technology conventions.

For example, as EVs generate a bigger and bigger share of the industry's unit sales, I anticipate that vendors for such ancillary equipment as chargers and other infrastructure to support EVs will occupy more and more of an auto show's display space. As long as range anxiety and the necessity of home-charging apparatuses remain, I expect that the auto shows will become laboratory showplaces for sophisticated customers who are the staunchest cheerleaders for green technology as embodied by EVs but who still want to have enough juice at hand to further their advocacy. In short, the car no longer will be the star—it will share the stage with the power source!

CHAPTER 24

"I'LL SUE!"

If the United States is one of the most litigious societies in the world, the car business is surely infested with more legal arcana than any other sector of American business—and probably with good reason. For not only are regular customers inclined to invoke legal counsel over sales and service charades by dealers but dealers also are just as apt to invoke counsel against customers, suppliers, municipal governments, and, of course, manufacturers. The customers, often quite rightly, must seek legal redress for poor sales and service treatment. Dealers, sometimes quite rightly themselves, spend a good deal of their time not only fighting back but also bringing actions against municipal agencies for tactics that are bound up in bureaucracy, precedent, or sheer stupidity.

However, a dealer's favorite target is usually a manufacturer. Why so? Because the manufacturers, for whatever poverty they plead, generally have the deepest pockets a dealer can access. A dealer knows that state statutes and motor vehicle associations will back them to the hilt in a legal proceeding, no matter how obviously guilty they may be. Therefore, a dealer who won't spend $500 per month on a janitorial service to clean their own showroom will spend $500,000 with a legal firm to stick it up the manufacturer's ass. Not surprisingly, an entire cottage industry has emerged within the legal profession of firms that specialize in a genre called dealer law. Since the early 1980s, this field of specialization has drawn to its ranks some of the most eminently eloquent, fervently fastidious, and tremendously talented barristers US law schools can produce—and with good reason. Dealers, particularly the good ones, have a lot of money. Their targets, the manufacturers, have even more money. Accordingly, this cottage industry has grown in visibility, importance, and, of course, wealth.

But it wasn't always this way. In the halcyon years of the auto business in the United States, specifically the late 1940s through about 1970, the dealers and the manufacturers enjoyed what may be called a collegial relationship—the dealers made buckets of money on the cars and parts the manufacturers provided. The manufacturers, thanks to strong dealer organizations that marketed aggressively and sold prolifically, made tons of money as well. As a result, nobody wanted to upset the applecart. Over time, as American society as a whole became much more litigious, the relationship between the dealers and the manufacturers followed suit.

One of the catalysts seems to have been the recession after the Arab oil embargo of October 1973. Everybody—the dealers, manufacturers, suppliers, vendors, transportation companies, and consumers—lost a boatload of money. Some lost everything. In the industry's first real postwar hiccup, everybody wanted to point fingers. The forthcoming actions became dealers versus manufacturers or captive finance sources. Less successful dealers, who simply did not have the financial wherewithal to withstand the ensuing recession, felt honor bound to recover something. Many spent more on legal fees than they actually recovered.

Then the manufacturers suffered the other pinprick: suppliers who had fallen on hard times and wanted the same compensation the dealers wanted. The manufacturers who survived the oil embargo and the recession remained too worried about recovering sales momentum to spend much time, or legal fees, messing around with what were, basically, insignificant lawsuits in the bigger scheme. However, a precedent had been established—tenured dealers had had their first huge scare, and it raised awareness among all dealers that the only people looking out for them were the dealers themselves.

After the 1974–1975 recession, the government, which had weathered its own scare, decided that the manufacturers needed some prodding as a cushion against the volatility of oil prices and the uncertainty of the future. With gasoline now twice the price it had been before the oil embargo and with the United States still importing upward of a million barrels of oil per day just to get by, the government took two important steps—one benign, the other inflammatory. The benign response was the establishment of the Strategic Petroleum Reserve, under which the government began to stockpile millions of barrels of oil in salt domes in Louisiana as a sort of rainy-day oil fund. The inflammatory response was the establishment of the Environmental Protection Agency (EPA) and corporate average fuel economy (CAFE) standards that dictated a level of mileage efficiency the industry, as embodied by the four manufacturers, should attain.

Chrysler, Ford, GM, and AMC reacted like rebellious bairns. At the time, the behemoth barges offered by the manufacturers averaged about fourteen miles per gallon. The mileage requirements dictated by the government called for considerably more efficiency, increasing those goals every year.

At the same time, the newly created EPA determined what everybody knew but wouldn't talk about—automobile emissions propelled by leaded gasoline was one of the major, if not the major, contributors of air pollution. The waterfall effect of the CAFE requirements and unleaded fuel pounded the auto and refining industries with a double whammy. The oil industry, accustomed to blending high-octane, fully leaded fuel, had to adjust quickly to the new fuel requirements for unleaded gasoline. In that transition, the auto industry had to incorporate new technologies, such as catalytic converters. A major component of catalytic converters was platinum, one of the most expensive, hardest-to-extract precious metals known to humankind.

Imagine the angst of auto executives in early 1975 faced with skyrocketing fuel prices, impossible fuel economy standards, and extra expenses for equipping their fleets with the required new technologies. Enter the attorneys for the manufacturers. These attorneys, in concert with a multiplicity of lobbyists, argued long and hard for a relaxation of the fuel economy standards or, at best, a delay in their implementation. The combined legal and lobbying efforts were surpassed only by the early 2000s tobacco control battles. In their defense, the manufacturers had good points. Since their factories were tooled for the production of the large gas-guzzling boulevard barges they had been producing for years, and since they kept losing billions in the ongoing recession, they saw no problem expending further millions in efforts to curtail these new impositions.

However, the government can be just as persistent as any lawyer. The CAFE regulations eventually stuck, and still stick, to the point that fifty years after the fact, the government, the environmentalists, and their lobbyists are close to making the whole CAFE argument moot by their advocacy of the electric car business. Although neither the dealers nor the consumers nor the manufacturers are truly ready for them, EVs are coming. The groundswell of support for EV from the government, environmentalists, and regulators has finally persuaded manufacturers to spend billions developing the vehicles and the infrastructure to support EVs. Case in point: In 2022, Hyundai has sunk over $5 billion into an electric vehicle battery plant in Georgia, of all places.

The legal battles that have ensued over the years pale in comparison to the fracas that's occurring now. Manufacturers have forced the dealers to pay for a substantial portion of the EV regulatory, compliance, and infrastructure costs. Cadillac, in 2020, mindful of the investment EVs require, has offered dealers an opt-out by offering to buy out Cadillac dealers who simply did not want to foot the bill. It was a sound strategy: Cadillac was already eviscerated to the point wherein its volume had dwindled to a handful of cars, and the once noble GM division wanted no part of a legal tug-of-war with its dealers, many of whom had been ready to throw in the towel for several years and who viewed the opt-out as a sweetener for a graceful exit.

What happens with the remaining manufacturers and their dealers will be even more interesting and entertaining to watch. Since the government and many states and municipalities have ordained that electrification is the way to go and since the costs are so high and the requirements for chargers, service, and components so complex, the legal squabble over financial responsibility is likely to be long and bloody. The dealer network is not prepared for the addition of EVs, although the manufacturers, cognizant of the momentum the electrification movement has generated and even more painfully aware of the billions they've spent to develop the vehicles, are aggressively nudging the dealers in the *right* direction. America's transportation system is still geared for the internal combustion engine—driving range (or, depending on the EV in question, the lack thereof) is still a primary concern, so the development of charging stations on the nation's highways is even more critical.

And while we're on that subject, who in their right mind believes that the oil companies, whose very existence depends on the internal combustion engine, will roll over and take this lying down? Since the costs of high-speed chargers and training for technicians are so egregious, many dealers still balk at the cost. Accordingly, the manufacturers may face some tough choices: Do they forcibly terminate dealers who don't sign up to be EV dealers? Or do they develop modified dealer agreements that allow some dealers to remain representatives of their brand for gasoline-powered cars only? Or, and this one is an even better question, will states and municipalities get so persnickety that they will not allow gasoline-powered vehicles in their jurisdictions at all? It's a bit of a slippery slope argument but feasible, I believe, nonetheless.

Furthermore, the EV debate is only the latest facility-related issue between manufacturers and dealers. The manufacturers have been after dealers to enlarge and upgrade their facilities for years. Sometimes part of the equation is the purchase of land on which to build these new palaces.

Land and construction costs vary widely across the United States, so tension between dealers and their manufacturers always ensues. Some of this tension will inevitably manifest itself in lawsuits. When a new dealer is approved, they have already spent millions to construct a branded facility for their manufacturer—well, most of the time. Sometimes the manufacturer will grant a dealer a term agreement in which the dealer pledges to construct a branded facility within a certain period—say, two years. Sometimes, as dealers will do, the dealer misses the deadline. If the dealer has begun construction and runs into delays not of their own making (a municipal permitting snafu, weather-related interruptions, or material shortage), the dealer and the manufacturer will get together and revise the term agreement, usually invoking provisions for just such eventualities.

If, on the other hand, the dealer has not even started building their facility, the manufacturer will send a letter to the dealer noting this fact and threaten the dealer with the termination of their franchise. Such action on the part of the manufacturer is increasingly rare, given the protections that state motor vehicle statutes afford most dealers. Never mind the fact that the dealer has violated a contractual agreement—the dealer is *local* and must be protected from the vagaries of the Big Bad Manufacturer. Accordingly, the tone of the letter from the manufacturer regarding the breach will be absolutely unfriendly and will recount the commitments set forth in the term agreement. Most often the letter will conclude with a demand that the dealer respond in writing with a revised timetable for completion of their facility project.

Over the years I have seen many such letters; they remain remarkably similar from manufacturer to manufacturer. I have also seen many responses from dealers to such letters, and *they're* all over the board. Interestingly, the type of response a dealer may offer up to a letter of this ilk seems to depend more on where the dealership is and less on the brand or brands involved and the dealer's profitability. In my experience, a dealer in the South or Southwest will call the regional executive or national staffer who has dispatched such a letter. In the Midwest a dealer will usually respond in writing to such a communication. In Florida, Louisiana, and the Northeast, the more typical response will come from the dealer's lawyer and not from the dealer. Most responses I have seen recite dealer's rights and the heavy-handedness of the manufacturer (usually piling on antidotes of perceived or actual manufacturer maleficence toward the dealer), but curiously, they will mention little of the dealer's breach or any details about how the impasse may be solved.

Eventually, the manufacturer responds to the dealer's attorney by very clearly redirecting the subject of the exchange to the original breach, which, of course, is that the dealer has not fulfilled the terms of his agreement. Only at this stage does the dealer really get concerned enough to (a) call the regional office and set up a time for face-to-face discussion on the issue or (b) accept a call from the regional office suggesting the same. A good dealer wishing to come to some kind of accommodation will opt for a meeting as soon as possible to resolve the matter. Only a really unintelligent dealer, and indeed there are many, will choose to pick a fight with the manufacturer over a breach for which the dealer is solely responsible. Such a stupid dealer might fire back with another knee-jerk response, once again detailing all the manufacturer's previous bad behavior toward the dealer and looking for redress of these grievances *before* renegotiating the terms of the original agreement.

Lawyers for both sides will be equally overjoyed in this recalcitrant stance by a dealer in breach. If a dealer is dead set against fulfilling his agreement, manufacturers will have their attorney file a motion (with the motor vehicle commission, state court, or federal court—it doesn't matter), and lo, attorneys for both sides are on the clock. Since it's been the manufacturer's desire all along to simply get the branded facility built, the manufacturer will look for the most expeditious way to bring the matter to a close. As mentioned before, while manufacturers hate spending money in general, they particularly detest spending money on lawsuits. Usually at this point, the dealer has forgotten the real meaning of the argument and is looking to merely stick it to the manufacturer any way he can.

Depending on the brand, these types of confrontations can get long and ugly. Few dealers want to rile the likes of Mercedes, BMW, Honda, or Toyota. They will grumble about the exorbitant facility demands that a Porsche building entails, but in the end, Cayenne and 911 grosses are pretty nice, so the dealer will knuckle under. Curiously though, a dealer will go to extraordinary lengths to avoid honoring a facility commitment to a brand with less cachet. That's why Mitsubishi, VW, and Suzuki (when Suzuki still sold cars in the US) have had such a hard time getting branded facilities built. Amazingly, a dealer for a second- or third-tier franchise will spend as much money on lawyers to avoid building a branded facility than the facility will cost in the first place.

And the list goes on. In fact, I can write a separate book on how these legal issues are resolved. But to summarize for present purposes, almost always, after months of depositions on both sides, pretrial motions, preliminary filings, and a lot of bullshit rhetoric, a state judge (or an administrative law judge if the matter ends up in the state's motor vehicle commission) will order the dealer and the manufacturer to mediate. Since all the manufacturer really wants is to get their branded facility built, they'll look to settle quickly by this point. The dealer, knowing they are indeed in breach of a contractual agreement, by this time is looking to get something from the manufacturer in exchange for the branded building the manufacturer wants. Like the issue of a new-dealer establishment or a relocation of an existing store, such action goes either one of two ways: (1) the dealer demands money from the manufacturer to defray the cost of the branded building, or (2) the manufacturer offers up a certain number of hot-selling units to the dealer as an inducement to move forward with the project. As always, the attorneys will milk this resolution for all it's worth—billable hours rule the day.

Customer complaints and EV issues and delayed builds aside, the worst legal imbroglios in my experience have been dealer placement issues.

Manufacturers constantly look for ways to expand their brands, and many times such practice involves establishing new dealerships or relocating existing dealerships to more advantageous, more highly visible, and hence more profitable locations. Sometimes these new locations, either in the case of a new dealership establishment or the relocation of an existing dealer, come dangerously close to another existing dealer of the same brand.

Given the huge investment dealers make in their facilities, personnel, and equipment, many remain as territorial as wild animals and will viciously defend their relevant market area (RMA). The RMA for a dealer varies from state to state and is a by-product of state franchise laws designed specifically to protect existing automobile dealers from competition. The wide variation in RMAs can utterly confound a manufacturer's market representation department. A dealer's RMA extends from the location of the existing dealership to a radius of five to fifteen miles around the existing dealership. To be sure, exceptions remain. In most states if an existing dealer goes out of business or is terminated by the manufacturer, the brand is allowed to reestablish in the previous dealer's RMA, provided the new establishment occurs within two years and within two miles of the previous dealer's location.

However, as indicated before, the state statutes vary. Connecticut, for example, affords a manufacturer only *one* year in which to reestablish within two miles of the previous dealer's location. If you're thinking that these guidelines sound restrictive and rather onerous to the manufacturer, you're absolutely right, and that is exactly what the state legislatures and state motor vehicle commissions are doing when they write these statutes—limiting the power of the manufacturer. Car dealers contribute to the political campaigns of state legislators who, in turn, in most states, appoint the faceless bureaucrats who staff most states' motor vehicle commissions. Accordingly, the legislators are (somewhat) beholden to the dealers.

Now that we've set up the duck, let's take a hypothetical example: A dealer in Texas who already has several franchises is being courted by a manufacturer for a brand-new dealership. The manufacturer, through its attentive market research, realizes that this dealer not only performs extremely well with their existing brands but also is situated in an area of extremely favorable population, with its household and income growth not far from one of the fastest growing metropolitan areas in the country. The manufacturer, familiar with this particular state's definition of "RMA," carefully considers the location of an existing dealer almost twenty-five miles away in the major metropolitan market mentioned earlier. The manufacturer looks at three important factors in considering the new establishment: (1) the huge potential for the brand represented by the proposed new dealer in this dynamic and high-growth market, (2) the subpar performance of the existing dealer almost twenty-five miles south in the metropolitan market, and (3) the likelihood that the existing dealer in the metropolitan market will raise a stink or file a formal protest against the manufacturer in the state's motor vehicle commission over the proposed new establishment. A drive-time analysis reveals that the proposed new location is indeed just over twenty-five miles from the existing dealer in the metropolitan area. Without spending several thousand dollars on a GPS survey to nail down exactly how far away the new location is from the existing dealer, the manufacturer makes its decision to move forward.

So far, so good, but almost every state has a notification procedure whereby the manufacturer must notify, in writing, any contiguous dealer of a proposed new establishment of a new dealer *regardless of whether that new dealer is within the RMA of the existing dealer.* In this case, the manufacturer, based on its own informal auspices and the fact that the new location is in a different county from the metropolitan dealer, gambles that the existing dealer in the metropolitan market will not object to the new opening. Further, the new-dealer establishment protocol in this particular state allows any dealer noticed of a probable or pending establishment sixty days to respond to the motor vehicle commission and the manufacturer with any objection to the proposed establishment. If no formal written objection is provided to the motor vehicle commission or the manufacturer during that sixty-day period, the manufacturer may proceed with the new-dealer establishment.

What almost always happens is that on the fifty-ninth or sixtieth day, the existing dealer has his attorney file the requisite protests of the proposed new establishment, and that is exactly what happens in this hypothetical case. You see, just as dealers believe that the manufacturers are truly as stupid as they appear, the manufacturers, in a combination of self-absorption and hubris, believe the same thing true about the dealers. In this case, the required notification in this particular state has to include not only the physical address of the proposed appointment but also the legal description of the property involved. Hence, the existing dealer in the metropolitan area, upon receiving written notice by the manufacturer of the proposed establishment, commissions a noted Austin civil engineering firm to perform a GPS survey (very common in the year 2000) of the actual distance between the southernmost point of the proposed dealership's legal property description and the northernmost boundary of the legal description of the property of the existing dealer. Voilà! The southernmost boundary of the proposed new location is within twenty-five miles by several hundred feet of the northernmost boundary of the property of the existing dealer. Logically the existing dealer then files a formal protest in the Texas Motor Vehicle Board against the establishment of the new dealer in the adjoining county, invoking the RMA statutes in Texas. Next, attorneys for the manufacturer *and* the existing dealer in the metropolitan area shout with glee. They're both now set for a big payday.

In another hypothetical instance, but using the same context as revealed here, attorneys for the manufacturer and the existing dealer meet. After several rounds of posturing, which may take several months to a year, an agreement is struck through mediation. This agreement can take any one of several forms: In one possible scenario, the manufacturer will agree to delay the new-dealer appointment long enough to allow the existing dealer in the metropolitan area to concentrate on the brand with enough good-faith effort to bring the brand's performance under that dealer into compliance with the manufacturer's standards. Many times this scenario is augmented by an order, signed off by all parties, that the manufacturer supply the existing dealer in the metropolitan market with (a) a certain number of cars to enable the existing dealer to hit the aforesaid performance indices, (b) an amount of money ostensibly for marketing purposes that the existing dealer will use to further the brand in his existing RMA, and (c) a combination of both of the above—a number of cars to achieve the manufacturer's required performance standards, plus marketing funds to help make this goal a reality. Another possible result is that (d) the manufacturer, with the concurrence of the proposed new dealer candidate, will agree to make a large lump-sum settlement payment to the protesting dealer to allow the new-dealer establishment to proceed. I have seen all four scenarios. In the case where a manufacturer pays an existing dealer for the privilege of proceeding with a new-dealer appointment, disbursements by a manufacturer can range from $100,000 to over a million dollars. If the amount is over, say, $300,000, such an amount is a true windfall for the protesting existing dealer regardless of what he has paid in legal fees.

None of these resolutions happen within a quick time frame. None of them are cheap. More egregious is the rancor that such a battle engenders between the manufacturer and the existing dealer—to say nothing of within the proposed dealer candidate. In some cases the proposed dealer candidate will be out several hundred thousand dollars because the manufacturer may insist that the proposed dealer share in some of the settlement costs. But even worse, the proposed new dealer may have lost one to three years of valuable time, during which he could have been planning and constructing a new facility or, in some cases, pursuing a new opportunity with perhaps another brand that may not be vulnerable to protestation.

Given what's at stake, new-dealer appointments or relocations of existing dealers that entail such legal challenges are the most injurious to factory dealer relations, and they engender the most far-reaching negative effects.

No one, the dealer or the manufacturer, comes out of such an experience without looking at the other in bad faith.

But all these in-house squabbles are dwarfed by the story of the guy who, having bought a lemon, comes back into the dealership exclaiming, "I'll sue!"

CHAPTER 25

THIS JUST ISN'T FUN ANYMORE, AND EVERYBODY IS UNHAPPY (PART II)

When the 2005 Dragonfly Green Saturn VUE gave up the ghost after at least ten years of loyal service to our household in 2020, we decided to look for a new vehicle. For weeks, we had known the end was near. The windshield leaked, and the carpet was as soggy as a ship's mop. The resulting moisture had shorted out enough of the electrical system to render the vehicle if not entirely inoperable, then most certainly dangerous to drive. Neither the air conditioner nor the power windows worked. Attempts to dry out the vehicle, conventional and novel, had failed to revive the patient. Time to get a new car.

My partner technically owned the VUE, so the transaction would actually be in her name, even if we'd planned to share use of the new car. However, since I was the one in the business, I immediately sprang into action. I called up a dealer I knew representing the brand for which I worked and told him of our plan: A purchase of a low-priced front-wheel-drive SUV via a thirty-six-month closed-end lease. I added that I would help with one thousand dollars for the "due at signing" portion of the transaction. "I've got it!" the dealer said with great enthusiasm. I then clarified the approximate price we expected. The dealer happily gave me the name of his representative at the dealership who would be shepherding this transaction through the process and said he would phone the rep personally about our pending arrival the following Saturday.

Given my penchant for thoroughness, I next called the rep myself to reiterate what I had told the dealer, hoping to streamline the process as much as possible. I emphasized to the rep that we had a good idea of what we wanted and especially that we didn't want to spend a lot of time at the store. Five seconds of silence followed, then I heard a sigh at the other end of the line. The rep said, "Well, the earlier you get here, the quicker you'll get out of here." That statement did not sound encouraging, though in the past I had heard that line many times, and I'd even uttered it myself. Surely, I figured a guy in the business could do better, could achieve more efficiency, yes? Probably? (Probably not!) We agreed on nine o'clock the following Saturday morning, the dealership's regular opening time. The rep said we should talk to a salesperson named Dave when we got to the store. I fought the urge to cross my fingers for good luck, but I was pretty sure the rep had, only behind his back.

I have mentioned prior in this book that, for many customers, a visit to a car dealership ranks about as enjoyable as a trip to the dentist or, worse, a visit to the county motor vehicle department. Although I spent most of my early career in dealerships as a salesperson or a visiting factory representative, the very idea of spending the day listening to a bullshit sales pitch, followed by the almost certain administrative interminable nightmare of completing the paperwork of sealing a deal, made me groan—aloud, which did not reassure my partner.

With this black acid coursing through my system, we arrived the following Saturday at nine complete with our COVID-19 masks. The showroom doors were locked, and though we could see various (also masked) employees milling about through the glass, no one noticed us. I felt a bit uneasy at this development—usually, a customer appearing at a showroom door on a Saturday morning is pounced on by one or more voracious salespeople. In lieu of making a spectacle of ourselves, I led my partner to the service entrance, and we walked past the service adviser, who seemed shocked (about the eyes, at least) to see a couple of unannounced customers casually strolling through his area. His glance gave me another moment of unease, as if I were invading someone's personal space. I could feel his eyes burning a hole through the back of my head as my partner and I proceeded through a service department door into the customer lounge, where four or five forlorn customers (nobody likes bringing their car to a dealership for repairs on a Saturday) sat, sipping coffee and leafing through some well-worn magazines.

We left the lounge to enter the showroom and promptly sat in two chairs at a random salesperson's (not Dave's) desk. We carefully sipped the bottles of water my partner had packed and patiently waited to be acknowledged. For yet another uncomfortable moment, I felt I was at a low-energy dud of a party to which I had not even been invited, but in less than a minute, a tall spare salesperson arrived and asked if we needed help. "We're here to see Dave," I mumbled through my mask.

And he responded, "Hi, I'm Dave, and you're the guy from Kia, right?"

I said, "Right," and introduced my partner. I explained that the vehicle would be hers, not mine. Dave asked us to sit at his desk, which was only a few feet away, and we dutifully complied.

So far, so good, I thought, despite the weird welcome. I mentally discarded a bit of my ingrained trepidation of being party to a retail car transaction. I wasn't gonna backtrack to bitch about the front doors being locked at opening time, and anyway, the guy *was* clearly expecting us bright and early. We were in the door, and the transaction process began.

Yet again, I explained to Dave what we were looking for at what price point, at what due-at-signing figure, and at what approximate monthly payment. Dave looked at my partner and said, "Okay, let's start with this guest sheet." Name, driver's license, insurance card, social security number—all were given. Then the flashbacks began: The collective memory of witnessing hundreds of such scenes, some as much as forty years in the past, was beginning to weigh on me. Research has shown that many customers detest the paperwork shuffle and retail gamesmanship so common in a lot of new customer transactions. As my partner worked her way through the guest sheet, I made small talk with Dave, not only attempting to establish my bona fides as a car guy but also trying to mask my irritation.

We already knew they had an ample supply of the make and model my partner wanted. Dave asked a few more questions, and the discussion started to get more specific; even within a specific model, countless combinations of goodies abounded. I should have foreseen the process unfolding: My partner had been riding with me in one of the more upscale versions of the same model, which included a sunroof, bigger wheels and tires, fold-in lane-assist mirrors, Apple/Android sound options, and, most importantly, heated leather seats. Even though I had spent a number of years as a distribution manager for car companies and had ordered hundreds of cars at a time, I began to seethe because I absolutely knew what came next.

Not surprisingly, the basic model Mr. Cheapskate (me) had selected had none of the features my partner really wanted. Since I had not, in fact, been a part of the retail process for many years, the myriad of choices and the cleverness of the manufacturers in bundling the most popular options in expensive, upscale packages had been lost on me. As I mentally bumbled for a face-saving alternative, my partner astutely took over, and I reluctantly followed her lead. Still flustered, I agreed that we might have to go toward a higher-priced variant to get the specific equipment she wanted. In mere minutes, Dave, a real retail pro, produced such a model with all the requisite amenities. But the monthly payment, even with three thousand dollars due at signing, was about one hundred dollars more than we really wanted to pay per month. My jaw tightened, and I could feel the blood pounding through my temples.

My pulse slackened, if only just a bit, as Dave brought us out to the vehicle for a thorough walk-around presentation. Dave asked my partner to prioritize her color choices. This she did, and the model Dave had his guy bring up was perfect. Right color, right options—but the price was just too high. As my pulse ratcheted back up, and this time another notch, Dave had my partner take a turn around the dealership in the new vehicle, and she really, really liked it.

When we went back inside, the sales manager appeared with a worksheet that confirmed that the price was, at least for a monthly payment, about one hundred dollars more than we wanted to pay. The sales manager presented a couple of other transaction models, which still were too expensive. I looked on nervously as Dave, to his credit, worked through these obstacles to present a more satisfactory proposal that encompassed the correct color, equipment, and pricing. Twice he gave us hands-on tours of different models meeting these criteria. Still there were gaps between my partner's requirements and reality. They needed more test-drives. Throughout, Dave remained cool as a cucumber and handled all our concerns expediently and thoroughly. My partner also maintained her patience and poise. Meanwhile, my loathing for the entire infernal process increased.

I was feeling less than friendly, but the friendly haggling took time. Hungry and restless, I looked at my watch to discover that it wasn't morning anymore—12:15 p.m.—and we were still not settled on the vehicle yet. This detail revealed how even a seasoned car guy could miss steps or fail to anticipate the little nuanced obstacles that could get in the way of completing a transaction. Shame on me.

My partner, bless her soul, and Dave, the salesperson, handled this entire transaction much better than I could have. When they came back from the third test-drive, I knew we were close. When the sales manager proposed the addition of aftermarket heated seats installed at the dealership and my partner exclaimed "yes," I sighed in relief—loudly.

Dave brought up *the* vehicle. He insisted that my partner drive the vehicle to be sure she was comfortable with the ride and feel of what she was about to lease. Off we went on my partner's fourth test-drive of the morning. The bright gunmetal-blue exterior paint, the luxurious leather interior, and the perfectly ergonomic instrumentation combined to send her into delighted giggles! As she drove farther, I could see she was sold.

Upon our subsequent return to Dave's desk, we settled on that model at a transaction price of about sixty dollars per month less than what we feared we would have to pay. Dave disappeared into the dark rear recesses of the dealership and emerged only a few minutes later with a couple of bottles of cold water and what looked like a munchkin doctor's medical bag. "I've got a gift for you," said Dave. "This is your Kia's roadside kit." By this time, it was exactly 1:10 p.m., and I thought I could finally relax a bit.

Not so. While my partner looked like a kid on Christmas morning, I felt the sinking feeling of *here we go again*. Dave pulled out the guest sheet and (again!) requested to see my partner's insurance card; then ensued a long-winded call between Dave and the insurance company. Between his clichéd niceties, the requisite inquiries, and several instances in which Dave asked my partner to speak with the insurance representative directly, another twenty-five minutes were lost to transactional bureaucracy. My annoyance, which had abated when we'd finally settled on the right car, returned and redoubled itself.

Afterward, as Dave gleefully pulled items from the roadside kit—a solar LED flashlight, driving gloves, a colorful bungee cord, and other assorted automotive arcana—the finance staff began putting together the guts of our deal. Dave eventually satisfied his preoccupation with the roadside kit and began issuing orders to the get-ready guy to prepare my partner's vehicle. Thus began the single most frustrating part of the transaction—the wait for the finance paperwork to be finished and the vehicle to be readied for delivery. I could feel my jaw tightening again.

Forty minutes doesn't sound like a lot, but when there is absolutely *nothing* for you to do, it becomes a long, long time. An oversize

Bavarian-style pretzel with spicy mustard, a collection of inappropriate car stories told by me and Dave to entertain my partner in the interim, and two more cold bottles of water later, we were, at last, summoned to the finance office. What a treat. My partner was excited, but after years in upper management, I long since had simply forgotten what a signing extravaganza awaited her. The disclosures, unmasking, and initializations, all on forms with near-incomprehensible legalese, went on for a solid thirty minutes, and although most of the transaction was handled by e-contracting, the finance manager could not resist the fun of pulling out a printed copy of the standard Kia Motor Finance lease contract, which was longer than my partner was tall. Not having seen one of these contracts in several years, I shuddered and thought, *If somebody like me, who is in the business, can get so utterly unnerved by this process, how does it actually feel to an uninitiated purchaser?* With near-screaming nervous fatigue, I forked over a credit card and one thousand dollars in cash to complete the day's activities.

Well, almost. My teeth were still clenched, and I could feel my heartburn rising. Dave still had to properly deliver the car to my partner. It was more than I could take. Since I had done several hundred deliveries myself and witnessed hundreds more during my time in retail over forty years ago, after ten minutes, I stood to take my leave. As expected, Dave, nothing short of a gentleman, wished me a fond farewell and seemed sincerely very happy to have met us and taken us through the transaction. I had two thoughts: *What a classy guy* and *Thank god we're done!*

I told my partner I was headed back to the house. A hot shower at full throttle and a large whiskey beckoned me. She was going to spend some time with her vehicle. It was 3:40 p.m. When I got in my vehicle to head home, I raised my right fist in mock triumph. Mission accomplished! I felt like Tom Cruise. (Not really.)

To recap, I had no right to expect the transaction to have gone any other way. Throughout the process the dealer, the sales manager, the finance manager, the get-ready guy, Dave, and my partner were nothing short of aboveboard, courteous, and professional to the end, despite my obvious impatience.

The whole point is, in a traditional car transaction, even when the vehicle is supposedly right, the customer and dealership are totally cooperative, the money, insurance, and other required documents are all in order, and finally the finance portion is conveniently completed via e-contracting, I still contend that *this just isn't fun anymore.* My partner will probably disagree—she's in a shiny new SUV from a great brand with the equipment she wants at a comfortable price point. Yet I will argue that she is in the minority of truly satisfied customers on the basis of how long the whole process took (not to mention she has the patience of a beatified saint, as demonstrated in this chapter). Sure, certain buying services and other processes can make the retail transaction more efficient. How quickly the dealership and the industry can streamline the transactional process will determine whether the current business model can and will survive.

Several months after my partner leased her new car, after my blood pressure had decreased and my nervous system normalized, I thought back on the experience, particularly on how fortunate I had been over the past forty-one years. With a couple of exceptions, such as buying an SUV for my first wife when she and I were foster parents and buying a used Toyota 4Runner for my daughter when she turned eighteen, I had stayed entirely out of the retail process due to a professional perk. For most of my career, I had driven a brand-new car of whatever make I happened to be working for at the time.

Driving a new vehicle is a definite bonus of working in the industry, at least on the wholesale side. A factory representative, particularly one with field or dealer contact responsibilities, drives a new car of their own brand. In addition, the company pays for fuel, maintenance, insurance, registration (if applicable), and regular car washes (a company-owned car should always be spotless inside and out). In my tenure I have driven countless new cars of several different brands, from a 1977 Chrysler Newport Custom to a 2014

Porsche 911. Besides the fun and status of always being in a new car, there is also the financial windfall—over the years I think I've received a quarter of a million dollars in benefits, even if they were taxable. All of us in the whole-sale end of the business still get high off the new-car smell. (We really do.)

CHAPTER 26

WHEN THE CORONAVIRUS HIT TOWN

The year before the pandemic hit was a good year for the car business. It wasn't the greatest year on record, but most dealers made money in 2019 regardless of brand. Most manufacturers hit production and sales targets, and everyone in the industry was thankful for a strong economy entering President Trump's third year in office. The Dow had just hit twenty-seven thousand, inflation was low, and interest rates and unemployment were at record lows. There were no bugs in the system, so to speak. However, nobody really paid much attention to what was happening in Asia, where people were dying by the thousands from a bug that no one had ever heard of. Secure in their roaring economy, most Americans couldn't see and therefore didn't care what was coming.

But come mid-March 2020, American business, along with the auto industry, had to hit the brakes. For the auto industry especially, the speed and severity of the coronavirus crisis was like nothing ever seen before. The 1992 recession was a romp in the park compared with all previous crises, and yes, the 2008 financial crisis was almost as scary as the recession in the early 1980s. But nothing, absolutely nothing, hit American business, and the auto industry in particular, with the blunt force trauma of the coronavirus.

The first terrible jolt for the automobile business when the coronavirus hit town was the forced closure by state mandate of retail automobile dealerships. Suddenly, with no revenue stream, dealers who had financial obligations of as much as a million dollars a month had hard decisions to make. The initial decisions involved personnel: With no customers, the dealers' first reaction was, "Why do I need all these employees?" As a controllable expense, salespeople, office workers, and fixed operations personnel became the earliest and easiest casualties. Rent, utilities, interest on floor plans, and mortgages on facilities all had to be paid regardless. Even then, dealers were left with hundreds of thousands of dollars of fixed costs, which even wealthy outfits could ill absorb. The good dealers, large and small, who had been through crises before had some cash reserves to withstand several weeks of closure, but everybody was feeling the pain by the end of March 2020. Accordingly, franchised new-car dealers turned to their manufacturer partners for help.

The manufacturers, who were in a more severe state of shock than the dealers, had the same concerns, albeit bigger and more far-reaching. The manufacturers didn't take long to mirror the dealer actions, though on a much larger scale. If dealers couldn't be open to *sell* cars, they certainly were not going to *buy* cars; practically every assembly and supplier plant was shut down overnight. With no revenue stream themselves, many manufacturers, besides furloughing or laying off employees, defunded all nonessential programs, suspended research and development, halted product planning, and froze capital expenditures. As March entered its final week, dealers, manufacturers, and the country as a whole looked to the government.

To its credit, despite many reports from the left-wing media, the federal government's response was measured, broad, and heroic. Spurred by President Trump, the Treasury Department, and a Congress that was just as scared as anybody else, the government acted with rare unanimity. With speed that surprised just about everybody, over a trillion dollars was pumped into the economy. The details were well documented. Hundreds of millions of Americans received $1,200 stipends; the notoriously tightfisted Small Business Administration (SBA) was urged, then directed, to speed up the processing of loans to small businesses. With the states largely handcuffed by the severity of the coronavirus crisis and still bogged down by their ubiquitous regulations, the federal government became everybody's savior. The states' knee-jerk reaction to practically shut down their economies made everyone conscious of the role the federal government was taking. After a couple of weeks, while the count of dead and sick increased, American business, though still worried about what was happening, remained hopeful that the crisis could be survived if managed properly.

The federal government's most visible and lasting contribution to managing the crisis was the Paycheck Protection Program, or the PPP, as it had come to be known. Every dealer who survived the coronavirus crisis had the federal government to thank—not that the dealers' own heroic efforts and business acumen, as well as the marshaling of their own resources and their own banking and business relationships, did not play a part. Just about any small business with more than a few employees took full advantage of the PPP, and some of the chief beneficiaries were the nation's automobile dealers. A retailer with several dealerships could apply for the PPP in the individual stores, though the formula for arriving at the amount to be disbursed to each store was complicated. Historically, the SBA had been a lender of last resort, due mainly to the complicated and burdensome procedures for applying. Any dealer with a solid relationship with a local or regional bank always went to that bank or to their facing captive finance source rather than the SBA. The federal government made clear to the SBA and the legislative branch that the only way an economic collapse could be averted was by fast action on the government's proposed response to the crisis. With speed that ran circles around the SBA's usual process, literally billions were disbursed to small, medium, and large businesses—from the giant airlines to the modest car dealers.

Still, there arose notable hooks in the whole business. Within weeks after the inception of the crisis, as mentioned before, many dealers had shut down completely and furloughed or laid off many of their employees. As part of the PPP, dealers had to pledge to hire back most of those employees and refrain from furloughing others. At this stipulation, many dealers grumbled all the way to the bank; however, given the choice between, in some cases, eight-figure money and rehiring valuable staff, the dealers invariably cashed the checks and brought a lot of their folks back on board, despite the cost of payroll in the meantime.

The effect of the pandemic was nearly instantaneous. April 2020 was one of the worst months for the North American auto industry in history. Sales collapsed, manufacturers and suppliers shut down more plants, and to add to the macabre mood, dealership and original equipment manufacturer employees began to contract the virus and die. Even older dealers, who could remember December 1979 and its 21 percent interest rates and 13 percent inflation, had never seen anything like the coronavirus crisis.

However, as the federal government money via the PPP began coursing through the veins of American business, conditions stabilized. American car dealers, always among the quickest, most resourceful entrepreneurs in the world, took their windfall and ran hard with it to the delight of the propeller-headed tech elements of the automobile manufacturers. Dealers began aggressive campaigns, digitally marketing to an extent never before seen. In many cases digital sales became their only revenue stream—showrooms remained closed well into May, and service business was largely by appointment only and only when parts could be procured. Many dealers, scared out of their wits by the double whammy of very visible sickness and death not only of their employees but also of those around them in their communities, obediently and thoroughly adopted state and federal protocols and adhered to the Centers for Disease Control and Prevention's guidelines pushed hard by state dealer associations.

Consequently, state governments began lifting restrictions on how business could be conducted at car dealerships. Accordingly, May 2020 saw some business improvement—while dealers wrote tons of red ink in April, dealer operations improved slightly in May. The stock market, which had tanked briefly in December, recovered somewhat in the late winter, and then all but collapsed in late March and April, began to show signs of real recovery. The wave of optimism cautiously grew. Curiously, in spite of continued infections and restrictions on commerce in most other sectors of the economy, car sales and dealer profits recovered in June. Almost defying logic, industry sales and dealer profits throughout July and August 2020 were some of the best ever recorded. While no one had a good explanation, everybody was so relieved that nobody looked too hard for one. In late summer, as state restrictions on dealers were largely withdrawn, sales and profits improved even further.

Yet strange inconveniences appeared in this new normal. No one, employee or customer, could enter a dealership without a mask. In some cases the restrictions on the number of customers who could be in a showroom at any one time remained in place. Service work was stifled a bit by the requirement to sanitize every car before delivery to the customer. On the manufacturers' side, production ramp-ups were slowed by the new protocols and physical distancing they had to comply with.

But overall, a cautious optimism wafted over the industry: Dealership employees, frightened at the prospect of permanent layoffs, were selling and delivering more cars than ever. Plant workers who had been called back to work to assemble respirators and personal protective gear were relieved to be back programming robot welders and bolting tires onto shiny new cars. Customers who had, by necessity, put off car purchases for several years were glad to get out of the house and into the showrooms to spend some of the money the federal government had disbursed in April.

As the coronavirus pandemic wore into mid-autumn, sales and profits at the dealerships managed to hold about even, but the situation was surreal. The headquarters, field offices, and other administrative facilities of the manufacturers remained closed, although the plants remained open, along with port facilities and component plants. The real administrative work was done by employees working remotely from their homes. It was a strange existence—employees, many of whom normally spent up to an hour and a half each day commuting to and from headquarters or a regional office, were now spending their day in front of a computer screen. Thanks to technology and employees' innate ability to grasp it and, consequently, to adapt and adjust their schedules, the administrative work of the manufacturers kept rolling along.

There was little else that could be done. State and local guidelines for social distancing made it all but impossible to open regional offices and headquarters. It was a curious delight to some workers who were normally crammed into cubicles that they now had the freedom to work at a pace and a schedule that fit very well into their homelife, with their commute cut from sixty miles on a freeway to twenty feet from their bedroom to their home office. Some took a perverse joy at knowing that their employers were paying tens of thousands of dollars a month for facilities, many quite new, that were scarcely being used. I was among their number.

By October, however, most of that novelty had worn off. The work-from-home routine began to take on a strange weariness. Employees with young children who were out of school and at home all day had long since tired of the constant impossible demands of simultaneous child-rearing and working. However, the employees grasped and mastered new technologies to keep American business afloat at its most challenging time.

To conclude, car dealers and their manufacturing partners deserve credit for preserving jobs and adapting their business models to a continuation of profitability. Different driving factors prevailed. The dealers, because of the hooks in the Paycheck Protection Program, had to retain employees or surrender some of the PPP money. Since most of the dealer revenues throughout the spring were solely deposits from the PPP, they remained viable until customers felt confident enough to come back into the showrooms and service departments.

The manufacturers, on the other hand, had no such inducements. Temporarily shutting down the plants was expected, but most of the manufacturers tried hard to avoid layoffs and furloughs. *Of course, in the midst of hard times, firings and furloughs did not make for good media copy*, noted the cynic in me. Still, the manufacturers were ultimately rewarded by resourceful and renewed efforts of employees grateful to have been able to continue working.

CHAPTER 27

THE SMARTEST DUMB GUYS IN THE ROOM

The title of this book is *This Car Sux*! Lots of times the reason this car sucks is that the car, indeed, sucks. More often than not, the reason this car sucks is that the managers, designers, engineers, marketers, and advertisers suck worse. Behind every successful product launch and model run is a series of visionary managers, competent engineers, talented designers, and brilliant, intuitive, innovative marketing minds—along with a certain sense of timing, accidental or intentional, and a good dose of luck. Behind every flop is a combination of the antithesis of all the above and no luck at all.

Let's start with the big product wins. Unquestionably, the most well-known success in the US industry was the Mustang. Conceived in the early 1960s by Lee Iacocca and a determined band of managers at Ford, the Mustang launch in 1964 succeeded in large part due to a great sense of timing, building on prior victories and strong situational awareness. After the short but nasty recession of 1957–1958, all the domestic manufacturers realized that their product ranges needed to be expanded beyond the boulevard barges with tail fins and V8 engines they had offered from the end of the war until the recession.

The range of product wins varied from manufacturer to manufacturer: American Motors Corporation, the smallest of the domestics at the time, had a lovely, modest hit with the Rambler. GM, entrenched in their past, couldn't quite capitalize on the opportunity. Before the Mustang, Ford had done quite well with a simple, no-frills, utilitarian compact called the Falcon. Somewhat relegated these days to fond memories by Ford aficionados, a modern-day rethinking of Ford's actions in the late 1950s revealed vision and innovation. Part of the whack the industry took in the late 1950s was due to pricing, as well as the fact that the product offerings at the time were just inefficient. The Falcon, on the other hand, was smaller, lighter, much more fuel efficient, and therefore cheaper. The product played perfectly into the sense of economy that most felt at the time. We'll delve deeper into this idea later, but because another Ford offering of the mid- to late 1950s (the Edsel) was such a flop, the Falcon proved that much sweeter a success.

In a similar but inverse manner, Ford built on the Falcon's success by developing the Mustang. The brilliant cadre of middle managers Lee Iacocca had gathered around him realized that the basic underpinnings of the Falcon provided the platform to capitalize on a resurgent market in the midst of economic optimism and general good feeling led by the Kennedy administration. America was on the move again: the economy was booming, more people were gainfully working than ever before, and more money was circulating—all due to higher wages, stabilizing prices, and a surging stock market.

After several good years of Falcon sales, these protégés of Iacocca understood that America's growing middle class was ready for something flashier than the utilitarian compact. These visionaries took the basic Falcon platform and added sharper, more angular exterior sheet metal, a somewhat longer hood, and a shorter trunk. The engineers then added front bucket seats and a palette of eye-catching colors and, by 1964, produced a must-have automobile that Middle America couldn't resist. The Mustang was such a rousing success that by the end of the first model run, Ford had built, and its dealers had retailed, over 417,000 copies, unheard of for a first-time offering. The car, the timing, and the market were all spot on, so much so that Lee Iacocca, on whose watch this automotive gem was produced, found himself on the covers of both *Time* and *Newsweek* in the very same week.

Iacocca also figured into a much later automotive success, albeit of much more modest proportions. In 1982, while chairman of Chrysler, Iacocca partnered with a Detroit specialty shop named Cars & Concepts to take the 1982 LeBaron coupe and put a convertible top on it. Since convertibles had been largely absent from the industry for over ten years, the LeBaron Town & Country convertible sparked much interest in the segment and furthered Chrysler's recovery from its near-death experience. The car proved so popular that Dodge dealers clamored for their own version, and the Dodge 400 convertible was born. The new offerings cost very little to produce and constituted a home run for Chrysler.

Shortly thereafter, Chrysler enjoyed another success with the introduction of the minivan, a segment that Iacocca and his old Ford managers had been excoriated for championing at Ford. The Plymouth Voyager and Dodge Caravan were complete game changers, the first mass-produced vehicles of their kind in America, revolutionizing the industry forever. Their introduction, concurrent with Chrysler's paying off its loan guarantee obligations seven years early, cemented Iacocca's place in automotive history.

In addition to Ford and Chrysler as the big domestic winners, Mazda, which never got a lot of credit despite its excellent engineering and innovation, enjoyed a smash hit later in the 1980s with its Miata convertible. Cute, compact, reliable, and just downright fun to drive, the Miata was interesting in that it was a very niche car in an even more niche segment for a third-tier import manufacturer, which never topped 350,000 sales a year in the decade after. On the positive side, the Miata, which has been in almost continuous production since 1989, still has a loyal following and remarkably good automotive press.

Other successes remained more fiscally important than the zippy Miata or the Chrysler convertibles—but they just didn't have the same panache. For example, Ford's introduction of the "jelly bean" Taurus and Sable sedans saved the company in 1985. VW's revival of the Beetle in the late 1990s similarly led a resurgence in the formerly popular German brand.

All the manufacturers had benefited from the rise of the well-appointed, high-profile sport utility vehicle. To be sure, the Jeep, Ford Bronco, International Harvester Scout, Chevy Trailblazer, and Dodge Ramcharger always had their followers, but before the early 1990s, these vehicles and the sport utility market in general were the province of the rugged off-road sector. Over the course of several years, manufacturers realized that by adding cushier suspensions, plush interiors, and premium sound systems, their rugged sports utilities could appeal to upscale passenger car customers with a lot of money to spend. Late to the sport utility party were the European manufacturers, who, with their stubborn self-absorption, maintained into the early 2000s that sedans and performance coupes were the only way to go. As a result, the beautifully engineered VW Touareg didn't go on sale until the third quarter of 2003. And in the final example of totally Teutonic hardheadedness, Porsche's internal debate over whether to even consider an entry in the sport utility segment nearly tore the company apart. The sports car purists were finally won over by the prima facie business imperative. As a result, over 55 percent of Porsche's US sales were sport utilities by early 2016.

For all the myriad automotive successes, we had seen just as many lukewarm launches, big disappointments, and outright flops. For an outfit as historically successful as Ford, the Edsel ranked as the most dismal failure of the modern age. Conceived in the mid-1950s to build Ford market share and take advantage of the sizzling economy, the Edsel's eventual launch suffered from woeful timing. Introduced about the time of the country's worst postwar recession, the Edsel never met its sizable expectations. Well designed, well built, and positioned nicely in the market, the Edsel, nevertheless, merely cannibalized sales from the company's other two volume divisions, Ford and Mercury. As Edsel sales declined precipitously in 1958 and 1959, the vaunted Ford Finance Department got through to Henry Ford II and succeeded in killing the line, not that Henry needed a lot of prodding—the vehicle was named after Henry's father, and the embarrassing association of the name and lousy sales sealed the car's fate. By 1960 the car was out of production and lived on in automotive lore as a name synonymous with failure. It took the Falcon and the Mustang to pull Ford out of the doldrums and into prominence for the 1960s. Curiously, the Edsel had an affectionate following among car collectors who put a lot of value in its quality, its horse collar front grille, and the speculation of what might have been.

Ford's subsequent flops had almost as serious ramifications for the company. The Ford Pinto of the early 1970s got such bad press from its rear-mounted fuel tanks, which tended to burn furiously in rear-end collisions, that it almost cost the careers of several highly placed Ford managers. Although it sold well as a compact in the post–Arab oil embargo environment, the Pinto gave Ford such a bad name that the resulting press totally negated the profits the car generated.

In the decades of the 1960s and 1970s, Ford wasn't alone in its automotive fiascos. GM had just as difficult a time with its mid-engine Corvair. Launched in the mid-1960s and billed as a sporty compact, the Corvair was riddled with so many design flaws that a young Harvard graduate named Ralph Nader wrote a book about it entitled *Unsafe at Any Speed*. GM only made things worse for itself with a bungled investigation of Nader. However, since GM at the time controlled about 60 percent of the US automobile market, the company was able, by its sheer size and scale, to survive this episode, albeit with a long-lasting black eye.

GM had more missteps to come. Its product-naming conventions could have used more extensive research. The Chevy Nova, most popularly produced from the early 1970s as a two-door compact, ostensibly was named after an astronomical term. The name took on a much more different and unintended meaning when the car was introduced in Mexico. In Mexican

Spanish, *no va*, as a generally spoken phrase, means "it won't go." The name aside, the vehicle had other unexpected product quirks—many times it *wouldn't go* because its aluminum engines simply failed. That and poor fuel economy made GM something of a laughingstock in the early 1970s. Stung by the criticism and the failures, GM improved the car and added a four-door model later in the decade, but the damage done by the curious naming pretty much doomed the vehicle.

And yet GM was not alone in its product-naming hiccups. In the early 1960s, Chrysler's Dodge division, in a response to the nation's penchant for smaller, more economical models, introduced the Dodge Dart. A delightful compact sedan of remarkable quality and reliability, the Dart featured Chrysler's 225-cubic-inch V6 engine, referred to still in this day as the Slant 6. It was spartan, even by the standards of the day, usually ordered with vinyl bench seats and in limited, nondescript colors. The Dart, with its affordable price tag, carried a family of six quite comfortably. However, Chrysler, which had a substantial presence in Latin America in the mid-1960s, should have done the same type of research that GM failed to do. Dart was a perfectly acceptable name in the United States and Canada, but throughout much of the Western Hemisphere's Spanish-speaking world, the term "dart" in colloquial slang implied impotence. Only the car's reliability and popularity enabled the car and the name to survive well into the 1970s in the United States and Canada.

Additionally, Chrysler presented a different take on why it was wise to be careful with product names. In the mid-1970s, as the country was recovering from the effects of the Arab oil embargo, Chrysler introduced a large sporty coupe, perfect for the times and perfect for the market. With its long hood, sleek body styling, and dual vertical headlights in addition to Chrysler's 318-cubic-inch V8 engine, the Cordoba garnered a great deal of attention. The name, however, drawn from the Spanish town of Cordoba, seemed to stymie many customers. In the spoken vernacular, the three-syllable moniker seemed, in many instances, to take on extra letters and syllables, even after Chrysler hired the noted Mexican actor Ricardo Montalbán to pitch its remarkable new offering. Indeed, I couldn't remember how many times a dealer or customer would call it "Cordobia" instead. Chrysler further enhanced its marketing campaign with Montalbán, who at the time was the star of a popular television series called *Fantasy Island*, by having the dapper actor pitch its luxurious new interior fashioned in "rich Corinthian leather." Although customers were fascinated with the car, the interior, and Montalbán himself, nobody at the company could truly explain what differentiated "rich Corinthian leather" from any other leather, but the association of the car with the actor and the interior was a wonderful, if coincidental, success for Chrysler. Despite some quality problems, the Cordoba sold well until the introduction of its 1980 offering, which had the misfortune of being downsized in the wake of the 1979 oil recession and a terrible economic environment.

Some manufacturers' reactions to business conditions, however well intentioned, simply didn't come off well. Take the case, for example, of the Chevrolet Chevette. Introduced as a subcompact right after the Arab oil embargo of 1973–1974, the car was intended to tap a market more focused on economy. What Chevy got instead was a poorly designed, poorly built small car that did more damage to the brand than anything else. Although indeed small, the car didn't get nearly the fuel economy that GM had projected. Further, as a small car, it didn't generate a lot of revenue either. Since the public quickly soured on the car, the net effect for Chevy was that the Chevette soaked up plant capacity and marketing and advertising dollars that could have been better allocated to some of Chevy's more appealing products. Hence, the model really never got traction as its one hoped-for advantage, its fuel efficiency, withered away as the US economy recovered in 1976.

At least the Chevette was a good-faith effort by GM to capitalize on the economy movement. Some manufacturers, though, developed and built oddball cars that just seemed to spring from the imagination of deranged product planners and self-styled marketing geniuses. Consider the Mazda MX-3 sport coupe. If there was ever a product offering more dead on arrival than the MX-3, it had been long forgotten. Launched in the early 1990s as what Mazda's marketing "geniuses" hailed as perfect for the youth market, the MX-3 was the antithesis of what a smart, sophisticated young consumer would want for their first new car. Short, narrow, underpowered, and utterly overpriced for its target market, the MX-3 was also utterly disgusting to the dealers. The vehicle languished on dealer lots, and when a dealer did sell one, they couldn't make any money on it. At launch Mazda compounded the problem by overordering several thousand vehicles in a hideously purple exterior paint color with a totally unappealing black interior. It didn't help that the exterior color matched the ubiquitous children's television character Barney the dinosaur. Young kids might have liked Barney, but their young parents couldn't stand the car. The overall effect of the purple feature car was to jinx any MX-3 of any color. After a model run of a couple of years, the vehicle thankfully died a natural death.

The Chevette and the MX-3 remained notable examples of a manufacturer not only not doing its homework but also failing to ask its dealers for input—in each case the dealers certainly could have told the manufacturers a thing or two about why these vehicles were losers. Additionally and more importantly, both vehicles consumed resources such as engineering talent, plant space, and marketing and incentive dollars that could have been more fruitfully applied to more successful models in the respective manufacturer's product lineups or, even better, used for the development of more competitive models.

The MX-3 flop was closely followed by another Mazda marketing gaffe. Mazda, which became closely tied to Ford by virtue of Ford buying a significant stake in Mazda in the late 1970s, inadvertently became a dumping ground for the two-door version of Ford's popular Explorer sport utility. Since Mazda had become more closely financially tied to Ford after its dreadful 1992 model year, Mazda was hardly in a position to refuse the two-door sport utility; the sport utility market was just heating up, and Mazda had no entry in the segment and no plans for one. Mechanically the vehicle was a duplicate of Ford's two-door Explorer; however, like most vehicles in the segment, the four-door version was much preferred over the two-door.

The initiative could have worked if properly thought out and executed, but Mazda made three critical mistakes in the launch of the two-door sport utility from Ford. Firstly, it failed to get an allocation of the four-door version of the vehicle from Ford. Secondly, it chose to name (here we go again) its two-door version from Ford the Navajo, which had a most egregious effect. Indigenous Americans (and not just the Navajo Nation) were outraged. Thirdly and predictably, the only television ad Mazda produced in support of the Navajo launch featured stereotypical Old West scenes that Native Americans found even more insensitive. Indeed, appropriative names had been used in the past by car companies, but Mazda's mistakes in this arena proved disastrous due to the changing cultural and political climate. Although the Mazda Navajo offered the latest technology, more than adequate power, and better than average fuel economy, it simply couldn't take the triple whammy of the two-door body configuration, the ill-considered naming convention, and the botched marketing.

Similarly, the European record on product launches had been mixed. Through the years, VW has had a real winner with the Beetle. The car even looked like a cute little bug, so the nickname stuck. Aside from that, VW's vehicle-naming conventions took on more peculiar characteristics: Golf was indeed an odd name for the successor compact VW introduced in the 1980s. While it was a hit in Germany and the rest of Europe, the Golf wasn't that popular in the United States, and VW's standing suffered greatly, even with steady Beetle sales. The goofy (or should I say "golfy"?) name exacerbated the situation throughout the 1980s. Renaming the VW Bus the Vanagon was not the best move either; unwieldy and overpriced (the German mark was extremely strong against the dollar throughout much of that decade), the vehicle suffered from product problems as well as the unfortunate name.

Another VW blunder occurred in 2003 with the launch of the luxury sedan the Phaeton. Besides sounding like a villain from *Star Wars*, this brainchild of VW chairman Ferdinand Piëch had no business being under the VW nameplate. VW had been and still is a mass-market brand. Its very name means "people's car." The Phaeton, on the other hand, was a luxury car so totally out of place as to be laughable. At the time, VW as a brand in the United States was just beginning to feel the onslaught of economical Korean entries like Kia and Hyundai. Most VW dealers and employees, including me, were absolutely convinced that the Germans had lost whatever sense they might have had left. VW's wheelhouse was well-made, economical, compact sedans like the Jetta and Passat. Interestingly enough, most of the rest of the automotive world felt the same way. However, such was Ferdinand Piëch's ego that he not only forged ahead with a $100,000 luxury sedan but also built an entirely new plant in which to assemble it.

The reaction of the dealers and potential customers was, "WTF?" It was a valid response. German luxury sedans were made by Mercedes and BMW. The VW group's own entry into the luxury market was through Audi. What was the business case for the Phaeton other than Piëch's one wild dream? The answer was there wasn't one, not that the car didn't have its admirers—the Phaeton's W12 engine ran beautifully. From the perspective of styling, handling, interior appointments, and reliability, the car was a very good luxury car. But how many people would have thought to go to a VW dealership for a luxury car? More than once I heard a customer say that it was a lovely car, but they just couldn't buy a $100,000 VW. And the truth was not many people did. Within a year it was obvious that however good the product was, it wasn't a fit for the VW lineup. By 2006 the car was almost an afterthought but lived on in the auctions as a good used car that dealers could make money on if they were lucky enough to snap one up at around $30,000.

Switching gears a bit, some ostensibly dumb moves in the industry really had nothing to do with the product. Here we'll go back to names for a second. For years Nissan had been marketed in the United States and other parts of the world as Datsun. After a rickety start in the United States in the early 1960s, the brand got some respectable traction through the import and sale of its compact pickup truck. Tough, durable, and well priced, the Datsun pickup carved itself a respectable niche particularly in the Western United States. Datsun's cars, on the other hand, had simply been too small and underpowered to get much attention in the American market. After the import market exploded in early 1979, however, *everything* Datsun sent to the United States literally jumped off the lots. During several months in 1979 and 1980, Datsun actually sold as well as both Toyota and Honda. By this time the quality of the cars had improved along with the power, styling, and range of offerings, and of course, the price remained extremely competitive. Datsun, overall, remained more than competitive with the other import brands, and thanks to Nissan's advances in engineering and technology, several Datsun models achieved Best in Class status. And thanks to the sales momentum generated just before the voluntary restraint agreement, Datsun got very favorable quotas when it came time for MITI (the Japanese Ministry of International Trade and Industry) to divvy up import percentages. Despite the limits on the number of cars it could import, Datsun remained second only to Toyota in import volume and popularity. Its commercials, conceived by the noted US advertising firm Chiat/Day, were also extremely well done and highly popular and advanced Datsun's brand image immeasurably.

And then the unthinkable happened. The Japanese decided to change the brand's name from Datsun to Nissan in the United States. At first glance this choice seemed practical, sensible, and commercially reasonable. Since Nissan used its corporate name in other countries as well as Japan, they thought it should work just fine in the United States too. There were, in fact, already examples in the industry of the trade name being different from the corporate name, with that information eventually coming to light with very little fuss. Mazda in the United States was sold for years before many Americans realized that the manufacturer's corporate name was actually Toyo Kogyo. In addition, Fuji Heavy Industries marketed its vehicles around the world as Subaru. Here's the difference, though: In the instances of Toyo Kogyo and Fuji, the companies were shrewd enough to keep the same already recognized brand names in the United States.

Changing the brand name from Datsun to Nissan proved more arduous. The difficulties went beyond changing out logos on vehicles and reprinting brochures, bulletins, manuals, and letterhead. Beyond changing out signs on buildings, factories, dealerships, and port facilities. Nissan was, whether they realized it or not, very clumsily tossing away twenty-five years of hard-won brand equity literally overnight. Since the late 1950s, the car had been known as Datsun. Now the company expected dealers, salespeople, mechanics, vendors, and customers to buy into a change of name that hardly any of them recognized.

Given the loss of ready brand recognition, in addition to the many different dialects of English spoken in the United States, what should have been a simple change turned out to be quite a chore. "Nissan," as a term, is relatively well known now, but it was almost totally unknown in 1984. And Southern Californians don't pronounce words the same way Southerners, Midwesterners, Texans, or Northeasterners do. For sure, "Nissan" spoken by a Floridian is a hell of a lot different from "Nissan" spoken by a New Yorker. Although Nissan spent millions of dollars on the changeover, including a new facility and signage scheme, as well as new dealership layouts and colors and ad tags, the change was clumsy, awkward, painful, and worst of all, long. It took until almost 1990 for all the dealership signage to be fully updated. Today an old blue-red-and-white Datsun brand sign in good condition will fetch almost as much as a VW lollipop sign on eBay.

Of course, almost thirty-five years later, the change from Datsun to Nissan has long since been complete. The public and most customers are now more aware of Nissan than Datsun. Even given the length of time it took the change to take full effect, it was (probably) worth the hassle. At least "Nissan" is easier to pronounce than "Hyundai" or "Daewoo."

Speaking of name changes, a tricky business in the auto industry, one of the goofiest, most poorly executed attempts at a corporate name change was announced even though it was never intended to stick. On March 29, 2021, VW issued a press release, just in time for April Fools' Day, stating that "Volkswagen of America" would be changing its name to "Voltswagen." Given the pending launch of VW's highly publicized electric vehicles, the change seemed highly plausible, particularly when VW's own public relations department answered, with all seriousness, inquiries from the automotive media and declared it all true. Even Volkswagen of America CEO Scott Keogh confirmed the story, fending off suggestions by some naysayers in the industry that the whole thing had to be an April Fools' joke. By this time the story had so much credence that practically the entire automotive media had bought into it. It was a clever, bold strategy, until the revelation that the whole thing was, in fact, not true.

Well, to be succinct, hell hath no fury like the media duped—particularly the automotive media. It seemed like every editorial manager and every automotive publication unleashed their fury at "Voltswagen." (I felt for you, Volkswagen.) Dave Versical, the noted editor of *Automotive News*, was particularly pointed in his editorial, explaining that one of the dumbest things VW could have done on the heels of its well-publicized diesel emission scandal of 2015 was draw even more attention to itself with another lie, however clever and whimsical their marketing firm and American executives thought it was. But by that time, VW had gotten what it wanted—plenty of buzz about its EV program.

Despite the vituperation of the automotive media, VW, predictably, refused to admit to a mistake. Questioned several days after the episode, VW CEO Keogh explained, "I would do it again. I would 100 percent execute it a little bit differently for sure." In summary, and as a harbinger of things to come, that was an interesting comment from one of the smartest dumb guys in the room.

CHAPTER 28

THE CUSTOMER

The driven entrepreneurs of the early twentieth century probably didn't intend to put the entire world on wheels, but once they could mass-produce the automobile, ever-increasing products (and corresponding profits) became possible. In the early days of the industry, before manufacturers perfected production techniques, problems with the cars themselves vastly outnumbered the issues surrounding how they were purchased; since in the beginning vehicles were mostly custom made, only the well-to-do could afford them. Accordingly, it's not surprising that over 120 years after the automobile's invention, thanks to mass production, better technology, and credit purchase, many problems that customers experience with their automobiles have as much or more to do with the buying experience and less to do with the vehicle itself.

To explain further, ever-advancing technology has evened the playing field for just about all manufacturers. From a quality perspective, it is very difficult to rate one brand of car or one model in a product line above others. Since the eastern Europeans are pretty much out of the game, the Americans, Mexicans, Canadians, western Europeans, and Koreans have all caught up with, and in the cases of certain brands actually surpassed, the Japanese. To be sure, complaints still arise over recall items, most of which are now handled under warranty. Aside from VW's classic diesel scandal of 2015, it appears that no brand has actively tried to pull the wool over the eyes of any customer or government or regulatory agency. (In the case of VW, the diesel scandal was another classic example of flawed Teutonic thinking; the Germans, with their typical superiority complex, actually thought that Americans, even the highly trained, highly competent engineers and staffers in the US government's regulatory agencies, were too stupid to detect the defeat device intended to fool everyone that the VW diesel engines were not emitting an excessive amount of particulate matter pollution.) Most automobiles today are excellent examples of technology, styling, engineering, and quality. Similarly, most manufacturers, using decades of examples of bad decisions, have learned that the slightest hint of deception in design, manufacture, and representation of their products is not the proper way to do business.

Customers, the manufacturers have finally realized, are the lifeblood of the industry. Without customers flush with cash or the ability to finance, no market for the technological marvels the factories produce exists. The fact that even VW has been able to recover somewhat from the bad faith of its diesel scandal indicates that customers will forgive, if not forget. Further, the fact that Chrysler has survived for years after taking a billion-dollar hickey for rust on the fenders of its mid-1970s Volaré and Aspen offerings solidifies the point.

Instead, what sends a customer spinning most often these days is bad treatment at the dealership level or, worse, a financing deal in which the customer feels cheated. A close second is difficulty in scheduling a service appointment or misrepresentation of a service problem. Time is money, and any disrespect of either is a valid reason for a customer to be dissatisfied.

In an earlier chapter, I explained the different financing options available to a customer buying a new or used car. I also explained how these myriad choices can confuse a customer and thus offer an opportunity for an unscrupulous dealer finance manager to (1) truly throw a customer into a fit, (2) mangle the dealer's reputation, and (3) turn a customer completely off the brand. Likewise, a service writer who gets overzealous on a multipoint inspection when a customer coming in for a five-thousand-mile checkup simply wants the basics and then to get the hell out of the service department can cause almost as much damage as a dishonest finance manager. Multipoint inspections are useful for pointing out maintenance needs; weaponizing multipoint inspections to pad a customer pay ticket is just not cool.

Therefore, since cars are being built as well as ever, when a customer complains to a regional office or headquarters, the natural tendency of the factory is to blame the dealer or their employees. Years ago, most zone or regional offices had a customer satisfaction representative. This individual, usually a recently promoted district sales manager or district parts and service manager, fielded calls from customers who felt, sometimes quite rightly, that they had been had. Over time this function has been realigned to headquarters, which is too bad for a couple of reasons: To start, whereas a customer satisfaction representative in a zone or regional office actually has dealer contact experience and, most likely, experience talking with retail customers, a person at a national headquarters quite often is a recent college graduate, possibly in their first job. Further, the customer service representative in a zone or regional office usually knows the dealer, may even know the finance manager or service adviser in the dealership, and can discern patterns of bad behavior and customer mistreatment. Despite all the sophisticated programs and voluminous efforts by the manufacturers to lean on dealers to shore up customer treatment, this gap in customer service remains one of the biggest challenges in the industry and leads to lots of verbal recriminations among dealers, manufacturers, and customers.

J. D. Power, the data analytics company that built an empire beginning in the 1970s by measuring customer satisfaction in the automobile industry, remains the gold standard by which manufacturers judge their dealers' competitiveness in the area of customer handling. However, after forty years of analyzing data and accepting billions of manufacturers' dollars to concoct surveys detailing who is on top and why, customer satisfaction remains as elusive as ever. To his credit, founder James David Power III has refined his surveys to reflect practically every aspect of a customer-dealer interaction, from the condition of the vehicle at delivery to parts availability to the courtesy of a salesperson or service adviser to the length of service wait time. J. D. Power, as a firm, deserves a lot of credit for effectively nudging the industry to take the whole matter of customer handling more seriously.

Interestingly, the issue of customer satisfaction had been parodied to the extent that the 2021 Super Bowl carried an ad from Vroom that was quite disparaging to car dealers. The used-car newbie eviscerated car dealers with an advertisement comparing dealerships with torture chambers. Unfortunately, the image lingered and was emblematic of how many customers had felt about car dealers for years. As Dave Versical wrote in his March 8, 2021, editorial in *Automotive News*, "The ad was grossly unfair and largely outdated. But as someone who once begged a car salesman to let me leave, I could relate." Versical then quoted a well-known New York City dealer who declared, "Darwin will take care of this problem."

Versical's 2021 editorial remains pertinent and may even be somewhat prescient. He not only gives a balanced view of the traditional sales process but also pinpoints where the process is likely headed. Clearly nobody—neither dealers nor manufacturers nor, least of all, customers—is in love with the current process. Customer handling, or the lack thereof, fundamentally defines the industry to many potential consumers, and careful innovation in this area is sorely needed to ensure the future of the car business.

As a case in point, one result of the COVID-19 pandemic was the manner in which the savvier dealers responded to the restrictions placed on them. Most dealers, as mentioned in a previous chapter, dusted off all the manufacturers' helpful information on digital retailing, retrained their managers and sales forces, and aggressively went after business online. Better still, I would argue that virtual retail platforms elevated the customer's experience by streamlining the retail process. Freed from the smarmier of the traditional sales practices such as long waits and endless negotiations, online customers bought in droves. In many cases the only time a customer saw an actual car in 2020 was when they arrived at the dealership to sign the final paperwork and take delivery of their new vehicle. The whole virtual process worked just like the manufacturers and the consultants had been telling the dealers it would for five years. In the middle of the scariest year of the twenty-first century, car dealers had their most profitable year ever!

With this irrefutable evidence, confirmation in print (and in the bank), the old car sales stereotype is done for—it's just a matter of time. With the memory of 2020 still fresh, customers will lead the "Darwinization" of the retail automobile business.

CHAPTER 29

THE WAY FORWARD

In the previous ninety-six thousand or so words, I have examined not so much cars themselves but more so the relationships among the three most important participants in a retail vehicle transaction: the manufacturer, who produces the car; the dealer, who, in the United States, is responsible for retailing the car; and the customer, who is supposed to reap the benefits of the relationship between the manufacturer and the dealer. For most of the last 120 years, the fundamentals of the relationship among manufacturer, dealer, and customer have changed little. The manufacturer builds the product, the dealer sells the product, the customer buys the product. The customer is reliant on a trusting relationship between the manufacturer and the dealer to provide: (1) parts and accessories for the customer's car, (2) training for the fixed operations personnel who help maintain the customer's car, and (3), eventually, updated new models when the car reaches the end of its life cycle or when the customer decides to trade the car in rather than selling the car on the secondary market. Not surprisingly, as we have seen, the intertwining relationships have had their ups and downs. For the most part, however, the system has worked satisfactorily.

Since the Great Recession of 2008 (which has seen what will probably be the last great shakeout of automotive brands and vulnerable dealers), the last few years have been remarkably good for manufacturers, dealers, and customers. Specifically, Ford, the only original equipment manufacturers not to take government money during the Great Recession, has thrived, largely due to America's obsession with expensive pickup trucks and SUVs. The Ford family and the company's shareholders still bemoan the company's share price, but nobody can argue with the profits. GM has emerged from bankruptcy in 2009 as a completely different company, more in tune with embracing technology than making money or cars. Chrysler, through a complex set of transactions that has found it mostly under the control of European influences (first Fiat and then through a strange alliance with Peugeot), has made the most spectacular recovery of any company, in the process taking its Jeep brand to the pinnacle of popularity and success.

The so-called domestic manufacturers are not alone in the latest joyride. The Hyundai Motor Group, comprising the Korean brands Hyundai, Genesis, and Kia, has made wonderful advances since 2009, to the point where Kia has supplanted Porsche at the top of the J. D. Power initial quality survey several years in a row. (Since I left Porsche and joined Kia when this spectacular event occurred, I have taken particular pride in this development.) The Japanese manufacturers—Toyota, Honda, Nissan, Mazda, Mitsubishi, and Subaru—have all recovered very well from the devastating March 2011 tsunami; only Suzuki, which has unceremoniously left the US market in 2012, is not around to partake in the current success the American auto industry enjoys. Only in a period such as the last dozen years can a bunch of boneheads like VW go from the highest market capitalization of any company on earth in October 2009 to a scandalous, insipid sinking in September 2015 due to the diesel incident, then still survive to pretty much limp along at about the same three-hundred-thousand-unit volume they've maintained since about the year 2000. Accordingly, VW is living proof that, somehow, *anybody* can make it in the car business. The other Europeans—Mercedes, BMW, Peugeot, Opel, and Volvo—have done quite well in the same time span.

For a while, in the late first quarter and early second quarter of 2020, it appeared as if the American car industry had encountered the one crisis it might not recover from. In a previous chapter, I examined the catastrophic effect the coronavirus pandemic had on the industry. Nothing—I repeat, nothing—had ever had *everybody* in the industry as scared as they could be as the pandemic. I went through the Arab oil embargo aftereffects of 1973, the Chrysler loan guarantee crisis of 1979, the dip after 9/11 and the dot-com bubble in 2001, and then the Great Recession of 2008, but nothing tested the resolve of the American automobile industry like the coronavirus.

But a funny thing happened on the way to automotive Armageddon; thanks to fast action by the Trump administration and thanks to faster action by manufacturers, suppliers, dealers, their employees, and customers, the industry responded with a resiliency and speed never before seen. In true American fashion, Americans overcame fear, doubt, and difficulty and reentered the market with such vigor that 2020 was one of the most profitable years for US car dealers. Despite the COVID-19-induced sales reductions of March and April 2020, the industry, overall, ended the year with more than respectable sales totals and a great deal of hope for the future. Some automobile brands had their best performance in years.

So while looking to the future, why will any dealer or manufacturer or, for that matter, any prospective customer feel any unease? Well, I'll tell you why. As I write these words, a groundswell of American popular opinion backed by the threat of government mandates and a storm cloud of political correctness fostered by the political left is bound and determined that before the end of my lifetime every car sold in the United States will be electric.

To be sure, all-out war has been declared on the internal combustion engine. The aspiration is noble but infeasible. The American industrial and motoring infrastructure is still very much geared toward gasoline-powered vehicles. Our entire transportation system, from motor vehicles to rail to aviation to marine commerce, is pegged to the discovery, extraction, refining, distribution, and heavy use of petroleum. Frankly, it tickles me when I hear a highly placed executive of an automotive company declare that their brand will be totally electrified by whatever year (and that is usually before 2050). I probably won't be around to see the full picture, but I sure as hell want to see the preview. Since the environmentalists, the government, and congressional pundits have decreed that the industry will be all electric at some point, somehow, and for some reason, the manufacturers have taken the hint and are all vowing to comply, though with some caution.

And since we're talking about the manufacturers here, note that while their dealers have very much adopted digital commerce and online selling, the manufacturers still insist that the dealers continue to build large, expensive facilities, such as opulent showrooms and service departments with more and more service stalls. This position flies in the face of the experts who maintain that customers will conduct more business online and that the flood of electric vehicles to come will require less maintenance. I'm not sure how the factory-dealer relationship will evolve to appropriately handle this conundrum.

As long as we're talking about the factory-dealer relationship, there is still a battle to be waged over the manufacturers' desire to inject themselves into the retail process. This spat will be a fun one to watch. Already, Tesla, currently the largest manufacturer of EVs, retails most of those vehicles directly to customers, absent a dealer network. In the winter of 2021, Volvo announced a subscription sales model that effectively relegates its dealer network to a very secondary role in the retail process. Not surprisingly, the Volvo model has quickly run afoul of the dealer associations and motor vehicle boards of several states. In short, the issues of electrification, new facilities and their costs, and the desire of dealers to keep the manufacturers out of their business have created friction in the factory-dealer relationship.

It is ironic that on the heels of having overcome perhaps the biggest crisis in its history, the American automobile business stands at the precipice of its most dangerous period of uncertainty since its inception. So strap yourself in—it's gonna be a hell of a ride.

ACKNOWLEDGMENTS

I had always fancied myself a writer. But beyond a thirty-thousand-word thesis for my graduate degree from St Andrews, I had never taken the steps to seriously put pen to paper.

All this changed one September day (which I mention in the prologue) when Donna Roberts and I were driving to a car show in Parsippany, New Jersey. Some knucklehead in an aged Pontiac cut me off on I-287 just south of Morristown, and I let fly with a frosty, "Bonehead! That's going in my book!" Having heard countless such expostulations from me over the years, usually in the course of my recounting stories from the early years of my career in the car business, she had enough. "OK, mister! Start talking," she yelled as she reached for her laptop in the back seat of my company-owned Kia Sorrento. She transcribed while I spent the next seventeen months talking off the cuff in a mostly linear narrative. I am grateful for the nudge she gave me that day and for all the nudges, love, support, and encouragement that followed.

Similarly, Donna's friend Mike Farragher, the author of six books and a couple of plays and a noted New Jersey–based contributor to the *Irish Times* and *Irish Voice*, encouraged us on this journey. Mike's connections with Project Write Now, a New Jersey–based writers' advocacy group, led us to

Courtney Harler, who from her base in Las Vegas provided much-needed editing and critique of the original manuscript. This book would not have been completed without the spark from both Mike and Courtney.

Brandon Coward and the staff at Amplify Publishing Group have been extraordinarily helpful and encouraging to a first-time author. Their professionalism and expertise have been indispensable.

Marc Clark, a colleague from my Chrysler days in Memphis and New Orleans, helped me tremendously by clarifying names, dates, and events from our joint automotive experiences in the early 1980s.

A special thank-you is due to Don Hughes, the finest boss I had during my career, and his wife, Vicky, and their daughters, Shannon and Mollie, for their steadfast friendship. Don is the best exemplar not only of a regional director but also of a solid car guy, husband, and father.

Finally, I gratefully acknowledge the sorely tested patience of my son, Patrick, and my daughter, Cate, both of whom managed to thrive while Dad was hammering highways from Houston to San Antonio to Victoria, Texas, or jetting from Berlin to Tokyo to Detroit to Jeddah—and a million small towns and big cities in between.

ABOUT THE AUTHOR

Randy Pressgrove is an automotive industry expert with more than forty years of experience, including sales and dealership development assignments across the world—from Memphis, Tennessee, to Saudi Arabia—with Mazda, Toyota, Volkswagen, Audi, Porsche, and Kia. He holds a graduate degree in Scottish medieval history from the University of St Andrews, which he has not found to be professionally useful. He lives in New Jersey.